GALLIPOLI CORRESPONDENT

Chas. Bean, standing in a communication trench on Gallipoli.
Photograph by P.F.E. Schuler. (AWM neg. no. PS1850)

GALLIPOLI CORRESPONDENT

The frontline diary of C.E.W. Bean

Selected and annotated by
KEVIN FEWSTER

George Allen & Unwin
Sydney London Boston

First published in 1983 by
George Allen & Unwin Australia Pty Ltd
8 Napier Street, North Sydney, NSW 2060 Australia

George Allen & Unwin (Publishers) Ltd
Park Lane, Hemel Hempstead, Herts HP2 4TE, England

Allen & Unwin Inc.
9 Winchester Terrace, Winchester, Mass 01890 USA

National Library of Australia
Cataloguing-in-Publication entry:
Bean, C.E.W. (Charles Edwin Woodrow), 1879–1968.
Gallipoli correspondent, the frontline diary of
C.E.W. Bean
Bibliography.
Includes index.
ISBN 0 86861 213 8.
1. World War, 1914–1918 — Campaigns — Turkey and
The Near East — Gallipoli. 2. World War,
1914–1918 — Personal narratives, Australian.
I. Fewster, Kevin. II. Title
940.4′25′0924
Library of Congress Catalog Card Number: 82-83579

Phototypeset in Linotron 202, 11 point Bembo
by Graphicraft Typesetters Hong Kong
Printed at Griffin Press Limited, Australia

Front endpaper: Detail from F. R. Crozier 1883–1948 *The beach at Anzac* 1919 oil on canvas 123.3 × 184.2 cm Australian War Memorial
Back endpaper: Detail from G. W. Lambert 1873–1930 *The charge of the 3rd Light Horse at the Nek* 1924 oil on canvas 152.5 × 305.7 cm Australian War Memorial

Contents

Abbreviations

AA & QMG	Assistant-Adjutant and Quartermaster General
ADB	*Australian Dictionary of Biography*
ADC	Aide-de-Camp
ADMS	Assistant-Director of Medical Services
AGH	Australian General Hospital
AIF	Australian Imperial Force
ALH	Australian Light Horse
AMC	Australian Army Medical Corps
ANZAC	Australian and New Zealand Army Corps
APM	Assistant-Provost-Marshall
ASC	Australian Army Service Corps
Aust.	Australia
Aust. Perm. Forces	Australian Permanent Forces
AWM	Australian War Memorial, Canberra
Battn Bn	Battalion
Bde	Brigade
BGGS	Brigadier-General, General Staff
Brig	Brigadier
C in C	Commander-in-Chief
Capt	Captain
CEWB	Charles Edwin Woodrow Bean
CGS	Chief of General Staff
CMF	Commonwealth Military Forces
CO Comd	Commanding Officer
Col	Colonel
Comm	Commonwealth of Australia
Commdt	Commandant
Coy	Company
CRE	Commanding Royal Engineers
DA & QMG	Deputy-Adjutant and Quartermaster-General
DAAG	Deputy-Assistant Adjutant-General
DDMS	Deputy-Director of Medical Services

DHQ	Divisional Headquarters
Divn Div	Division
DMS	Director of Medical Services
DOW	dicd of wounds
Gen	General
GHQ	General Headquarters
GOC	General Officer Commanding
GSO	General Staff Officer
Hd HQ	Headquarters
hosp	hospital
Inf	Infantry
KIA	killed in action
Lanc.s	Lancashire
Lieut Lt	Lieutenant
Maj	Major
MEF	Mediterranean Expeditionary Force
MHR	Member, House of Representatives
MLA	Member, Legislative Assembly
NCO	Non-Commissioned Officer
NLA	National Library of Australia, Canberra
NZ & A Div	New Zealand and Australian Division
NZEF	New Zealand Expeditionary Force
NZMR	New Zealand Mounted Rifles
PRO	Public Record Office, London
RAN	Royal Australian Navy
Regt	Regiment
RMC	Royal Military College
RMLI	Royal Marine Light Infantry
RTA	Returned to Australia
S/Sgt	Staff Sergeant
Sec	Secretary
Sgt	Sergeant
SMH	*Sydney Morning Herald*
temp	temporary/temporarily
VC	Victoria Cross

Acknowledgements

THIS book could not have been produced but for the gracious agreement to its publication by CEW Bean's widow, Mrs Ethel Bean; the assistance of the life-long friend of Chas. Bean, Mr AH McLachlan; and the support provided by an Australian War Memorial Research Grant and the Monash University Publications Committee. I am deeply indebted to Mrs Bean, Mr McLachlan, the Council of the Australian War Memorial, and my colleagues at Monash.

For the past seven years I have based most of my research on the unsurpassed riches held in the Library at the Australian War Memorial. I owe a special debt of thanks to the library staff for their friendliness, guidance, and patience over this time. In particular, I thank the Australian War Memorial Librarian, Michael Piggott, for his friendship and assistance. I am also grateful to my family and friends, Mark Cranfield in particular, who have helped and encouraged me with this project. Alec Hill offered many thought-provoking suggestions, as did Geoff Serle. It was especially valuable to read the Gallipoli chapter in manuscript form from Dr Serle's now published biography of Sir John Monash. Belinda Probert provided much needed advice and support at the times it was required most. My thanks, too, must go to Julie Prince and Elizabeth Relf for typing and retyping the manuscript so efficiently and always so cheerfully.

All photographs are reproduced by kind permission of the Australian War Memorial. The maps were prepared and drawn by Wendy Gorton.

Introduction

More than 50 000 Australian troops saw action on the Gallipoli Peninsula between April and December 1915. Nearly 7 600 of them were killed in action and now lie buried under Turkish soil. One man, a civilian, probably observed more of their deeds than did any soldier, and viewed them at least as highly as did any general. The troops held him in the highest regard. As the official press correspondent with the Australian Imperial Force, Charles Edwin Woodrow Bean landed at Gallipoli on that first, fateful morning of 25 April. Bean had started a diary of his doings and those of the soldiers on the day he sailed from Melbourne with the first contingent of Australian and New Zealand troops, off to fight for Britain, Australia, and the Empire against Germany. He kept the diary in Egypt and throughout the long months at Anzac Cove. By the time he left the Peninsula (only a day before the last troops were evacuated) his diary had grown into a most comprehensive personal account of the campaign — an intimate record of the bravery, stupidity, and camaraderie which have given Gallipoli a special place in the history of warfare.

Bean almost missed the chance to accompany the Australian troops. When it became clear in early August 1914 that war would soon start, Australia notified England that it was prepared to send a military contingent to assist the 'mother country'. Bean immediately wrote to the Commonwealth Minister for Defence asking that he might be permitted to accompany the troops to England as a newspaper 'eyewitness' reporter. The Minister replied that Bean's application would be considered if the opportunity arose to send a press correspondent.[1] That same day, 13 August, a cable was received stating that the British Army Council would permit each Dominion to have one correspondent accompany its expeditionary force. For reasons known only to himself, the Minister disregarded this instruction and invited the two major Australian newspaper combines, the *Sydney Morning Herald*/Melbourne *Argus* group, and the Melbourne *Age* and

Sydney *Daily Telegraph*, each to nominate a representative. They selected 'Banjo' Paterson and Peter Schuler (the son of the editor of the *Age*) respectively.

In the meantime, however, the Liberal Party had been ousted from office at a Federal general election. The incoming Labor Minister for Defence decided it would be more equitable to adopt the original scheme and appoint one pressman to represent the entire Australian press. He asked the Australian Journalists' Association to nominate a suitable person. The Association organised a ballot of its members which Bean, an employee at the *Sydney Morning Herald*, won narrowly from Keith Murdoch, the Melbourne representative of the Sydney *Sun*. Although he had had no previous experience as a war correspondent, Bean's extensive journalistic experience in Australia and overseas suggested he would prove a most suitable choice.

Bean had grown up in a strongly Imperial environment. Born on 18 November 1879 at Bathurst, New South Wales, he was the eldest of Edwin and Lucy (née Butler) Bean's three sons. Edwin Bean had been born in India, educated in England, and resident six years in Australia as headmaster of All Saints' College, Bathurst. Lucy Butler had grown up in Hobart. In 1889 ill health forced Edwin to resign his post and return to Europe where, after two years spent mainly at Oxford and Brussels, he became headmaster of Brentwood School, Essex. Young Charles attended this school until 1894 when he entered his father's old school, Clifton College. Charles was very happy there. Nicknamed 'The Run 'Un' for his Australian accent, he recalled as his fondest schoolday memories, acquiring 'a real interest in literature, & in the classics' and playing cricket. He was, as Ken Inglis has put it, 'a schoolboy in love with England and Empire'.[2]

In 1898 Charles won a scholarship to Hertford College, Oxford where he read classics, graduating in 1902 with second-class honours. He took up law and was called to the Bar in 1903. The following year he returned to Australia and was admitted to the New South Wales Bar. For a time he supplemented his income by writing articles for the Sydney *Evening News*. During the next three years, while travelling in New South Wales with the circuit court, he kept notes of his impressions of returning to his native land. The *Sydney Morning Herald* published these in a series of eight articles in 1907. Bean now decided to foresake the law in favour of journalism. In January 1908 he joined the *Sydney Morning Herald* as a junior reporter. He was sent in 1909 as special correspondent on HMS *Powerful* during the Australian visit of the

United States Great White Fleet. The next year he explored outback New South Wales for a series of articles on the wool industry. Both assignments impressed on him the opportunities facing his young nation and the fine, resourceful people it was producing in these outback areas. He developed these articles into three books: *With the flagship in the south* (London 1909), *On the wool track* (London 1910), and *The dreadnought of the Darling* (London 1911).

In 1910 Bean went to England as the London correspondent for the *Sydney Morning Herald*, returning to Sydney early in 1913. His parents left England for Hobart in December 1913. Charles was now leader-writing for the *Herald*. When the war broke out he undertook a 'War Notes' column. He, like almost everyone else, thought it would not be too long before Britain and her Allies defeated the German menace. A few days after his appointment as official correspondent, he wrote to his mother that he expected to be away '12 months or so' with the expeditionary force.[3] This confidence was reflected in his decision to pack French and German dictionaries and a Rhine guidebook in his luggage.

A special niche was carved for him in the expeditionary force. He would remain a civilian but could wear a close copy (minus badges) of an officer's uniform and would be regarded as an honorary captain in the mess. The Army undertook to supply him with a batman, a horse and rations. His £600 salary (set at that of a major) and expenses were to be met by a levy on those newspapers which used his articles. Initially papers were charged for each article they took, but later were charged a fixed annual subscription arranged on a sliding scale according to the city in which they were published.

Great things were hoped for from the Australian troops . . . and their press correspondent. As the force prepared to sail one paper wrote:

> No journalist in Australia, or, one may venture to say, elsewhere, has a more picturesque and graphic style in describing scenes of peace, and the spirit animating his fine book, "Flagships Three", . . . is sufficient assurance that he will be equally at home in writing of war.[4]

Bean was now a 34-year-old bachelor. His press correspondent's licence described him as 5 feet 11½ inches tall, of slight build, with red hair, blue eyes and glasses. The troops soon dubbed him 'Captain Carrot'.

Bean was one of three press correspondents to witness the

landings on 25 April. Their presence was in direct contrast to the strict embargo prohibiting journalists from the Western Front. Lord Kitchener, British Secretary for War, was highly suspicious of the press and flatly refused to allow correspondents to be attached to the armies in France. Sir Ian Hamilton, the Commander-in-Chief of the Mediterranean Expeditionary Force, did not share these suspicions and, unlike most of his peers, consciously strove to foster amiable relations with the press. Bean and the representative from the London dailies, Ellis Ashmead Bartlett, watched the ANZAC operations while the other English correspondent, Lester Lawrence, followed events at Cape Helles. From the outset, Bean established a work routine totally unlike that of either of his English counterparts. They spent most of these early days aboard the warships, watching the battles from a safe distance and relying heavily on the reports from GHQ and interviews with the evacuated wounded. Bean, on the other hand, went ashore at the first opportunity. One result of this was that he tended to view the campaign more from the standpoint of the frontline soldier than from the somewhat detached perspective common among staff officers. It is revealing of Bean's approach that he is rarely mentioned in the diaries of other Gallipoli correspondents and fails to appear at all in the published diary of Sir Ian Hamilton. Moreover, it might not be coincidence that of the twelve journalists who reported on the campaign, only Bean was wounded at all seriously.

Several factors account for his singular approach. First, and probably most important, he worked on Gallipoli in the manner he knew best. People fascinated him. He moved around Anzac Cove observing and talking with men much as he had roved across New South Wales collecting information for his articles. The characteristics he perceived in the soldiers tallied with what had so impressed him in earlier years with the men of the outback. This could only have further encouraged him to stick by his methodology. Encouragement came also from a somewhat unlikely source, Major-General William Bridges, the Commander of the 1st Australian Division. Bean later wrote of Bridges:

> he treated me throughout as one of his staff except in this, that he gave me no orders & left me free to write & do what I pleased . . . I obtained a chance such as no journalist in this war, or probably any other, has had of going absolutely where he liked, in the line (or indeed in front of the line, if I had wanted) without any restriction so long as I was with our own troops.[5]

Another factor which may have played an important role in forming his routine was the imposition of an embargo on his writing in the first phase of the campaign. It was planned for the first convoy to sail to England, but during the voyage the ships were rerouted to Egypt. Bean's press licence gave him authorisation only for the voyage to England. Therefore, when the force landed in Egypt, he had to seek a new licence. This problem was still unresolved when the troops set off for the Dardanelles. Bean was granted permission to accompany the force only on condition that he refrain from despatching any articles until the licence question had been settled by the authorities in London. Thus, Bean went ashore knowing that he would not be sending any stories for some days. There was little point in his writing copy which would be outdated once authorisation was finally granted. Hence, while Bartlett and Lawrence (both of whom were authorised from the outset) battled to outscoop each other, Bean had to make do with watching rather than writing. This must have been infuriatingly frustrating for a journalist observing the greatest single event in the history of his nation; yet it gave him the opportunity of gaining a familiarity with the pattern of events which no other correspondent approached. By the time he received authority to publish, he had established a daily routine that might never have evolved had he been empowered to send copy from the first day of landing.

Bean's method on Gallipoli also reflected his perception of the function of the war correspondent in modern war. While he held strongly that the correspondent should be briefed as fully as possible on events at the front, he did not agree with those who contended that it was the journalist's place to question authority or criticise strategy. Bean firmly maintained that his rightful role was to report, not criticise. Nor did he see it as his place to sensationalise his copy or 'scoop' his fellow correspondents on any story. He kept to these principles throughout the war. Thus, he advised his assistant in December 1917 that the duty of the Australian official correspondent:

> is to give Australia a knowledge of what the men and officers of the force are doing, and what is really happening in the war as far as they are concerned in it consistently [*sic*] with (1) not giving information to the enemy (2) not needlessly distressing their families at home.
>
> The rule of the censorship also forbids criticism.[6]

Of course, his desire to report the daily lives of the men rather than rely heavily on official communiqués from GHQ placed large demands on Bean's time. It required that he visit the frontline whenever possible, as well as liaise with HQ, and write regular articles and cables for the morning and evening papers. In addition, he had set himself the mission of keeping a diary.

Before leaving Australia Bean had discussed with the Government the possibility of his writing an official history of Australia's part in the war. The idea remained with him throughout the long years of the war. He kept the diary as 'a detailed note of what I saw, heard and thought'[7] in the hope that it might one day form the basis for his history, and, with this end in mind, he had packed 'a plentiful supply of notebooks'[8] in his luggage. He was not to know that over the next four and a quarter years his diary and notes would fill 283 such books! His dated diaries number about 120.

The diary was usually written up at night from shorthand notes he had taken in the line during the day. Often the entries were written either in poor light or darkness and were thus most untidy. In such cases he would later transcribe them into small notebooks or school exercise books. When transcribing, he frequently added fresh comments, reflections, sketches and maps. Thus, while the diaries generally gave a day-by-day account of events, they often also contained his more considered judgments. 'Often, especially at Gallipoli,' he reflected later, 'I sat at my diary during most of the night because that was the time of least interruption. Sometimes daylight found me still at it — occasionally, by some strange process of mental effort, falling asleep at each full stop and then waking to write each successive sentence.'[9]

His prodigious output was made possible only by the great assistance given him by his batman, young Arthur Bazley. The two first met only a few weeks before the first convoy sailed. Bean had mentioned to his friend and fellow journalist, Archie Whyte, that he would require an assistant to type his articles and perform other clerical duties. Whyte suggested Bazley, an eighteen-year-old junior clerk at the *Argus*. Bean found him 'a youngster who is awfully keen to go — who was a boy scout & a good cook, knows how to look after a horse, [&] is a gunner in the artillery . . .'[10] But there was a problem: the minimum enlistment age was nineteen and Bazley's father was opposed to his boosting his age. Bean duly visited the recruiting office and arranged for Bazley to state he was the requisite nineteen years old.

Bean could not have chosen a more diligent or loyal assistant. When in 1917, for example, Bazley was offered a safe job in

Bean's diaries and notebooks (almost 300 volumes) laid out for work on the *Official history*. In the background, his staff A.W. Bazley (left) and J. Balfour. (AWM neg. no. H19501)

London working with AIF Records Section, he confessed in his diary: 'Although I would like it, I feel I ought to be over in France with Capt. Bean... I would only take it on if I were likely to assist Capt. Bean by doing so'. He did eventually accept the position, but only after Bean had persuaded him to do so. Bazley's admiration for Bean is perhaps best summed up by a comment, made early in 1917, when Bean decided to produce a book of his war articles and donate all profits to a fund for blind Australian soldiers. Bazley noted in his diary: 'He is a white man, if ever there was one'.[11]

Bazley's assessment was shared by almost everyone who watched Bean in action. Peter Schuler, the *Age* correspondent who sailed with Bean aboard the *Orvieto*, wrote later that Bean 'of all men was the most enthusiastic, painstaking, and conscientious worker that I have ever met'. Keith Murdoch, another Australian journalist who briefly visited Gallipoli, echoed Schuler's tribute:

> I have seen [Bean] . . . at work, and heard his work discussed by those who, in their work of directing our armies, find it of the utmost service. No accounts of actions could be more accurate than his — no description of the men's suffering and gallantry could be more sympathetic. He is always in the place where he can see and help most, however dangerous it may be.

At least one Australian soldier was equally impressed by Bean's bravery. A signaller from Western Australia wrote home after seeing Bean during the night attack at Cape Helles on 8 May: 'There are some heroes in this world, and Bean ... and [the Australian medical officer] Dr. Matheson [*sic*] are two of them ... [Bean] is an honour to Australian journalists'.[12]

Nor was such praise forthcoming only from Australians. One British field censorship officer who oversaw much of Bean's work in France believed the official Australian correspondent had a special facility to 'bring out the relation of facts to humanity ... Mr Bean's cables were perfect; he would watch a battle from a shell hole with his notebook in hand, and he would describe the special features of each fight like an impressionist painter.'[13]

The great integrity which shone through Bean's approach to war correspondence arose out of his total dedication both to the work and the men he was reporting on. This commitment made him persevere when others might have flagged, and drove him into dangerous, exposed locations on the battelfield simply because he chose to stay with the troops. However, although it was also widely believed that Bean's work displayed an absolute devotion to truth, this claim seems open to challenge. Bean himself admitted in 1917:

> The correspondent ... has to take very great care not to write matter which may be valuable to the enemy even though the censor might not realize it. A change of date or place (which is immaterial to the facts related) sometimes makes it safe to relate facts which if given with the true date and place would be dangerous.[14]

A more significant criticism is that he was often selective in what he presented as truth. As his ship was steaming towards Imbros in early April, Bean wrote a note of warning for newspaper readers back in Australia: 'it is quite possible that my letters & cables during some periods in the next few months may have to deal with safe subjects quite apart from news. There are certain periods in a war when the publication of news could become so risky that it is best suppressed altogether.'[15] At several later points in his diary we can sense the moral dilemma he experienced when forced to choose between truth, devotion to the Empire, and loyalty to its often incompetent military leaders. He invariably chose to keep his criticisms to himself.

In self-censoring his work, Bean was no different from most of the other war correspondents of the Great War. Few ever attempted to expose the futility of the carnage or the appalling leadership they so often saw at the head of the armies. Ashmead Bartlett and Keith Murdoch did try in September 1915, but even they sought to do so first through official, rather than public channels, and achieved a measure of success only because senior British politicians were sympathetic to their wish to see the Gallipoli campaign ended. In the main, the correspondents were prisoners of their profession and times. For the previous half century, war and war correspondence had been seen by the British as a jolly adventure, full of bravado and romance. More often than not, the war correspondents of 1914–18 tried to maintain the image of old, even when this meant grossly distorting the horror which confronted them. They went along with the earlier tradition, firm in the belief that the people at home should be spared the gruesome actuality of modern attrition warfare. Their silence served only to make the field censors' task more easy, and the soldiers', more severe.

Not everyone was impressed by Bean's apparent commitment to accuracy and detail. Some found his style too clinical, lacking the colour which people liked to associate with battle. A *Bulletin* correspondent, for example, thought Bean's articles 'as precise a specimen of journalistic horology as I have ever seen'. The writer cited one article in which paragraphs began '3.45, 3.50, 3.57':

> there wasn't a thrill in a column of it. It ended with the . . . detached and impersonal statement that owing to his having been wounded he would have to leave until later the verification of certain details. Such a man could do algebra while Rome was burning . . . [D]espite his slickness in getting the news, Bean pants bravely along the track with a millstone about his neck and a padlock on his soul.[16]

Bean was well aware of such criticism and admitted there might be some truth in it (see p. 156). It was yet another illustration of the romantic flavour still associated with war. Possibly his regard for detail and accuracy was a residue from his legal training.[17] No matter what its origin, he had the good sense to accept that he could not, nor should, attempt to alter his style radically by over-dramatising his copy. In any case, on most of the occasions that an Australian newspaper did criticise his methods, it subsequently received at least as many letters praising Bean as attacking him.

There are other points where Bean's work on the Peninsula might be questioned. In view of his well-known dedication to observing battle 'at the sharp end', it comes as something of a surprise to read that he visited Quinn's Post for the first time on 24 May — a full month after the landing. Quinn's was the hottest spot in the line, with the distance between the opposing trenches sometimes as little as six yards. Situated at the head of Monash Valley, Quinn's was generally regarded as holding the key to the entire Anzac Cove area. Why Bean took so long to visit it remains a puzzle.

The diary reveals time and again the special bond Bean felt with the 1st Division, AIF. In many ways this close association was to be expected: Bean had left Australia with the 1st Division and hence knew its officers better than those of later convoys. More importantly, the officer commanding 1st Division (Major-General Bridges) was also in charge of the entire AIF. Bean, it should be remembered, was able to land on Gallipoli only by becoming attached to Bridges' staff. He built his dugout close to 1st Div. HQ. Consequently, he spent more time mixing with 1st Div. than with other AIF units. Rarely, by comparison, did he visit 4th Brigade on the left flank. Certainly he was far less familiar with its officers, and this possibly clouded his judgment of their performance in the August offensive.

Anyone reading this diary should keep in mind the statement of caveat (see p. 22) which Bean insisted be attached to each volume when he deposited the diaries in the Australian War Memorial. The diaries were never intended to be, and should not be read as a definitive account of the campaigns. But they are probably the pre-eminent record of the Gallipoli campaign. The Peninsula theatre was so confined, especially at Anzac Cove, that both sides could scarcely avoid becoming familiar with the habits of the enemy. Bean, like the soldier in the line, developed a familiarity and respect for 'Johnny Turk' which could rarely occur across the much wider No-Man's Land on the Western Front. This facility, even if limited, to develop some feel for the whole front is only one of the Bean diaries' many special features.

As the official Australian war correspondent, Bean was uniquely placed to observe the campaign. Unlike correspondents from specific newspapers, he was answerable neither to editor nor proprietor. He could roam virtually at will through the lines and report on what took his fancy. His bravery at the front and keen attention to detail quickly won him the confidence of officers and men alike, and he frequently became privy to the hopes and doubts of those around him.

Many soldiers at Gallipoli kept diaries. Bean's is different in one crucial respect. He was paid to write, not fight. In his role as participant observer, Bean was frequently able to detach himself from his surroundings and analyse his emotions in a manner rarely available to the soldier under fire: his descriptions, for instance, of his first experiences of shrapnel and rifle fire are highly graphic. Soldiers would generally write their diaries during lulls in battle. Bean, by comparison, was expected to record the action. On occasions he drove himself to write much as the fatigued soldier motivated himself to continue fighting. The level of detail falls away slightly only at the August offensive, precisely because Bean suffered the fate of a soldier and was wounded. As soon as his strength returned, he went out collecting notes, unit by unit, to rectify the gap in his records.

Many factors suggested to me that this book should limit itself to the twenty-five diaries covering the period October 1914 to December 1915. My selections constitute possibly one-quarter of the material written in those diaries. I rejected the idea of condensing all 120 diaries into one volume as this would have necessitated editing on a scale that could not possibly have retained the essence of the great task Bean had set for himself in keeping the diary. Furthermore, there are significant differences between his lifestyle and diary on Gallipoli and later in the war. In France Bean lived at a chateau with the other correspondents and travelled to the front. His experience of life in the line and the 700 photographs he took on the Peninsula and earlier are only two of many features which distinguish Gallipoli from the Western Front. When the AIF moved to France it was supplied with official photographers and artists to document its activities. No such facilities were available when the first convoy left Australia nor, for that matter, on Gallipoli, so Bean took it upon himself to compile a photographic record of the campaign. All the photographs reproduced in this book were taken by Bean, unless there is a statement to the contrary. We thus have a unique visual and written record of one man's war.

Gallipoli is also of pre-eminent importance as it was the first great test both for the AIF and Bean. It was here that the traditions of the AIF were forged. It was also here that Bean established his reputation as a war correspondent of the first order. The impact of the campaign on developing Australian notions of nationalism has been widely discussed by historians. Some contend it forged Australia into a nation, others claim it only cemented the existing bond to Britain and her Empire. Bean took to the war popular British middle-class ideas about war, sacrifice, racism, and imperialism, as would have most of the officers and many of the men in the AIF. Gallipoli sharpened his belief in what he saw as the specifically Australian values and characteristics of egalitarianism, a strong democratic spirit, and a national sense of sturdy self-sufficiency. Whatever the changes in perception the war may have wrought in Bean — as in other Australians — clearly there could be no return to the political and social assumptions of pre-war Australia.

There can be no hard and fast rules governing selection criteria for a book of this kind. Often I was uncertain exactly why a particular passage seemed to justify inclusion. I just knew it had to be there! Having said this, I was conscious of several self-imposed, loose guidelines as I worked through the diaries. First, I did not want the book to read like a potted version of Bean's *Official history*. It was, of course, necessary to include much military detail but, in the main, I have included personalised entries ahead of historical and operational details collected essentially for an official history. Readers may, nevertheless, care to compare his diary entries with accounts proffered in the *Official history*.

A second criterion was to select extracts which tell us something about Bean the man: in particular his attitudes to Australia, Britain, and the Empire. The genesis of Bean's Anzac Legend lay in his travels through outback New South Wales and the books he wrote pre-1914 about those experiences. Gallipoli clarified his thoughts. The process of exploration and confirmation can be traced clearly through the pages of his diary. By the time he left the Peninsula his ideas on the Australian *vis-à-vis* the British character and future prospects for the Empire were set in clear focus.

I have deliberately striven to keep my editorial intervention to a minimum, allowing wherever possible the continuity to flow from my extract selection procedures. Throughout the extracts from the diaries textual annotations appear in square brackets. As anyone who cares to read the page reproduced from the original diary (see p. 203) will be aware, Bean used his own system of abbreviations when writing. This shorthand has been reconstituted and occasional grammatical slips corrected wherever I felt ambiguity might otherwise arise. On the whole, however, his variations in abbreviations and spelling have been allowed to stand. I have, however, corrected misspelt names except where alternative spellings were given and it has not been possible positively to identify the person referred to.

Bean deposited his Great War diaries and papers in the Australian War Memorial in 1942 upon completion of the last of his six volumes in the series *The official history of Australia in the war of 1914–1918*. The diaries and other material in the Bean collection were first made available to the public in 1979. They may be read in the Library at the Australian War Memorial, Canberra. Three pages of the Gallipoli diary (9 November) remain closed to the public under Australian Archives' regulations.

Bean died on 30 August 1968. A few years earlier, he had toyed with the idea of producing a book of extracts from the diaries entitled 'Unofficial history'.[18] Old age and his activities in other fields have denied us this book. My hope is that the book I have produced does justice to this remarkable man and his work.

Readers should be aware of the following note which Bean insisted be attached to each volume of his diary:

These writings represent only what at the moment of making them I believed to be true. The diaries were jotted down almost daily with the object of recording what was then in the writer's mind. Often he wrote them when very tired and half asleep; also, not infrequently, what he believed to be true was not so — but it does not follow that he always discovered this, or remembered to correct the mistakes when discovered. Indeed, he could not always remember that he had written them.

These records should, therefore, be used with great caution, as relating only what their author, at the time of writing, believed. Further, he cannot, of course, vouch for the accuracy of statements made to him by others and here recorded. But he did try to ensure such accuracy by consulting, as far as possible, those who had seen or otherwise taken part in the events. The constant falsity of second-hand evidence (on which a large proportion of war stories are founded) was impressed upon him by the second or third day of the Gallipoli campaign, notwithstanding that those who passed on such stories usually themselves believed them to be true. All second-hand evidence herein should be read with this in mind.

16 Sept. 1946 C.E.W. Bean

1

Australia Will Be There

ON 3 August 1914, as the threat of war in Europe loomed, the Australian Government notified Britain that it was willing to despatch an expeditionary force of 20 000 men should the need arise. The offer was accepted with gratitude. In September, while this contingent was still being raised and trained in Australia, the British War Office invited each Dominion to attach an official press correspondent to its force. George Pearce, the Minister for Defence, asked the Australian Journalists' Association to nominated a representative for the position. The Association organised a ballot of members which Bean, then writing for the *Sydney Morning Herald*, won narrowly.

It had been intended that the Australian contingent, named the Australian Imperial Force, with its New Zealand counterpart of 8 000 men, would sail for England in early October. Bean and Arthur Bazley, his eighteen-year-old assistant, were to leave with this convoy. However, several German warships, the *Scharnhorst*, *Gneisnau*, *Konigsburg* and *Emden*, were known to be cruising somewhere in the waters around Australia. Consequently, the departure of the troop ships was postponed until adequate naval convoy escort vessels could be provided. The convoy was to rendezvous in King George's Sound, off Albany, Western Australia.

Bean and Bazley were assigned to make the voyage on the Orient liner, *Orvieto*, with General Bridges and his staff of the 1st Australian Division. The 36-ship convoy would be escorted to Europe by the RAN light cruisers, *Sydney* and *Melbourne*, the Royal Navy cruiser, *Minotaur*, and the Japanese cruiser, *Ibuki*.

October 21

Said goodbye to mother at "Northampton", 27 Acland Street.[1] Taxied to Port Melbourne with father taking luggage... Archie Whyte and father came to Port Melbourne, and after being held up on pier managed get on to wharf through Colonel Wallace and

Major Dowse. Father left at 1.10 with Archie. Crowd in afternoon broke line of sentries and rushed wharf. Sailed at three. Watched St. Kilda pier for father and mother and thought I saw them waving a white handkerchief...

October 26
Reached Albany, wind rising... Eighteen ships were in port when we came in — in lines about 6 in each. We three made 21. Two or three arrived since...

October 27
Moved into harbour — coaling. Spent most of day writing...

October 28
At about 9 a.m., moving out of the inner harbour we noticed one, two, three — 13 distant ships on the horizon. They were clearly the New Zealand transports and convoy which New Zealand had demanded to bring them over. One smoking heavily moved in first, close under hills to west. She had a Japanese flag — *Ibuki* — a much thicker set ship than any of ours in the Pacific except the *Australia* — broad funnels (3?). She anchored close under the hills...

October 29
Censorship of letters established in consequence of orders from Melbourne... Letters must not bear date or name of place. Unless letters from Albany also are censored this won't be much good. Papers have already had composition of this force and New Zealand force. *Sydney M. Herald* had names of transports if I remember right (or most of them), still its perhaps better late than never...[2]

October 31
21 men taken ashore tonight for refusing to be vaccinated!!! 35 sick (mostly those men found to have syphilis)[3]...

November 1, Sunday
This day at 6 a.m. we up anchored. Schuler[4] and I went to bed very late; he was up first and called me. Ship was getting in anchor as I went up on deck. *Minotaur* and *Melbourne* already moving out. We steamed slowly down line... The *Southern* was dressed when we passed her, but we weren't dressed in spite of the fact that a convoy order had been given that ships were to be at attention

when passing other ships. This was hurriedly made good; troops were called to attention (in the bows — they couldn't hear down in the stern), when passing some of the other ships. No New Zealand ships observed any formality. I don't mind betting the *Euripides* will have stood to attention and had the ship properly lined with men. One can't help thinking a lot is omitted that might be done to give the men in this flagship a pride in themselves. There was a great chance in Albany to get a spirit of competition going between this ship and others which would have interested the men and given them a right pride in themselves as Victorians and Australians, especially as against the New Zealand people. MacLaurin and MacNaghten in the *Euripides* have done something of the sort — you bet they would, and I would stake a good deal on theirs being the smartest battalions when we land. But we seem to miss these opportunities through not thinking of them. They ought surely to encourage the Victorian troops to think themselves the best. They are splendid chaps, most of them — both officers and men...

Left:
Some of the well-wishers who broke through the military guard at Port Melbourne pier before the *Orvieto* sailed, 21 October 1914. (AWM neg. no. G1539)

Right:
Peter Schuler, the *Age* special correspondent, standing on a Pyramid, New Year's Day 1915. Beneath him is Mena Camp. (AWM neg. no. G1651)

We altered course about 7. De Bucy told me earlier in the day that we were making for South Africa. Afterwards he told me the course had been altered 2 hours after he had mentioned it to me and we were now going to Colombo. I don't know how far this is authentic...

One can hardly realise that we are off now on a really huge, hazardous experiment. There is distinctly a hazard in it... The Admiralty — no doubt rightly — has decided to take such chances as exist. Any day or night, later on, we may meet the *Emden*; or the *Konigsberg*, if she is still in this ocean and cares to take a sporting chance... [It was known that the *Scharnhorst* and *Gneisnau* had left the area.]

November 2

News of war being declared by England and Russia on Turkey. Shall we be stopped in Egypt?...

November 7

Today at dinner, after the King's toast (proposed by the General), Captain Gordon Smith proposed sweethearts and wives. As we were sitting in the lounge after dinner the lights in the whole ship went out. This was done in ours and every other ship for $\frac{1}{2}$ hour; in order to practise steaming absolutely without lights. The lights were cut off in the engine room. The men immediately tumbled up on deck to their stations and stood there. Even cigarettes and pipes had to be put out, by order from the bridge. It was quite difficult to make one's way along deck. I trod on several bare toes, and finally climbed up to the smoking room roof. The fleet was in absolute darkness except for an occasional signal light...

November 8, Sunday

A cruiser of the enemy might guess we should go this way and wait for us here. Accordingly the *Melbourne* is showing no light and instructions have been given to the ships to show none either. So far, the result has not been very successful. The difficulty is to convince people like the smoking room steward in this ship or the men (or even most of the officers) in any of them that there is any need for precaution. I doubt if anything short of keeping them standing on parade would prevent a man from striking matches if he wanted to light his pipe. The *Euripides* looked like a floating hotel till her lower deck lights went out at 9.30...

November 9
Slept on deck last night in case anything were seen of the *Emden*. A beautiful night — quite a bright moon. At midnight the lights on the other ships had disappeared and only the dark hulls of the convoy and the black smoke of the Japanese ship could be seen. The air was beautifully mild. The only sound was the "fist fist" of some valve in the engine room and the occasional noises of the stokehold. Woke at 5.30. An exquisite rosy fingered dawn — the faint pink and blue distances behind the grey clouds...

At breakfast a rumour was going round the table. "If it were true, they wouldn't let it out," said someone. "No, I suppose it's a leakage." "The *Sydney's* gone off, anyway," said another. However — it was true. By the end of breakfast I heard that a warship had been sighted on the other side of the Cocos [Island, some fifty miles west of the convoy].

Officers gathered in groups outside the saloon entrance on the port side of the promenade deck. There was by this time no trace of the *Sydney* although officers were continually searching the skyline in that direction with their field glasses. The question was: would the *Sydney* find the warship (we could get no news of whether it was the *Emden* and whether the calls were to other German warships — she might be meeting the *Konigsberg* or the merchant cruiser supposed to be in these waters) and how she would get on if she did find her?

At about 9.40 it gradually went round that the *Sydney* had signalled that she had sighted the enemy. About a quarter of an hour [later] I heard someone say something about "fighting". Then "Yes, the *Sydney's* in action now — she's signalled us to say she is fighting them."

Just then we noticed that the *Melbourne* was moving out from ahead of us into a position out on the port side. She was passing fairly close to us when somebody said, "Look at the *Ibuki*." The Japanese ship was moving up on the other side of us, where she was stationed, in order to cross our bows and get on the port side of us also. She was stoking up; the smoke was pouring from her funnels thicker than ever — the wind carried it away from us so that the ship appeared nestled into the black masses of it. She passed us a few minutes later — prepared for action. Her decks were naked — a few white figures were clearing away or fastening down the last few encumberances. Her upperworks — both bridges, and I think, the fire control stations were neatly padded with rolled hammocks. One huge Japanese ensign was flying at the peak planted fair against the black smoke cloud. And just as she passed us she broke from the mainmast head a second great ensign of the rising sun — her battle flag. She was moving fast by this time — punching great masses of white out of the rich dark sea, spreading the seas wide on either side of her bluff bows as she went. There were few men showing about her — one or two white figures trotted up the gangway to the bridge. A little later someone noticed that the big guns were being moved. One knew by that that the guns crews were in the turrets going through the normal preliminary to going into action — testing the turret gear and the guns...

About the time when the *Ibuki* and *Melbourne* were reaching their final position we learnt that the *Sydney* had reported that the chase was making off to the northward. This would bring her, as it happened, straight into the convoy. This was why the *Melbourne* and the *Ibuki* had taken up their position between us and the point from where the enemy would first be seen...

We lounged over the rail like spectators in the gallery looking down over the glassy sea — the transports steaming steadily on their course at their usual snail's pace. Just over the horizon someone was being done to death, in the midst of crashing steel work, burning decks, sudden flashes of flame. We ought to see something of it at any moment. The ordinary training of the ship was going on on the deck below us and on the boat deck too, exactly as if there were no cruiser nor anything close within a thousand miles of us. The men knew something was happening — but not many knew any details. A friend of Peter Schuler would come up to us every now and then during a stand easy in the work. "Hey, Peter" — then when Peter nodded — "What do you know, eh?", he asked in a stage whisper.

About 11.15 we heard that the fight was practically over. The enemy had been stopped before she even came within sight of us. "Enemy run ashore to save sinking", said the message...

Early in the afternoon one heard a series of cheers bursting out from under various parts of the awning foreward and aft like so many exploding shells. The message had come through at last. "*Emden* beached and done for"... Later came a much louder cheer. The men had got a half holiday. So it was the *Emden*. Her business had been finished in about 25 minutes that morning — done whilst we waited...

It was all very sudden, this fight in the morning — the *Sydney* had raced off, killed them, and was ready to return as swiftly as a terrier would kill a cat...

November 15, Sunday
The land was in sight from the first light... Reached Colombo at about 2... Took a boat off to the *Sydney*...

Capt. Glossop told us . . . [there was] no objection to our coming on board and getting the story provided
(1) We got it only from officers and did not publish anything that we got from the men.
(2) We sent it by letter to Australia, and did not send either by cable or to the local papers anything that we got...

After getting the facts as far as they can be known we had supper on board and came back to the *Orvieto*... I stayed up dictating to Bazley until 3.30 and then turned in...

November 16
Finished two articles (morning 2, evening 3) by 3 p.m. and got [them] away just in time to catch the 3.30 shore boat[5]...

Several local people spoke rather feelingly about the behaviour of the New Zealanders in town last night and we certainly saw numbers of them laid out in all directions on the landing stage. They have only dry canteens and they are liable to break out at every port they come to...

November 17
Today at 11.30 we sailed...

November 21
All sorts of reports today. One is that we land at Suez or Port Said to fight the Turks. Schuler tells me no arrangements have yet been made for this voyage beyond Suez or Port Said, and that we definitely stop at Aden...

November 23
Began letters for papers and posted diary up to November 17th... Sent it to father marked confidential and only to be shown to close relations who are not likely to repeat what they read there...

November 25
Slept on deck. On waking up at about 5.30 saw land very faintly outlined ahead — one big peak of it, and presently a coast line to starboard — also mountainous. That coast was an enemy's country; the hill ahead was Aden... [The *Orvieto* docked later that morning.]

Glasfurd took me through part of Aden after lunch picking out the various types as we passed them. He has fought and hunted in Somaliland and knows India and it is wonderful with what certainty a man who knows them like that can pick out the various types. "That chap is a Somali — lazy beggars but good shikarris; this fellow is an Arab — they are magnificently made men; this old bird is some sort of a Greek or Armenian or a half breed dago; that old bird in the shop door who took off his hat is a Parsee, Mr Somethingjee Jeejeeboy. That man driving the taxi is a native of India; these two fellows with their beards parted and tied up are Sikhs, Muabee Sikhs — pioneers, the highest caste of Sikh will not do manual labour. That thin chap with the fair yellow skin and long hair I expect is a Persian."

Certainly the Arabs are magnificently made chaps — with legs beautifully moulded like Fijians — not a match stick stuck into a boot like the average Indian. He is almost fair — yellow, except when much exposed to the sun when he becomes black; and his smile is invariably bordered with heavy lines running from his eye right to his chin. We haven't many Arab soldiers, but the French have, and they must be excellent.

It is curious that of all these chaps the one who seemed far more akin to us than any other was the Indian. It may be that he is a colonist here like ourselves, or that he is the most educated and belongs to a half-western civilisation when he comes from places like Bombay. Whatever the reason one could not help classifying the taxi driver with ourselves — one of the occupying race in a region of half savages...

November 26
Early this day we left Aden...

November 27
I have decided to make this diary my chief personal record of the war. A classification of items under subjects — such as I generally make — is not suitable for this job — not yet at any rate. The diary has drawbacks; but after all, where the events are mainly historical, and later events put the nose of earlier events out of joint, the diary form is useful. Generally I have had to describe and explain merely a state of affairs which have already become facts — the wool trade; the life in the bush or on the rivers. Here it is a series of new facts every day. There are strong points against a diary. It is not always easy to find from it the facts you want when you are afterwards writing up some particular subject e.g. our men — the British officer — the problem of our sea-transport. It would be

easier to write these things up if at the time when the points are noted they were noted under that heading (as I have usually done). I try to do this too. But the main record, I can see, will be most conveniently kept in diary form.

The chief drawback is — as I have found ever since I joined the press — that writing or acquiring information takes so much of my time that I have almost ceased to read. Other ways of learning have to take the place of reading. I have been writing almost ever since we left Aden, and tomorrow I shall have to start getting together the facts to be written up the following days and posted at Suez. Since Colombo I haven't had one day at the Roman novel and have only read one book. Well — one can't have everything. It is a great life and after all one is learning half the time even if not from books.

November 28

As I was coming up from breakfast this morning I heard that a conference was held at 2 a.m. at which it had been decided to land in Egypt...

Undoubtedly this is wise. It will save at least three weeks of sea voyage alone — will probably come cheaper in ship hire — will give us at least two hours more of daylight every day for training — and save us at least two or three days per week on which the weather would have made it impossible to do any useful training in England — our men will spend the worst of the winter in a climate they are accustomed to and we shall probably save about 300 horses at the very least. Above all we shall begin to count as of value from the day we reach Egypt — the spectacle of 30 000 white troops marching in all in one body with guns and everything complete (probably the best equipped force that has ever left any country) can't help affecting the Egyptians who only know an army of occupation of 6 000 in peace time; and if the Turks do come along we are there with the Indian troops, a pretty considerable army, to defend the canal, which the Turks would have to reach across 100 miles of desert...

Final test match, Australia v England on boat deck. We crumbled in the first innings and England won easily...

November 30

At 3.30 we entered the [Suez] canal... We had about 2½ hours of light before us ... and we began to see the defences of it before we had gone a mile. On the right hand side, opposite the first of the canal company's stations, was a row of white tents cuddled about

Bean changed into his war correspondent's rig as soon as he heard the contingent would be disembarking in Egypt. Photograph by Peter Schuler. (AWM neg. no. G1561)

half way up the bank... On the bank were several Native Indian soldiers, some of them digging with shovels. Our men began cheering and cooeeing as we came up to the fort and at once the whole camp was alive to the fact that a troopship was passing; they came racing across the enclosure in strings from huts and tents, as fast as they could go, to the top of the bank. I think at first they thought it might be more troops from India, white or native. When they found it was the Australians they cheered and our men cheered and cooeed and they cheered again until the cooees and cheers got out of range of one another. A signaller was wagging a flag for all he was worth — "Good luck to you boys" — a message from the British officer in charge. As we passed along the canal, at every few miles we found a post like this on the Eastern bank...

All through the night (except for a spell before midnight when we were moving through the bitter lakes) we were passing at intervals these little fortified posts on the canal side... The same scene happened again and again through the night — always about a company of silent tall dark figures which turned out at once on the sight of a soldier; and always a white chap — generally he seemed a mere boy — shepherding his flock of warriors...

December 1

In the hurry that followed this — packing, landing, getting into camp, arranging for cables, and the preparation of a pamphlet for the troops (to be published by one of the newspapers — at first I thought the staff would do it as it contains rules of health, places to go to etc.; but it took me too long) I have let this diary go for a month. This is the first long break in it. I have always before written it up either on the day with which it deals, or within two, three, or four days... [All profits from the sale of the booklet, *What to know in Egypt ... a guide for Australasian soldiers*, went to the Red Cross Society.]

December 3

Early this morning we were off Alexandria and entered about breakfast time... There were a few natives on the quay; and here it was we first had an object lesson of the way in which native policemen in this country deal with crowds. Some seller of newspapers or drinks managed to get through the line of sentries and disobeyed the policeman to an extent which he considered above the limit — so he went for him like a tiger. He had a short horsewhip of cane or hide in his hand; and he fairly lathered the man with it. Hit him over the head, arms, and body, kicked him, pushed him, hit him until one would have thought he would be really badly hurt. The men in the *Orvieto*, who were all watching like a crowded gallery, couldn't understand this sort of thing at all. They called out to the policeman to stop, and really their temper began to be worked up to a pretty high pitch... It seems almost the only way of dealing with the rabble here. They have no restraint and no morality of our sort; and although they have considerable virtues of their own you are apt to get disaster when people with their morality meet with people of our morality unless the two are kept apart by a hard and fast division. The two moralities overlap as it were; they are slack in some things where we are strict. And our people coming into contact with that slackness are apt to go all to the dogs unless the distance between the two is maintained. It is interesting to see how after a little stay here, that distance creates itself. Our men were cheek by jowl with the natives when they landed — as any good democratic Australian would be. I was inclined to be so myself. Within a month or two the trouble, if any, is that we are inclined to be too intolerant of them...

We disembarked about three in the afternoon into a train which was standing almost alongside of us... This country we went through out of Cairo was full of sights that were as strange as a picture show to Australians. Low pasture cut up into little squares by low dry irrigation furrows — all as a Chinaman's garden. Occasional high grey mud dykes wandering across the country like long black dusty snakes; and stalking along the top of them, often silhouetted against the sky, like figures on the frieze of a wallpaper, a constant stream of people that might have stepped out of the bible; tall peasants whose dress seemed to consist of a towel wrapped round their head and a long blue cotton night gown; big fat proprietors with rich coloured cloaks over their white under shirts, riding solemnly on white asses; women as straight as those that sometimes bear up the roof beams of a Greek temple, draped in one flowing dress of black with earthenware pitchers on their heads and hiding half their face with their hood as we passed — when they had not a yashmak. Small boys squatted on dusty black buffaloes which looked as though their home were the mud and they were sorry they ever left it; camels loaded on either side with such huge parcels of Berseen (native lucerne), or maize, or sugar cane, that it looked as though a small haystack had somehow come to life, and had managed to get a camel's head and tail attached to it; small weedy duncoloured native cattle; occasionally an Arab horse, very poor, but with a prettily arched tail and neck which even when their ribs are sticking out gives them a certain beauty when first you see them. Every now and then we passed an old dry grey dust heap with a few rags fluttering about it, which if you did not see that various humps in the heap contained windows and that there seemed to be a maze of passages though it, you would take to be the dump about some mine, or the dry mud thrown up alongside a dam. These were native villages — and even after two months in the country it is still a mystery to one what sort of existence these people manage to support there.

It was dark before we reached Cario... The streets of Cairo, with their dazzling electric lights, big white shop fronts, gardens of palms, clang of trams, and clatter of cabs along the asphalt, struck one as exactly like those of any big French or Italian city...

By the end of a fortnight ... the different parts of our force had shaken themselves loose. The Light Horse Brigade was in its own camp at Maadi, the first Australian Division was in its own camp at Mena under the Pyramids; and the New Zealanders were in camp about 5 miles N.E. of Cairo at Zietoun, near Heliopolis and Abbasia where most of the British Territorials were congregated... [Bean based himself at the Mena camp, sited some ten miles from central Cairo.]

About Christmas time our men certainly began to play up a bit. We were inexperienced and had not yet realised the system necessary to stop it; and I think the police system has been a bit inefficient from the first. The same old wasters would break camp every night and as they were therefore the men Cairo saw most of we began to get a bad name in Cairo... Probably General Birdwood who arrived at this time to take command of ourselves and the New Zealanders under the name of the Australian and New Zealand Army Corps, and who had his Headquarters at Shepheards [Hotel] could see more of it than our staff — and so could General Maxwell...

January 1, 1915

[Bean's younger brother, Jack (nicknamed Jock), had travelled with the first convoy as a medical officer in 3rd Bn.]

Jack's birthday — 34th I think. I walked down in the morning to wish the old beggar the best of luck — many times to be repeated I hope. He put in an extraordinarily strenuous day and finally threw himself on his bed and went to sleep quite exhausted. That was his way of enjoying his birthday. His regimental lines are (thanks to his never tiring of getting about at any hour day or

Left:
Lieut.-General Sir William Birdwood, GOC ANZAC. (AWM neg. no. G1222)
Right:
Major Jack Bean, 3rd Battalion AIF. (AWM neg. no. G1536)

night to see things himself) a model to the camp, and he has been told so. His nice corporal . . . who is such a splendid chap when sober, is off on the scoot — and went into Cairo with leave yesterday and has not returned. I believe this breaking of leave is getting a serious matter. Between 200 and 300 of our men at this present moment are somewhere in Cairo — their whereabouts are not known. I know this from conversations Peter Schuler has had with the men — to be partly due to the inexperience of the officers. In a force like this, hastily raised, there is no uniformity in the way in which the officers treat their men. A fellow who is breaking leave will tell you "Well, look here, I got back half an hour late last week and went into camp past the main guard and gave myself up squarely — and the Colonel gave me a week's C[onfined to] B[arracks] for it. And then a chap in the next lines breaks camp and stays out two days and is caught getting in at the back of the Pyramids and only gets two days. I'm going to do something to get punished for this time." The slackness of N.C.O.'s is another cause. Our N.C.O's have very little idea, some of them, of their responsibility — they were all mates out back, and they will often do what they think is a good turn to a chap by giving him in as present when he is absent. But when all is said and done the chief cause of trouble is the tone amongst a certain section of old South African soldiers, and men who have been through the Imperial Service. I have noticed this myself and I have heard it on every side; so much so that if one sees a chap in trouble now, drunk or brought up a prisoner, or if one sees a dirty untidy soldier going without his belt in town or in a crumpled field service cap (which looks sloppy and is against orders) one looks automatically for the South African ribbon...

When I got back from Cairo the other night General Bridges told me he had had a letter from General Birdwood on this point, and he would show it to me. From what he said I take it that he would not take it amiss if I sent a letter and a wire to give people in Australia some idea of how things are; we shall be probably getting rid of a few of these old hard heads — sending them back to Australia. And it is just as well Australians should have an idea of why some of them are returning or else they will probably treat them all (on their own representation) as heroes. It must be pretty awful to be sent back at this stage. I believe one of the first men intended to be sent back was an officer. I see that an officer has asked leave to enlist as a private in his own corps — so this is probably he. He has been allowed to do so, and it is the best way out unless a chap is in absolute disgrace...

Well we are going to settle down to work and eschew all this and high time too, to my idea. A guard is to be placed on the bridge ¾ mile out of camp on the road into Cairo and no one will be allowed over it who has not a pass. There will be three pickets in town instead of one and they will deal at once with any man whom they find drunk or misbehaving himself. I believe the system is now in force and that accounted for the comparative quietness of Cairo last night...

January 7

I hear that all leave is to be stopped tomorrow midday, so that any man found in Cairo will be a man breaking camp. Pickets will be sent in to round them all up. Some of them I suppose have been in there for days or even weeks. A few may be at Port Said or Alexandria — goodness knows where. We have been so comparatively lenient (rightly, I suppose) up to the present that it would be impossible to shoot these chaps — in fact it wouldn't be just except in cases of most serious crime (of which I don't personally and definitely know of any). But they recently shot 3 Indians for trying to get away from the Canal on a pilgrimage to Mecca. This was to stop a "rot" from setting in, as we say in cricket...

The pickets in town this night had orders to arrest every Australian they saw. Leave had been stopped some time before and no one had any right to be in town except on urgent business with a special pass. There were a good number of Australians arrested (a New Zealand officer told me they got over 100 Australians and only one New Zealander, but I don't altogether trust this). However, there are a certain number of men still unaccounted for. They are mostly pretty wary old birds, I fancy. Anyway, when they saw there were no men coming into town they suspected something was up and at once began I suppose to lie up, like hares, in various haunts round town. They got to know that the pickets were all carrying side arms, and I believe some of these deserters managed to raise side arms from somewhere and started to venture abroad in them. The pickets caught a few and of course from that moment the pickets began to suspect that every man they saw wearing side arms was a deserter in disguise. The consequence was that the pickets spent most of the rest of the night arresting other pickets...

January 9–30

From this time on, although there was a great deal of [venereal] disease amongst our men, which they brought on themselves by their indulgences in Cairo, the discipline steadily improved. The disease is simply deplorable, but apparently quite unpreventable. Cairo is a hotbed of it — in particularly serious forms — and some of the cases are simply tragic; young soldiers, really fine clean simple boys who have been drinking and have found themselves with a disease which may ruin them for life. In one case which I heard of, the youngster was said to have been made drunk by two older soldiers — the beasts that old soldiers will sometimes make of themselves inclines one to wish that we had not a single example of them in the force[6]...

The third week in January the *Kyarra* (an Australian coastal steamer of 7000 tons) arrived painted (but not otherwise fitted) as a hospital ship and containing two general hospitals (base hospitals) two stationary hospitals and a clearing hospital...

The authorities have decided to do what was clearly the best thing — to send back to Australia by this ship about 500 or 600 men who have been found to be endangering Australia's good name by their behaviour; or who have (generally in the case of the old soldiers) shown themselves drunkards or shirkers; or who have made themselves unfit for service by incurring disease. Some of these last cases are hard ones in that the men going back were merely more unlucky than most of those staying behind. Still, they must have known in most cases the risk they ran. Along with these there are going back (on Feb 1 from Suez) a certain number of men who are ill or incapacitated through no fault of their own.

There is being sent back with the men an account of exactly what they are being sent back for — a medical report in the case of each disease — and so on. The Government will therefore know (and if it likes, can publish) exactly the reason why each man is being returned. [In fact, the *Kyarra* sailed for Australia on 3 February, taking 169 invalids and 132 disciplinary cases.]

There was a time about Xmas when the sights in the streets of Cairo were anything but pleasant for an Australian who had any regard to the good name of Australia. There was a great deal of drunkeness and I could not help noticing that what people in Cairo said was true — the Australians were responsible for most of it. There were rowdy noisy British Territorials and rowdy drunken New Zealanders, but my own observation was that the Australians were easily the most noticeable[,] and the most frequent offenders were Australians. I think we have to admit that our force contains more bad hats than the others, and I think also that the average Australian is certainly a harder liver. He does do bad things — at least things that the rest of the world considers as really bad; but it is equally true that he has extraordinarily good points — more I should say, than the English soldiers here and than the New Zealanders. If he is unrestrained he is also extraordinarily generous and openhearted. He is not in the least colourless or negative — you don't often meet an Australian who is without a character. He often has strong positive vices but he more often has strong positive virtues also; and the virtues are so good and so attractive that I think the Australian will have to rely on the good things he does to wipe out the bad ones; and I think the sum will come out on the right side when it is all totted up. That is my great comfort when I wonder how I shall ever manage to write up an honest history of this campaign. I fully expect the men of this force will do things when the real day comes which will make the true history of this war possible to be written.

Except in a very few cases neither the Australians nor the New Zealanders have acted offensively towards the natives. They have managed to get, I am told, into lower quarters in Cairo than are visited by the British troops and have run the risk of making the Egyptian despise them — which is said never to have occured to British soldiers before — but on the whole they have been kind to the natives. I have heard of a few vile exceptions of Australian and New Zealand bullying — presumably through drunkeness. One big Australian is said to have walked up to an Egyptian sitting quietly at a table outside a cafe and hit him hard under the ear knocking him on to the pavement. The soldier was drunk and his friends were trying to get him away. But I don't know if these things are true, because I didn't see them myself and didn't get them from a man who actually had seen them. On the whole our men, if they have erred, have erred on the side of being over familiar with any class of native who simply wants to exploit them[7]. . .

[A]bout January 20 I was allotted a horse. . . Just after I had got him we went for a 10 mile route march in order to see that the Headquarters was ready to move. One third of the division . . . marched out of camp at 9 with every baggage wagon packed, and the horses properly loaded, exactly as if we were ordered off to the Canal. . . The march was well carried out — the only thing being that the Artillery started 4 minutes late owing to Colonel Hobbs' watch being wrong (which shows how important official time is); and that when the Infantry struck the soft road after leaving the Pyramid Road they lost step and were apt to straggle. The result was a big gap between the Infantry and the part of the column ahead of them.

The other two thirds of the Division went out on other days and the staff published in Orders afterwards its comments on their marching. On the whole there was little fault to find. The improvement in the men is noticeable — and never more noticeable than when the "second lot" arrived.

Just after the Turks turned up in the Canal our "second lot" were due to reach Egypt — a new Infantry Brigade, the 4th, with the 13th[,] 14th[,] 15th and 16th battalions of Infantry; a Light Horse Brigade, the 2nd, with the 5th[,] 6th and 7th Light Horse. And about 3 000 reinforcements — 10 000 in all. We have heard that they are a big fine lot, mostly country men owing to the new method of selection by which a man can be selected in the back blocks by the police without coming to Sydney or Melbourne or the other capitals to try his luck. The system is so obvious that I wonder it wasn't tried at first. We hear the second lot has a big proportion of these men, and letters have been received that they painted Colombo red. A hundred or so of them got ashore without leave, and made a name for Australia in Colombo. (Some of the officers in the force since they have arrived tell me the thing was exaggerated; others say it was not.). . .

They came in next day after lunch. The first ship we saw was the *Themistocles* and the first incident we saw as we stood on the wharf was the ship's police running down the wharf side to catch a private who had slipped down a rope in the bows and was making for the town. Four others got away before the military police got them. The ship was crowded with men ... who hooted the police...

One couldn't help thinking that we were in for a hot time in Cairo if they are going to be all like this. The *Ulysses*, however, the flagship, which came in just after, seemed to contain a much steadier lot. As she came in we could see Charlie Smith, the *Argus* representative standing there on the promenade deck in a big khaki helmet and a nice fitting suit of light khaki. And to my great surprise, up on the bridge, next to Colonel Monash, the brigadier commanding the troops in this convoy, was Major (now Colonel) M'Glinn, of Sydney, who has come as brigade Major. I had not heard he was coming.

We went on board and had a long yarn with Smith, and afterwards with M'Glinn and Colonel Monash who were exceedingly kind and made us stay to dinner with them...

February 6

The Turks have been seen on the Canal for some days. The first actual contact with them was on January 26 when our patrols were fired on East of Kantara at long range by a body of Turks with mountain guns. This was one of several bodies of advanced troops which we have located... And now they are just beginning to brush up against our outposts and patrols along the Canal... [Engineers from 3rd Field Coy were the only Australians engaged in these skirmishes.]

Since the arrival of a Turkish force off the Canal I seem to have noticed a change in the attitude of the people here. As one walks through the streets remarks are made behind one's back which one can't understand — but I think they are probably cheeky. There is a perceptible insolence in the manner of some of the inhabitants. In Cairo in one of the picture shows the other day, there were shown films of all the nations at war. The audience sat glumly through the pictures of French and Russian troops; when it came to the Germans they cheered. The Kaiser's portrait was cheered and that of the King of England hissed. Some of our officers and military police were there, and there was a bit of a row over it...

Today, I sent the first cable dealing with the part our troops take in the war — a cable to say that so far we had taken no part in it. These cables have to be very limited at present, because the Turkish main attack is likely to be made before long and the one thing they want to know at present is where to make it...

February 8

I went in today by arrangement to see General Walker, chief of staff to General Birdwood, about my position. He says that Maxwell's staff see no reason why my position is different from that of any other journalist in Egypt — which if it is true is simply thickheaded because there are clearly only three other journalists in my position in the British Empire, and none of them is in Egypt, that is to say, "Eyewitness" whom the British people is allowed to have with its soldiers; the Canadian "Eyewitness" appointed by the Government of Canada; the journalist who will be appointed by the Government of New Zealand; and myself who have been appointed by the Government of Australia. I think Walker saw the point before I left him[8]...

I had a very curt intimation from Captain Newcombe of the local Intelligence Department today, saying that as Lord Kitchener had asked for all communiques to be wired to him before publication, and they would be published in London, I would not in future receive copies. This means, in conjunction with Maxwell's decision to the effect that my position is the same as that of all other correspondents, that I simply can't do the job the Australian Government sent me here for. As my work could not by any possible flight of imagination be considered as doing the least vestige of harm to the minutest military interest, I don't mean to accept the position without, if necessary, a reference to the Australian Government. I have to get the story of the war for them for subsequent publication and I can't possibly do that without seeing something or hearing something more than I am at present allowed to do under these restrictions...

March 2

That article which I sent last Christmas about the troops being in danger of losing their good name through a rowdy element which ought never to have been allowed to enlist, or at any rate to sail, has got back here and is causing a quite unexpected amount of feeling amongst the troops. I have read it and re-read it and I can't see a word in it that anyone in the force — any decent man at any rate — can object to. Most of the men on the staff thoroughly agree with me in this; so do most of the officers of the Engineers, many artillery officers, and several amongst the men who have spoken to me about it. But the great majority are inclined to be quite bitter about it and I am clearly in for a rocky time. There seem to be two reasons for this: (1) their wives and families have misunderstood the article — or perhaps only heard it at second-hand — and have written to them about it. (2) The Sydney *Sunday Times* which does not apparently go to the expense of buying my articles, borrowed this one, instead from the Melbourne papers and tried to make a scare out of it. They said it was my first article; as a matter of fact it was my 18th. But the men, who can't be persuaded I didn't write the *Sunday Times* article and I don't suppose ever will be, think it is the first I wrote and that I have done nothing but abuse them. A poem written to that effect in camp — rather a good one, I believe has been sold to the extent of 2000 copies.

March 4
I have done two things to try and put things as far as possible right, with regard to that article. There is no doubt it is exceedingly unpopular and I don't suppose it will be forgotten for a week or two by the 1st Australian Division. Today I got things shouted at me sometimes when I went through the camp . . . "Do you read the *Argus*?" and things a good deal warmer, occasionally, than that. . .

I don't know that I'd have written it if I had thought any Australian people would have twisted it into scares about their absent soldiers and that wives and relations would so hopelessly misunderstand what was so clearly written. I believe that article has done and will do good — anyway my job is to tell the people of Australia the truth. When things go wrong — and they looked like going very wrong at Christmas time — my job is to see that at any rate the blame is put on the right people and that the innocent don't get a bad name for what they didn't do. When things go right I have to try and see that the Australian people knows the right people to get the credit. If they want someone to feed them on soft pap, only to tell them good and pleasant things whatever happens, than I am not the man for the job. I am not going to shift any part of the responsibility for this article on to other shoulders. I have told no one except Jack (although some of the staff knew it before) that the General asked me to write this article. . . In order that anything said in my article may not affect the reputation of the force outside Australia, I have got Reuters correspondent here to telegraph an immensely appreciative (and to my mind perfectly true) summary of the work of the A.I.F. here to every paper in

Great Britain. I know it has had some effect in Australia because we have had a telegram from the Defence Minister there (which has been published in Orders) congratulating the troops on the report. I have seen that this also got into the [Cairo English language newspaper] *Egyptian Mail*...

March 7, Sunday

Today Colonel Patterson asked me in to see two officers — Major Maygar and Major Clarke, both of the 4th Light Horse — who had come up to place before Headquarters a letter complaining of my article. It seems the old South African soldiers had a meeting some days ago at which Maygar and others were present. They were tremendously annoyed at my article and made up a letter to be sent to their Secretary in Melbourne. Maygar would not forward it on unless it was first sent to Headquarters. Colonel Patterson told them my letter was justified (though he was an old South African war man himself) and said they ought to think themselves under an obligation to me for helping to rid the force of the men who were ruining the name of the South African war veteran — or words to that effect. I read my letter to them — neither of them had read it and understood it before; and in the end both agreed that every word of it was true and I think Major Maygar and perhaps Clarke too (in a half measure at any rate) admitted that there was a reason for publishing it. Maygar asked me if I would come down and meet the South Africans and read the letter to them and tell them, as I had done to themselves, just why it was written and how the innocent men going home were amply safeguarded. I said I certainly would...

March 14, Sunday

Over at Heliopolis again... When I returned I saw clearly that there had been some sort of an intimation received that we were likely to start. Also I knew that Birdwood has asked General Maxwell to cable home asking whether I could go to the front and has received the answer that "press correspondents are not to leave Cairo at present. The date when they can do so is not yet settled." That means that the British Government or War Office is determined to treat me as any other Press Correspondent and of course it is a slight to Australia — though I don't suppose they realise it — that the man the Australian Government chose to send with their force to give some sort of account of it should be treated by the War Office as if they couldn't see any difference between him and the correspondent of any English newspaper. They make a big difference in the case of their own "Eyewitness" and the Indian Eyewitness and I believe Canada had an Eyewitness too. White who has more genuine sense in his little finger than many War Officials have in their small minds knows that I can do no harm and may do much good. There's no question of my attempting to evade censorship. I'm the representative of my country and not of a newspaper. But the War Office is unlikely to grasp the difference...

March 15
Wired to Sir George Reid, with White's consent, asking if he would get the consent of the War Office to my going off with the troops on condition that I write nothing until authorized...

March 24
I hear the 29th Division is at Alexandria — part of the Expeditionary force; 40 000 or 60 000 French. Some say that 30 000 British are already at Lemnos. The expedition may consist of one or two British Army Corps and one or two French corps; and two Russian corps. These last may perhaps push in through Asia Minor. Peter tells me he hears that the [C-in-C] Ian Hamilton is already here in Cairo staying with General Maxwell and that Birdwood has left... [These troops, and the ANZAC forces, were to form the Mediterranean Expeditionary Force and launch a major amphibious assault against the Dardanelles and Turkey's Gallipoli Peninsula.]

March 25
Clearly we ... [do] not start for some time. They are encouraging officers to take a few days leave and New Zealanders are arranging excursions for their men to Luxor...

March 28, Sunday
Went out with the three boys from the 5th to Marnak... We saw the Ramesseum and then the Colossi again — in order to make sure of the inscription of Mr. William Boggie of 1820 whose name lies squeezed between those of two early Greeks. We crossed the river with a party of Light Horse Officers. In their luncheon basket I noticed, besides the remains of a lunch a mildewed mummy head and a mummy foot. That night in the train our three friends of the fifth (who still contrived to make the journey in a reserved 1st class compartment in spite of the fact that about 40 New Zealanders were travelling 2nd on the same tickets)

opened a picnic basket and showed us a mummy head, a mummy hand and some bits of painted mummy case. The former two they bought, I think, for 1/6 and the latter they were given...

March 31

Arrived at Alexandria and found the Hotel Majestic full. I managed to get a room in the Savoy and found that Ian Hamilton was staying there. Sent up my card and was told he would see me this morning.

I saw him immediately after breakfast. He told me that he believed a pressman could do the necessary press work in war better than an "Eyewitness". There are points a pressman would notice of great interest to the public and perfectly harmless which eyewitness is apt to miss. He thought that as we had this Eastern show in English hands the Government would let the people have a little more information — or rather would give the journalist a little more scope. In France as one consequence of that "damnable question", he said, "I don't mean a system of compulsory service like you have[9] — they can simply tell the people to go hang — they don't trouble whether they need news or not"...

April 1

About dinner time there seemed an air of something happening. One of the Army Corps staff (Lesslie, I think) was out here to dinner. I heard the General's voice in his room remarking cheerfully, just after dinner — "Well, thanks for bringing us good news; that's the most cheerful thing we've had happen to us for a long time." Shortly after, when Jack was in here and my cousin, Jack Butler, who had come over to see us (he is a signaller now) Foster passed me a note. "All leave stopped". One knew of course what that meant. We — or rather they, the Division — were off. A little later I saw McLaurin coming up the stairs grinning. His holiday was gone. Men who were catching the Luxor train were stopped. Tonight a cable came for me from the High Commissioner to say that the question of my going to the front had been referred by the War Office to the Admiralty "for early decision"[10]...

Good Friday, April 2

There was to have been general leave today; and as the Division is not to embark until tomorrow leave has been granted to 25% of the men.

I believe that quite early in the day some slight trouble occurred.

But it was not till about 5 that matters grew to the stage of a serious riot. It is hard to ascertain the facts.[11] But as far as I can do so they are as follows:

Some New Zealanders who had picked up certain diseases [that is, venereal disease] in a particular street near Shepheards Hotel seem to have made up their minds to go in and pay the house back for what they got there. About 5 o'clock this plan first began to have visible results. Mattresses and bedding were probably torn up inside the house or houses first — but the first the public knew was when this debris began to be piled into a bonfire in the street. The Australian Town picket (which happened to be from a Light Horse Regiment) under its officer was called up; the officer found that a lot of damage was going on in certain houses and he concentrated his efforts on stopping the bonfires as soon as they started and trying to clear the men out of the house or houses that had been attacked. In doing so he arrested five men.

All this had of course collected a bigger crowd. The Greeks in this street and others like it habitually sell vile doctored liquor to the soldiers — (the Cairo authorities are to some extent to blame for never having stopped this) — and some of the men were very drunk. Of course most of the men were onlookers, the majority of them by now being Australians there to see the fun (there are three times as many Australians as of any other force in Cairo). The men who were actually fighting and smashing furniture were a handful. But the crowd wouldn't let the picket get away with its prisoners. Four of them were rescued and the picket carried off one. The officer of the picket was hit heavily on the hand by a big New Zealander who was holding a staircase — he dodged in under the New Zealander's arm and was hit with some iron implement.

The officer of this picket, or else some other authority who was dealing with the trouble, called in the military police — or red caps, as they are called by our men from the colour of their peaked forage caps — English soldiers, who are selected for this special force; they are mounted and carry pistols. They are bound to turn out if called on; the whole posse, perhaps 30 in all, trotted through the streets to the quarter in question. Australians and others, seeing the police trotting, of course ran along with them — as they would after a fire engine — to see the fun... [The British military police attempted to disperse the rioters by firing into the crowd. Several soldiers were wounded.]

I myself went in about 10 p.m. and the space in front of Shepheards [Hotel] was then kept clear by a square of [British]

Territorials drawn across the road. This particular lot was armed only with side arms but the others were marching into the square armed with rifles whilst I was looking on. The town was quiet again but the disturbed street was a wreck. I didn't see it but I'm told one public house was burnt out. The men were tremendously bitter against the red caps and a few fools would have tried to lynch some of them after the firing. I heard every side argued by Australians who were in it...

There is no question that in this scrap a leading part was played by the New Zealanders. I myself saw several drunken New Zealanders about Cairo that night. Both Australians and New Zealanders were pretty well in it. Many men are very sick at it having happened at all, as it will get Australia and New Zealand a hopeless name in Cairo. At the same time I have known rows of exactly the same sort at Oxford and Cambridge, carried through in precisely the same spirit; and people only called it "light-heartedness" there.

The men mostly heard a story that a Maori had been stabbed in one of these houses and that was what started it. Our picket was under the impression that a Maori had been hit with a bottle. The Maoris did not seem to be involved in the fighting afterwards to any extent, and some of the men, mostly outsiders, do not think the Maoris had anything to do with it.

April 3

Dear old Jack left camp today with his regiment for the front. They say that there is likely to be heavy fighting before they land — somebody at the hospital said they expect 30% casualties. Well, if it is a difficult landing I should say these fellows are just the men to carry it out. Whatever they can do they can certainly fight...

As Jock was very busy I arranged to come back at about 6.30 or a little before and have dinner with him... I found old J. with a line of about 8 or 9 men in front of him, with their kit and rifles. They were men of whose strength he was doubtful and he had to recommend that they should be left behind. It was most difficult work — the men were so bitterly disappointed. One or two who had been sent for were not there. He knew they were dodging him — they would try by hook or crook to keep out of the way till the battalion and they with it were well on their way.

(The General tells me that 100 men got out of hospital today and 100 more tried to, [so as to accompany their units into battle]). By 7 o'clock Jack managed to get away for some dinner. There were several ladies dining in the old flowery red white and blue patterned mess tent that night — two friends of the old Colonel and another I think a friend of Major Bennett. Jock and I could not get seats together and so sat at opposite corners of the table. Major Bennett shouted us champagne...

April 4, Sunday
Packing most of the day in case I get the word to move. Still no word.

April 5
Took Jack's luggage and my own into Cooks — it is expensive storing the things there but nothing else seems feasible. Left my diaries and notes for the book and copies of past articles with Dr. Ferguson of the Medical School. If he leaves Cairo he will hand them to the British Consulate to keep for me until I call for them on my [way] out after the war. This is safer than sending them from here to Sir George Reid — besides which the Diary is private and not written for the Defence Department. If ever it were used it would have to be used most carefully. For one reason, it contains a good deal of criticism; the bright side has to be written up in one's letters and that leaves a great deal more than the due proportion of criticism for the diary — I can't write everything here as well as in my letters...

April 8
I was writing up the last few days of this diary this morning when the General sent for me... "I've been talking to Skeen about you, Bean", he said, "and I think you had better wire to Sir George Reid to say you must have an answer within twenty-four hours." I said I hadn't done so (although I wanted to) because I had not wired to indicate that the expedition was likely to start. "Well, you can say just that", he said. That delighted me of course because I knew I should get an answer now. The General added, "What Sir William (i.e. Birdwood) has said is that you will come as an officer attached to my staff and will not write anything." I took it, of course that this was the arrangement all along suggested, that I should write nothing until authorised. I sent the wire off at once.

A little later Bazley came in. I had sent him with a message to the Head Quarters Australian Section Base and he came back with a big envelope. It contained a message from the General Staff in Egypt telling me to report at once to the staff of the M.E.F. in order to obtain instructions "as to your further disposal". (The wording seemed unnecessary anticipation — it may come to that, but I hope not)...

Colonel White showed me a signal. By instructions from G.H.Q. (I think that is the War Office) I am allowed to go attached as an officer to General Bridges' staff on giving a written undertaking that I will write nothing until permitted. It is the chance of a lifetime. It means that I shall eventually be able to give the Australian people an account of one of the most interesting events in history from a position closer than that of any observer who has been allowed to write his impression in the present war...

April 10

Reported to Army Corps Headquarters last night and they told me to report to Divisional Headquarters. I saw the General last night [and] he said, "Well Bean, you here. You're on my staff now, you know. I believe I have to give a guarantee or something that you won't write until authorised." Colonel White told me that I was to deal with Major Blamey [the Division's Intelligence officer]...

We sailed [on the *Minnewaska*] at 7 o'clock this morning. About 11 o'clock I heard the Captain say: "I've just opened my sealed orders. Forgot all about them until we'd been three hours at sea. Then I thought, why, bless me I'd better open 'em and see what they say. I found we were going to the right place."

The Army Corps Headquarters have the music room for their office; we have the Divisional Headquarters in the drawing room opposite — an excellent arrangement. The two staffs have two long tables in the saloon — it gives them a good opportunity to get to know one another. Last night the maps were handed out — of course that settled in my mind what we were going to do. All the confidences half whispered in Cairo by the Army Corps people (or supposed to have originated in them) must have been started as a blind if they were ever started at all. I notice that just before these starts are made "well informed" rumours always get round that the destination is some astonishing place. We have had perfectly smooth weather all day — another bit of luck...

I had a yarn with Colonel White — and he tells me that he thinks it is an extraordinary compliment the Australian troops being chosen to make the present attempt on the Dardanelles. They have got the very best British regular troops they could — the 29th Division — the best they could find, so he said; and here are the first Australian Division and the New Zealand and

Australian Division chosen to start the ball. "They wouldn't send us unless they thought we were competent", he said.

As for me, I am in luck if ever any pressman was. This is perhaps the most interesting operation in the war — one of the most interesting in history; a business of this sort on this scale has never before been attempted. And I am nearer to it than [any] journalist has been to the actual firing line since the beginning of the war. Dear old J. will I suppose be right in it. Well, if we come through all right, we shall have had an experience that will last us our lifetime...

2

Into Battle

THE moment for action was finally drawing close. The Australians and New Zealanders were to form part of a 75 000 man amphibious assault force to be launched against the Gallipoli Peninsula, Turkey. The objective was to gain control over the strategically vital Dardanelles Straits. It was a most tempting prize. If the straits could be taken the way lay open for the Allies to strike at the Turkish capital, Constantinople. Turkey might thus be forced out of the war, thereby reducing the pressure on the beleaguered Russians. Germany, in turn, would be threatened by Allied forces at her rear. In short, the Dardanelles seemed to offer good prospects for success and an escape from the now deadlocked trench warfare of the Western Front.

The military landings (under the command of the British general, Sir Ian Hamilton) had been decided upon only after repeated attempts by British and French warships in February and March 1915 had failed to neutralise the line of Turkish forts guarding the narrow seaway. The landings would be made by a combined force of British, French, Australian and New Zealand troops.

April 12

This morning early, when I woke up, we were coming up a strait between two lines of hills covered with green grass. I suppose I ought to call them "bare" hills because there were no trees on them. But one simply cannot bring oneself to call any place where there is grass "bare" — that is the effect of four months in the desert. Everyone was delighted to see the green. "I'm coming back here to take up land", I heard one officer of the 1st Battalion say to another as they looked over the rail.

There were three or four ships following us and ahead of us were a sloop or yacht of some sort and a torpedo boat. We followed round up the harbour entrance — and there inside we saw some war ships, some other ships, and a village. On the hillside near the village were some tents. A fine harbour opened

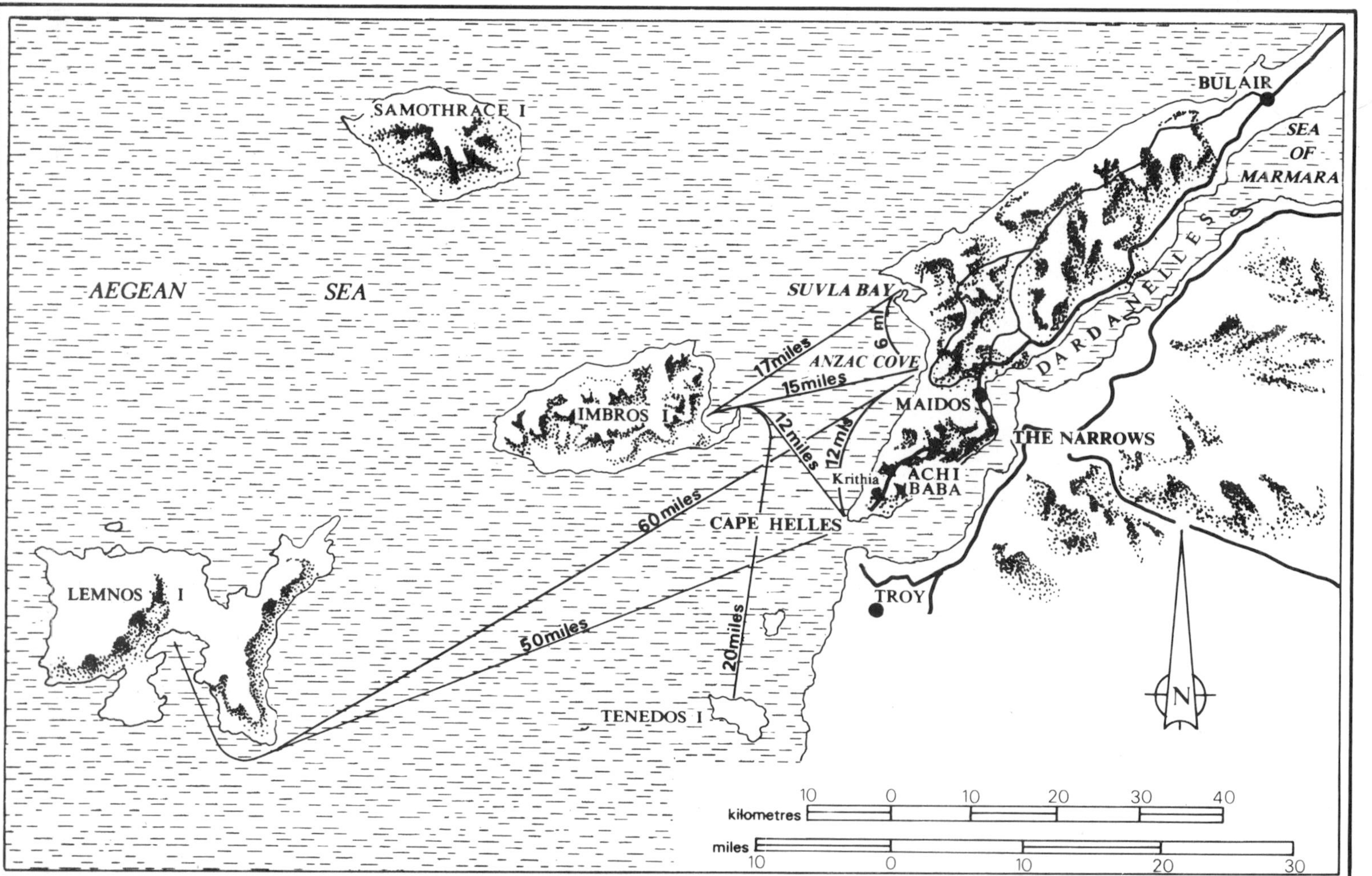

Dardanelles region

up, larger and larger as we went in... [This was Mudros Harbour, Lemnos Island, some 50 miles from the entrance to the Dardanelles. By 20 April more than 200 ships were assembled in the harbour ready to carry the Mediterranean Expeditionary Force to the beaches of Turkey.]

April 21

A wild wet night; raining and blowing hard this morning. Shortly after breakfast quite a considerable conference was held in our saloon. The New Zealand staff came over from the *Lutzow* or wherever they are. Our own staff ... trooped down with naval officers, the staff of the army corps, the commanders of our artillery brigades. There was a map on the wall and as a lecture of sorts was evidently going to take place I cleared out to the divisional office in the lounge upstairs...

There are some last moment shocks: for example the *Ionian* at the last moment says she has no water. Then the *Armadale* suddenly announces that the material for the tressle pier bridge or landing stage which she was supposed to have on board, was not all loaded at Alexandria. Part of it is in Alexandria still — and it was urgently needed... These things always seem to happen even in the best regulated shows...

April 22

Still in harbour. If things had gone as proposed I think we should have made our move this morning. The wind is fresh. The day is fine...

(This day we were to have landed at 3.30 a.m. but there was a heavy breeze and it was impossible)...

April 23

There is a great difficulty in getting around this harbour. The only private boat you can get are the bumboats which come out with chocolate, cigarettes, figs, and bread which they sell to the men at whatever price they can get — I heard them asking 1/– for a small loaf today but there were no bidders. The boats belonging to the fleet or transports are far too much in demand to go where you want them to and if you do get one touching at a particular ship the chances are you cannot get one back. I have learnt that the best way is to get hold of the first bumboat that you can persuade to take you, and keep him and pay him whatever you may have to.

I got one of the interpreters to bargain with a very small boat this morning... We got her in the end for 5/– an hour... We started at 10 a.m. for General H.Q. on the *Arcadian*. The walnut thumped across there somehow, taking, I suppose, half an hour. On the *Arcadian* I asked for Maxwell. He was in the general staff room (the gymnasium). He came out at once and was very nice. He had heard of me. I told him that authority might come for me any day, and asked what were the arrangements. He said that so long as we were at sea everything was to be censored in the *Queen Elizabeth*; as soon as we landed everything would be censored by the Army Headquarters. He himself, an old war correspondent who was in Belgium at the beginning of this war, is censor with the rank of Captain... I don't think he will be a difficult censor to have dealings with...

I got back just before dinner. As I reached the gangway a warship steam launch was shoving off. It was taking Gen. Birdwood and most of his staff to the *Prince of Wales* — the battleship from which they and the divisional staff and a part of the men of the 3rd Brigade are to land. The Divisional staff was not leaving the *Minnewaska* until after dinner...

The greater part of the officers of the 1st Battalion, and those of the divisional staff who are going to stay (as I am) on the *Minnewaska*, were down at the end of the promenade deck looking over the rail at the gangway — which leads from the 'tween decks where the horses are — and at the small steam boat from the *Prince of Wales* which was waiting with her lights lit fidgeting in the black water besides the gangway. White made his way through them — with his pistol in its case on his belt, his haversack packed, and a little blue enamelled pannikin tied onto the end of his swag. "Goodbye, White". "Good luck old chap!" said various officers as he passed... The boat cast off and slowly moved past underneath the ship's side... The men on the decks near the gangway gave three cheers for General Bridges; we from our corner gave three more cheers...

Until just before the staff was going I thought that tonight was the night on which we were to land. But before he left Blamey said: "You know there's to be nothing till Sunday." I don't know if this is a postponement owing to the sea being too rough; or whether it was already arranged that the movement would take two days[1]...

April 24

This morning at 5 I was waked by a motion in the ship. The screws were turning and she was slowly swinging round to go out. I put on my warm jacket and overcoat — even so it was cold up there with a north wind blowing. A good number of officers came up to see us move... A great number of transports were still in the harbour and about 20 or 30 large ones outside...

Staff officers have been advised to take off their brassards whilst in close touch with the enemy — so the bright colours have for the moment disappeared. I am keeping mine — dark green; it's not very conspicuous, and in any case it is best to conform with all the rules. Otherwise the chance of a non combatant being shot if captured is pretty good. I don't possess a pistol or any arms of any sort...

Just about sunset today we saw steaming slowly along the horizon to the west a squadron of 5 warships: *Queen, Prince of Wales, Bacchante, London, Majestic* — or vessels of those classes anyway. They were at 2 cables, except their leader, and steaming very slow with a long trail of smoke behind them. They were on their way to the job we are bound for...

One sometimes is inclined to think of the utter hopeless wastefulness of this whole war. But once a nation adopts the philosophy of Treitschke I suppose war is inevitable. Our people is a peace loving people and one knows this for certain, that if war could have been avoided with honour, we should have avoided it.

I heard one officer say: "I think of the job we're going to sometimes a little before breakfast and sometimes a little after dinner." Of course some people have been a little thoughtful tonight — because we know what a tremendous job it is, this assault on a strong fortress. But the Australian troops and officers are pleased with the compliment that has been paid them; and the 3rd Brigade most of all. Col. [Sinclair-]MacLagan who is a fine British officer and a capable one told the 3rd that "few if any finer brigades had ever taken the field." [Units from the 3rd Brigade had been chosen to go ashore first.]

The men — except for getting their ammunition handed out to them — have spent the day exactly as they spent every one before it — a parade; playing "house" (a troopship gamble) on the deck; reading; yarning about the war. It's a great gamble the whole thing really — a lot of bits of metal in the air; and just a chance whether you stop one or let it pass. A lot of men at one end of a machine throwing things into space with a deadly swiftness without the least idea what is going to be the effect of each discharge: it may mean a tragedy in some little cottage home in Tasmania or in an English country house; it may kill or wound or take out an eye or take off a leg. And a lot of Australians — boys who began life on the Murray or in a backyard in Wagga or

Bourke or Surry Hills will be left lying in Turkey. It is a curious business. However — for 8 months we've been training to get up against a front which we can't pass except by forcing our way through it at all costs — and now we're there. Some of the positions tomorrow I believe have to be taken "at all costs" — I believe that is an order to the 10th Bn.

The lights in the ship will all go out presently. Before then I want my little brandy flask filled. So this interesting analysis of feelings must close. I shall be in a devil of a funk tomorrow; but so will many others although they won't show it — and I hope I shan't also. I have rolled my coat, stuffed my haversack with 2 days iron rations and one day's bread and cheese — and now to bed.

April 25, Sunday

[The Allied assault had been planned as a multi-pronged attack. The 1st Australian Division would be landed at first light on the beaches near Gaba Tepe. The Peninsula at this point narrowed to only four miles wide. In order to retain the element of surprise, no naval bombardment would precede the landing. Shortly after this division went ashore, warships would blast Cape Helles (the toe of the Peninsula) preparatory to British forces disembarking there at five separate beaches. If all went to plan, the ANZAC force would sweep eastward to Maidos and the Narrows while the British pressed up from the south. In order to further confuse the Turks, simultaneous diversionary feint attacks were to occur near Bulair in the north (by the British), and across the straits at Belike Bay and Kum Kale in Asia Minor (by French units). In all, 75 000 Allied troops would be landed against 84 000 Turkish defenders.

Bean was to go ashore with men from the 1st Battalion, AIF, some hours after the initial landings had been made and a beach-head established.]

12 midnight: The ships have sailed from Lemnos. I have a cabin, the last in the passage, with a port hole opening onto the well deck. The port hole is just above my head as I lie in the upper bunk. Outside on the deck, amongst all sort of gear and under some of the horse boats to be used in landing, are some of the men of the 1st Battalion tucked into corners of their overcoats. They are talking quietly — two mates — outside the port hole. One has just waked.

"What time is it?"

"Ten past twelve — she's sailed. Where have you been?"

"Me and Bill have been down below having a farewell yarn."

Some sleepy chap along the deck is singing — The words were somewhat as follows, punctuated with yawns:

"What oh for a life on the sea.
So give it a chance
Come and have a dance
Come and dance along with me."

The voice breaks off into some snatch of another song: "When I am dead and in my little grave" and then the singer having rewound his rug around him tucks his head back onto his pack and snuggles down for another sleep. I must not oversleep — this night is too good to miss.

12.30: Came up on deck to see which course we are taking. We have just 50 miles to go and the Island of Imbros lies directly in our path...

Out on deck. It is a perfect moonlight night. We are passing the Northeast point of some island probably Lemnos. I can see the dark shape of the mountains on the soft grey satin on the sea. On the end of the point a pin point light is flashing three times every five seconds. Ahead of us is a simple small stern light always motionless. Away to the left — far on our port bow I can see two other lights — one after the other. Astern of us is another ship. I can see the faint glow of some cabin or galley lights; otherwise she is simply a black shape. We are heading almost due Northeast. Aft of the smoking room out of the breeze the guard is tucked away on the deck in deckchairs. Some are curled along either side of the promenade deck — one can just see them rolled up like grubs in their white and grey blankets and waterproof sheets. One has to look carefully not to step on them as one picks a way along the deck. One huge chap is sprawled on his face at full length without great coat or blanket, fast asleep like a boy — most of them are in overcoats and balaclavas. "Aho, its chilly" says one yawning. And so it is.

The young officer of the guard is there on a deck chair talking to one of our interpreters. He has orders to wake the troops at four [a.m.] All lights are to be turned out altogether when we get off the mainland — Gallipoli. We wonder whether the British have landed yet. Some say they landed during the past day — I fancy they land this morning. The Turk does not realise what is in store for him during the next few hours.

2.30: Came on deck again. The moon is almost down now. Our

third brigade has to land in the little interval of darkness between the moonset and the dawn. They must be getting near there now — 10 miles ahead of us perhaps.

We are steaming just north of a high coast line — it must be Imbros. There are clouds on the high velvet black hills. Other land, which must be Samothrace, to the North. Wonder if anyone sees us from Imbros. The light on the point of Lemnos is far behind, still winking. Two white stern lights still directly ahead of us. As I lean over the rail below the bridge watching them there is a flash on the foc'sle, a prolonged flicker of light. Some prize idiot lighting his pipe. Nothing will ever make some individuals forego that luxury.

3 a.m.: On deck again. All lights have been put out since last I was here.

3.30: We are clearing the last point of Imbros. The moon is down and it is much darker. I cannot see the land beyond although I know it is there — the distance is only 12 miles. Far on our right, either on the point of Imbros Island or on some ship stationed in the channel between there and the land are two white lights, one above the other and a little aslant as if on a mast. I shall not go down again. A colonel of the Army Corps Staff in his overcoat is leaning over the rail beside me.

Suddenly a circle of hazy misty white light appears behind some land far away to the right of us. I cannot see the land but I know it must be there because there is something hiding the actual light from which that glare comes. There is no mistaking it — a searchlight. It must be somewhere in the Dardanelles, south of the peninsula. It sweeps in a scared sort of way to right and left, shifts up a bit; fidgets and suddenly disappears. That must be one of the lights on the Turkish forts in the straits. It is just on 4 a.m. Wonder if they have heard anything — equally suddenly another searchlight — further in the straits. We can only see the haze of this one also searching round like the startled eyes of some frightened animal. There is the old searchlight again.

And just at that moment I first notice that dawn is slowly breaking right ahead — just the first faint rim of grey. Presently I look that way and the dawn is no longer there. The fringe of grey is away on our portside. We must have turned suddenly in southwards. The line of the land, a high line of hills, can be seen straight ahead and away to the left of us. We are moving in between two flanking ships, merchant ships, evidently stationed there to give us the position. It is well past four — just the time when our 3rd Brigade ought to be rushing out of their boats somewhere up the slope of those grey hills ahead. There is no sign yet of action.[2]

It is still too dark to see what I am writing. But the dawn is slowly growing. A line of officers is gradually lining the rail under the bridge, a ship's officer or two as excited as the rest. Down on the foc'sle forward the men are beginning to cluster to the sides. Another idiot strikes a match and immediately a torrent of words bursts over him like a shell from the bridge above. Five minutes later a British officer beside me — newly arrived from England — does the same.

4.25: Still no sound. We have passed between the two ships. There are three of our sister transports ahead and we are moving in between two of them to make up a line of four. Past us on our port beam slowly moves a destroyer dragging two long wrinkles across the silky water as she moves — It is light enough to see that now.

Suddenly, (4.37) from low down on the line either of sea or shore a signal lamp flashes. We can't say if it is on some small boat close in or on the shore itself. One of the ship's officers next [to] me takes my telescope and looks long through it.

"No I can't say which it is," he says.

Then at 4.38 for the first time, listening eagerly, I catch faintly on a gust off the shore a distant knocking as of someone who held up a small wooden box and knocked the inside of it with a pencil. It comes again and again continuously, like the knock-knocking of an axlebox heard very far off, very faint, through the bush. To my mind there is no mistaking it whatever. It is the first time I heard the sound, but I have no doubt on earth of what it is. It is the distant echo of rifle firing — first few shots, then heavy and continuous.

I told the ship's officer next me to listen. He heard it too; he knew what it was. There was some doubt amongst others. But within five minutes there could be no mistake. Heavy firing was going on in the hills ahead. We could not see the flash...

4.53: Just now there was the sound like a bursting rocket high in the air a little aft of the ship. A small woolly cloud unrolled itself. Below it a small circle of the surface of the silky water was lashed up as if by a very local fierce thunder rain. Presently far away on the face of a small promontory about two miles to the south of us is a brilliant pinpoint flash. Some seconds later a curious whizz through the air — a whizz on a descending scale just the opposite to the whizz of a steam siren. The long drawn out whizz sinks and sinks down the scale. There is a flash high in the air a quarter of a mile in front of us this time. Then a bang, the whirr of a shower of pellets sprayed as if from a watering can, the whip up of another circle of sea below and another white fleecy cloud slowly floating overhead. The wondering crowd on the promenade deck says to itself "So that is shrapnel". "Look mate," says a voice on the foc'sle, "they're carrying this joke too far — they're using ball ammunition."

4.45:[3] There was a bang which shook our ship — a huge bilious yellow cloud for a moment sprang out from the side of one of the warships just south of us. Far down on the point where that other flash came from a huge geyser of yellow black earth lifts itself — a lurid red flash just showing through the cloud of it. The Infantry — they are New South Welshmen — on the deck below run to the side, cheering, delightedly.

"Whew! that's Pat", says one excited boy waving his cap.

Several of the other ships begin firing, but the shrapnel still bursts ahead. At five o'clock one seems to burst fair over the stern of a transport ahead of us carrying a battalion of the Second Brigade.

Three minutes later we ourselves start moving in to take up our berth. Four of us, in line, are passing slowly in between the warships. Just on our port side we look down quite close upon the deck of one battleship — the *Prince of Wales*, I think... On our right the *Triumph* and *Bacchante* are firing round after round — the two big turret guns of the former roaring together.

Not a sign yet from the beach. Only that ceaseless knocking, knocking, knocking. Presently a curiously oval object floats past us low in the water. It is a small rowing boat bottom upwards. That was the first sign we saw.

Now at last as we moved in we could see on the sea, just below the line of the beach, a swarm of small boats — small boats everywhere. They seemed to be going each on its own and going every sort of way — rowing, not being tugged some were stationary — or seemed so. It is hard to tell at this distance. "I don't like the way they're all scattered about," said a staff officer near me. Some seemed as though they might be helping others in difficulties.

The warships are firing more heavily now — there go two great turret guns together. The enemy is still scattering his shrapnel over the water but always between the ships or just short of them.

5.15: Two shells pretty close to us. Those small boats returning for all they are worth each on its own — we can see them much clearer now — makes one just a little anxious. Why are they going

1st Division Headquarters Staff wade ashore at Anzac Cove on the morning of 25 April, see page 67. (AWM neg. no. G903)

so many ways — digging out for all they are worth[?] Has the landing been beaten off — is this the remnant[?]

At five o'c. the men went down to a hot breakfast. That firing is still going on in the hills. Whilst it continues one can scarcely think of eating. "You'd better come," says someone. "Never know when you may get a good meal again." It was a very hurried breakfast the officers took — 50 or 60 of them there at the saloon tables. Shells were falling near the ship; any minute one might come through the side. You can see plainly the flash, flash of the warships' guns — the glare flashes through the portholes like lightning. The stewards very willing this morning.

Up on deck again after a cup of tea and plate of porridge. The knock-knock — still coming heavily from the shore — the hills resound with it. But look ever so hard you can't see a flash. "I'm afraid they've not got very far" says a staff officer. There is one comfort. The small boats which are rowing back are surely returning to their ships. There are no soldiers in them — just four seamen with another sitting at the tiller — rowing for all they are worth to their various ships. So our men must at least be on the beach. The warships are supporting them for all they are worth — great shots are shaking this ship every 10 or 20 seconds. Far down south on the neck of Kaba [Gaba] Tepe I can see the smoke of our shrapnel bursting over the point where we must have located their guns.

Close in shore one can just make out the low shapes of one or two destroyers. They were to take in the men from the ships further out and transfer them to boats. The boats were to take them from the destroyers in shore. Others were to land straight in boats from the ships. Those destroyers in shore must just be discharging the second batch now. Another is swinging round three hundred yards away from us. It must be the first to discharge us. She was due at six o'clock. It is exactly 6.3. A geyser of foam rises beside the *Galeka*. I think it is from a gun on the big hills far away to the South. It was not far off. The shrapnel is now bursting in the air a little south of the transports; 3 shell this time. Now another three! Those must be from guns to the South of that promontory [Gaba Tepe]. We are just outside their extreme range.

The destroyer is alongside. Some men on her decks are standing round something which they have protected with a little nest of hammocks. It is a wounded man. One seems to be an Australian — another is a sailor, his face turned away from them very white and still. A seamen sits by him, holding his wrist. Now that one sees them there are half a dozen wounded men on that destroyer. Another has drawn alongside our other beam. She has a dozen wounded on her. Some of the small returning boats come along the destroyers. They lift a wounded man or two out of them also.

Still that rattle, rattle all along the hillside. It doesn't sound as if our men had got far. The ships are roaring whole broadsides now...

Two cruisers are round the South West of that obnoxious promontory shelling it — and the [battleship] *Triumph*. Just this side of it lies the four funnelled *Bacchante*... Far to the South is the *Queen Elizabeth*, signalling with some brilliant light. Our men must at least have got a footing on the land for those enemy guns to the S. are shelling the right hand shoulder of the nearer hill in front — four of them were shelling it some moments ago. There only seems to be one now.

6.45: The infantry from our own ship are climbing slowly down rope ladders into their destroyers — or rather into one of them. The *Derfflinger* has just got her first destroyer away. I watch it — old Jock is in that lot. The *Michigan* has got her two away. Astern of us one can see in the distance transport after transport coming up...

Suddenly — from high up on the further hill — there twinkles a tiny white light — very brilliant. What on earth can it be? We can

Men of the 1st Battalion transferring from the *Minnewaska* to the destroyer, *Scourge*, about 8 a.m. on the first day of the Gallipoli landings. (AWM neg. no. G897)

hardly have got our signallers right up there, headquarters properly fixed and the signal communication opened up by this time! "It can't be no — must be the Turks" is the general opinion. But what do the Turks want to helio towards us for — must be signalling to their men on the nearer hill.

Ten minutes later someone sees men upon the skyline. The rumour gradually spreads round. At 7.17 I heard of it. Through the telescope you can see them, numbers of them — some standing full length. Others moving over it. Certain ones are standing up, moving along amongst them. Others are sitting down apparently talking. Are they Turks or Australians[?] The Turks wear khaki, but the attitudes are extraordinarily like those of Australians. Just below them, on our side of them a long line of men is digging quietly on a nearer hill. They have round caps, I think clearly you can distinguish that round disc-like top. They are Australians! and they have taken that further line of hills! — three ridges away you can see them; the outlines of men on the furthest hill; men digging on the second hill; and the white flags of signallers waving on the ridge nearest the shore... [Eight thousand Australian troops had gone ashore by 8 a.m.]

8.30: The second destroyer (*Ribble*) is alongside — she has many wounded on board — men come to me and say that her decks are a sight — simply slippery with blood. I didn't go to see — somehow if that sort of thing has to come it will come of its own accord; no need to go and look for it. They don't seem to be hurrying about loading the *Ribble* — not a man is getting on to her although lots are on board waiting. I wonder why...

9.20: Another burst of firing on hills.

The ... *Ribble* is alongside. Put on my packs (i.e. overcoat and 1 ration and towel and [waterproof] sheet in an infantry pack; 2 rations in brown canvas satchel which Myers gave me — also most of my papers and some chocolate; rug and leather lining to overcoat in roll). Went down onto foc'sle deck with Capt. Griffiths — got the packs slung over into the destroyer and then climbed down rope ladder.

9.40: Moved off. Waved goodbye to Bazley... Most of the batmen with our sleeping bags, horses, grooms, the French interpreters, motor cars, Maj. Watson and the pay office people remain aboard until our landing is established. Some say they may be off in 2 days — some a week. Of course the horses may be longer.

As we are going ashore some heavy battery fires a big shot at the *P of Wales*. A monstrous fountain of foam rises beside her.

Landing boats returning to the destroyers as Bean is rowed towards the beach at about 9.50 a.m. on the first day. (AWM neg. no. G900)

Second shot at *P. of W.* Then 3rd big shot right over the *Queen* near the *Hessen*. They'll be sinking her if our people don't look out. I believe i.e. quite expect to lose a transport or two and it looks as if any minute we shall see the beginning: 4th big shot alongside *Hessen* — she's a German steamer, too. I wonder when they'll get her moving — they're frightfully slow. No, she's thrashing out at last — screw very high out of water.

Then a big shot — 5th — close alongside *Minnewaska*.

Next a shot close alongside a destroyer — it seemed to explode on touching the water — wonder if it went through her — it would sink her surely. You can see a white powdery patch on her black side, where the explosion dried the spray on it, I suppose. A sailor went straight to the side and looked over to see if any damage had been done. If it had she'd have been sunk by now — so I suppose it just missed her.

[The Turkish gun (later dubbed 'Beachy Bill') behind] Kaba Tepe[4] has fired a shot at us as we came ashore — at least I suppose they were firing at us. It fell good way short. Another destroyer was moving in parallel to us, carrying troops from other transport. About 200 yds from the shore the destroyers stopped. There were some very big empty ships' boats coming alongside and we clambered into them — Gellibrand and most of our party got up into the bows to be out of the way. I don't think anybody in the boat worried about shrapnel. Somebody says another shell burst between us and the other destroyer — not far away; but I didn't notice it. I was busy taking photos of the boats and the hills.

The sight of the hills as we got in closer and could see what they really were made one realise what our men had really done. I remember someone saying that the map ought to have been made more precipitous, that it didn't really give an idea of how steep the hills actually were — and I understand what they meant.[5] The place is like a sandpit on a huge scale — raw sandslopes and precipices alternating with steep slopes covered with low scrub — the scrub where it exists is pretty dense. There seems to be a tallish hummock at the N. end of the beach and another at the south end. We are landing between them.

The boat grounded in at 2ft. of water. We jumped out — got used to this at Lemnos where I saw many a man spilt by his heavy pack, so I got out carefully, waded to the beach, and stood on Turkish soil.

I took a photo of two of the fellows landing and then turned round to see the beach. It was a curve of sand, about 1/2 mile long, between the two knolls before mentioned. Between them, high above us, ran back a steep scrub covered slope to a skyline about 300 feet above us. One or two deep little gullies came down the mountainside, each with a little narrow winding gutter in the depth of it; these gutters were about as deep as a man, sometimes deeper, not more than 5 or 6 feet wide, more or less covered in the low scrub (largely arbutus) and so splendid natural cover against shrapnel whether it came from N. or S. On the beach some seamen were rigging up the first pole of a wireless station; infantry and engineers as they landed were being lined up and marched off at once — mostly, I think, towards the south end of the beach. Foster and Casey met us and took us off in a southerly direction to the 2nd gully where they said the general [Bridges] had decided to make his divisional H.Q. The place they chose was the bottom of the gully just where the gully opened out onto the sand. I chucked my pack and haversack down with others on a bunch of bush in the middle of this gully. Shrapnel had been dropping here thickly.

I think the General was away when we arrived — anyway Foster couldn't say definitely if this would be the place for the camp; so we waited on to see where H.Q. would be. The General was there shortly afterwards. White, Glasfurd, Blamey, Howse and Foott were all ashore before us.

10 a.m: The mountain guns have just landed. There is continuous firing.

10.30: The wireless is up. The boys are digging out a place for Headquarters in this gully near the beach. The signallers seem to have been allotted a bit of the gully just above us and the artillery just above them. A Turkish prisoner is being examined at H.Q. . .

We saw a few wounded men, a very few, limping or carried along the beach. I think about half a dozen poor chaps were also lying there dead — with overcoats or rugs over them. Most of these were carried away round Northern point of the beach, and away along the Northern beach where they were laid out together, about 30 of them . . .

I didn't want to get in the way at H.Q. so as Col. Hobbs was going up to see if he could find a position for his guns I asked if I might go with him. The Artillery staff scrambled up the gutter at the back of our H.Q. winding in and out under the leaves, dragging one another up the gravelly banks until we got to the top of our ridge. When about half way up I noticed an insect with a soft rustle of a flight, like a bees, flying over — I could hear them and looked once or twice to make sure. Then for the first time I realised it must be a bullet. It was so feeble, that sound, and so spent that it was quite comforting. One had expected something much more businesslike. As we got higher up the whistle did become louder, but I hadn't any idea whether they were near or far.

At the top we got into a path — I don't know if it was ours or Turkish, but our engineers were building quite a fine path lower down — which led us for about half a dozen yards over the beginning of a plateau and then a shallow trench crossed our path, running from right to left; so we dropped into it. There were several men in it and I think they were chiefly engaged in passing ammunition along it. We crept along it, passing a certain number of men — Col. Hobbs seemed rather desperate of getting any artillery up this way. As we went along this trench there was a dead Turk lying in it and there was one of our own men, dead, lying just outside the trench. Some parts of the trench had a very nasty smell — there was no mistaking it — the Turks must have used it for purposes of sanitation as well as of protection — I believe their trenches serve for every purpose. Finally we got to where the trench finished abruptly on the other side of the plateau in a V shaped cut through which you could see down into the valley and across to the other side of it. Col. Hobbs went on and had a look out of the opening and as he could do no good here we all returned to the beach. I stayed for a bit to talk to some of the men in the trench. One could hear occasionally a burst overhead and a whizz which I took to be shrapnel; but in this trench one was reasonably safe.

By the time I got out of the trench the road up to the entrance of it seemed to be nearly finished. Men bringing up ammunition were resting there for a moment. A certain number of infantry were sitting down there also for a breather. The ammunition men didn't get down into the trench but went straight on across the plateau — where to I could not see. It was a big labour bringing those boxes up the hill — but I knew it was awfully important.

Presently 4 guns from the N started shelling the road up N. edge of the hill, up which the troops were continually moving — or else these shells were meant for the troops landing, I couldn't say which. As I sat on the hillside above the Northern knoll — just at the Northen edge of the hill-slope up from the beach — they were coming over my head, high over, in salvoes of 4 and bursting rather high over the beach and the water in front of the destroyers. I can't say I like shrapnel although it seemed to be quite familiar by this time. I sat watching it by the road for some time and then walked down through the scrub towards our gully. On the way I saw several of the men of Jock's battalion carrying ammunition. They had a depot in the scrub there and a sergt. who evidently recognised me was in charge of it. He said the doctor had been attending to men on the beach, he thought, for a time and had now gone on with his battalion.

Then I came down to the beach and had a little lunch — that is, some biscuits, a little chocolate, and some water.

The General was there — they were making him a dug out on the right hand corner of the mouth of the creek as you looked towards the hills...

After lunch I went up the hill at the back of the beach for a bit, and finally decided to go and see if I could find old Jock. I went up to the communication trench on the hill top and through it, inquiring where Jock's dressing station was. Several men had told me if I went over that way I should find it down in the gully. I asked several in the trench (along which ammunition was being passed) the way, but they told me they didn't know — they were mostly 10th Bn. but also some 1st... I... went along the trench to near its exit on the further slope. I got a photo from this exit, but a man seemed to be sniping in at it from the other side of the valley — the men at the exit were well tucked into the sides of it — so I didn't stay there. I waited tucked up in the trench — and the

Australian troops going into action across Plugge's Plateau (the first point captured after the landings). Bean took this photo while standing in a captured Turkish trench overlooking the beach. (AWM neg. no. G907)

shrapnel began to plump in salvoes of 4 shots regularly into the backs of the men lying out on the opposite side of the valley. You could hear the shots going overhead and see the burst, I think, sometimes. It went on with monotonous regularity — apparently neverending and one began to think the chaps there must be having an awful time. I couldn't get a man from Jock's battalion — every other sort seemed to go through the trench. A number of N. Zealanders came along it and filled it up, with some officers and orders seemed to be passed along from a Col. Plugge at the back. There was a signaller in the trench, the reader in the trench with a telescope and the sender somewhere on the face of the slope outside. I knew — I don't know how, but one guessed from the way those guns were firing, unhindered by any firing at all of ours, that the troops were being very severely tried. It was sickening to hear it. I thought there was only a party of troops on the further ridge but it was the main line of our men really. One could tell something from the messages passed along. A request came back (from 1st Brig. I think) to know how the other landings were getting on. That meant they wanted something cheerful to tell the troops, I knew. I am not sure it didn't come along twice...

The afternoon wore on and I suddenly saw men crossing the trench a little way to my right — amongst them was Col. Owen. I wished afterwards I had gone alone and spoken to him — that was really my chance and I should have found Jack; but he was some way away and I didn't. The shelling went on and on — of course a good many bullets were nipping over head — you heard the whistle and the low scrub just above the trench bank looked pretty dangerous . . .

It was getting on towards evening so I decided to go on and find 3rd Bn., if I could, myself. I went along the trench to near the mouth, jumped out, and ran across the top and at once found myself in a little dip in the front side of the hill. There were a few men there, all lying down under the brow of the slope. On the edge of the slope was standing — I think he came up at that moment — Evans, the machinegun officer of the 3rd Bn. . . . and I told him I was glad to see he wasn't hit. I lay down under the cover of the edge of the ridge — it was slight cover — but he sat up on the edge of it all by himself, treating the bullets as if they did not exist, and they were pretty thick. The men were lying down pretty closely and I did the same. He didn't know where Jack's dressing station was and the men of the 3rd Bn. with him didn't either. (I think it must have been in that very place to start off with). As I lay there a lot of New Zealanders came up the hill and lined this ridge to left and right: the firing seemed to be heavy away to our left all the time and I couldn't help thinking that the Turks were getting round our left flank . . . As we were lying there six guns just behind us somewhere opened over our heads with a delicious salvo. It was like a soothing draught of water to hear those guns blaze at the Turks . . .

I went down and found H.Q. about dinner time. I thought I noticed the fellows seemed rather quiet with me — I couldn't help wondering if they had heard that anything was wrong with Jock. After dinner — I forget what time — Col. White told me that he had seen Jack "He was very cheerful — I don't think Howse thinks he's been badly hit," he said. That was the first I heard of it. Howse told me he had seen him and he never saw a wounded man better — not the least sign of collapse. "I don't think the bullet hit any important part," he said. "It was still in — but I don't think it hit the intestine." He said Jock had gone off to a hospital ship — he didn't know which. It was about 4 o'c. in the afternoon J. was hit. He was the only medical officer wounded.

When I got down to the beach I found that almost everyone had a dug out — a sort of ditch cut, something between a grave and a cave, into the creek side. The general's was pretty well finished. Next it was a little one which Glasfurd was sharing with Casey —

they asked me to sit in it — a sort of little kennel place. They were awfully kind. . .

I presently got my things and started on a dug out for myself. I started first up amongst the signallers. Several of them were lying cooped up there in little half circular places, not unlike tiny sandpits. I found a vacant corner — only a few feet for the whole place was covered with these dug outs especially on the south side (for protection against Kaba Tepe). I started to dig. The man in the dug out next door strongly objected — I don't know who it was. "What do you want to keep a man awake with that damned digging for?" he asked. "Haven't you got any bloody consideration?" I thought that was a bit humorous — a chap who was safely cuddled up in his dug out objecting to me making one on a night like this. I went on — but I presently got a better place on the other side of the creek a little way up the bank, just above the beach. As I was digging Ramsay and Murphy came up and gave me a hand — it really was a welcome help for I was fearfully hot. When they finished the dug out looked quite well — we heaped the earth on the Kaba Tepe side of it, which would keep out shrapnel bullets. But after they had finished I went on and dug and dug until it seemed to me ordinarily safe against gun fire from either flank — Kaba Tepe might get your boots, but not much else. . .

I don't know what time it was — perhaps 10 — when the dug out was finished. The staff were mostly sitting somewhere around not far from the general's dug out. In front of it was another dug out for the office which was also used as a mess room — tea was going there at meal times. But I, like most others, never felt in the least hungry and needed very little to drink. After the dug out was finished I fetched my pack, haversack and things there. . . The following morning first thing I went out and cut some arbutus branches and spread them overhead with the waterproof sheet over them for a roof. I had a post across the top and Riley helped me heap sand bags there for a bit of head cover — very heavy work but it made the dug out reasonably safe and was certainly needed for the roof was hit with shrapnel pellets. The dug out was never wide but it was safe. I used to write there at night after turning in — scribbling notes into the notebook from which I am transcribing this. The nights were moonlit and fortunately one could see to write by the light of the moon (for I had no other light) on most nights. But on Sunday and Wednesday nights when it was wet, and before the moon rose or after she went down, one could only guess at the position of the words one wrote, and I found pages afterwards scribbled over with lines written one on top of the other. One had not many hours of sleep — 3 or 4 this Sunday night, — perhaps from 10 to 4 the following nights. There was a cup of tea at 4.30 and breakfast at 7. This continued for about 4 or 5 days when the hour became 7 o'c. breakfast, 1 o'c. lunch and about 6 or 7 o'c. dinner — I was always very irregular so I never really knew what hours these meals were. I was out the whole day and wrote at night what little I did — bare notes. It was the 3rd day — or perhaps the second evening before I discovered that the mess was going for I was out nearly all day long. My meals until then consisted of chocolate and biscuits and water. (I generally took the water bottle to the trenches in case the men might like a drink). You filled your water bottle at some large tins on the beach into which water was pumped from a barge through a canvas hose. An A.M.C. man stood over these tins and there were several pannikins for ladling water out. There was also a low trough or tin for the mules. After the first few days these water tins, which were opposite the end of our gully, just on the edge of the sea, became very exposed to shrapnel and they built up sandbags in front of them. The water was taken up to the firing line in petrol or kerosene tins painted khaki and carried 2 on each side of a mule in wooden paniers... [The men] knew the value of these mules though they never liked them. As you went along the jostling crowded beach, a kick from a mule was very easy thing to get. You avoid them! A man would say — I'd rather have a bullet than a kick from a mule any day.

A pile of the kerosine tins and a pile of biscuit boxes gradually began to rise in front of my dug out — high and wider every day. The kerosine tins often had water in them and both they and the biscuit boxes provided shelters for the men on the beach when shrapnel came, although the working parties usually disregarded the shrapnel altogether...

Of course the beach was fearfully congested. As the night went on a great number of these stragglers were organised into parties to carry water, ammunition, and food, up to the lines. I have heard their number put at anything from 600 to 1 000. They many of them came down with wounded men. This is an offence in war, but few realised it at this early stage. The helping down of wounded did not really begin until about 4 or 5. Then it began to reach fair proportions — 6 men came down with one wounded officer. It is very easy to persuade yourself that you are really doing a charitable soldierly action in helping a wounded soldier to the rear. In later actions this has been chiefly done by the wounded themselves — one wounded man helping another — the men now realise that it is not right to leave the firing line. They were raw soldiers on that first day...

I went to sleep at about 11 or 12 for a couple of hours or less — I don't know if I even dropped off. The firing on the ridge above was tremendous and incessant and it sounded as though it were on the ridge above our heads — in fact many down on the beach thought it was — but it was not. There were every now and then a few specially sharp cracks and bullets whistled softly through the air...

I thought I could not tell how important these hours or the first night might be — and I particularly wanted to know how the artillery was landing; so I got up again and sat down by D.H.Q. with some of the others. General Godley had been in there earlier in the evening as the guest of our general. Howse was standing outside, talking to Col. Giblin. Watson of the Signal Coy. was there and clearly something was in the wind. In a minute or two I had what it was — some question as to whether we were to hold on or to embark at once.[6] Col. Howse unquestionably thought it was likely that the casualty clearing hospital would have to move off at once...

It was two o'clock then. I couldn't help looking at the sky to see if the dawn were breaking. One knew that it might have been possible to embark part of the force before daybreak if we had begun at night — but there were only 2½ hours of darkness left. It would have been sheer annihilation to attempt embarkation then — I was sure of that — the only possible way would be to hold on all next day, prepare all possible means of safeguarding the retirement and then embark next night without the enemy knowing what we were thinking of (if it were possible to deceive him). Even so the last part of the force covering the retirement would probably be sacrificed. I waited there sitting on the sand slope with some companion in the moonlight — with Howse and Col. Giblin talking in front of us. The General had gone somewhere — I don't know where — but one understood that the decision would be brought back by him. At two thirty either he, or some message, came back. There was a general stir in the small crowd which was in the know.

I heard a message being read out from the general's dug out for sending to all the units out on the ridges: "Sir Ian Hamilton hopes they will dig . . . and that the morning will find them securely dug in where they are... The Australian sailors have just got a submarine through the Dardanelles and torpedoed a Turkish ship."[7]

April 26
That clearly settled it... The group about the signal office broke up and everyone seemed to start digging — they were digging in the moonlight above the D.H.Q. office; clink of shovels everywhere — there was just 2 hours to daylight. The warships were firing all night and the two on the N. and S. flanks kept their searchlights steadily on the low country on the flanks. It was raining slightly but a waterproof sheet overhead and a drain leading out of one's dug out kept the rain from making much discomfort. I went back to the dug out as most others now did, and got a snatch of sleep before dawn.

It was the early grey of morning when I got up again. I walked along the beach in my overcoat to see if the guns had been landed yet... On my way down the beach I met Gen. Birdwood... Birdwood told me that he had been all round the line last night and seen all the men — they were fairly comfortable now. But he was obviously most disappointed by the result of the venture. "First there was the mistake of landing us a mile and a half north of where we should have landed," he said, "in this ghastly country. And then there's this enormous line. The troops very gallantly took an enormous extent of country against 500 well entrenched Turks." He was confident they'd hold it...

I think I went to sleep again. Anyway when I got up — perhaps 5 o'clock — the day was breaking properly. Everyone was getting up. I saw Col. White buttoning on his revolvers and his belt with a look up the valley behind him and it seemed to me that there was a general air of expectancy about the camp. In fact I'm sure that many officers there, when that morning broke, quite expected that we might be defending ourselves on the beach by evening and I think the whole lot were resolved that the Australian Divn. should not leave the beach — it would either stay there or cease to exist...

Well, the first surprise to me was that the expected bombardment did not come. Daylight came — but no bombardment. The sun got up... I went off after breakfast, on Col. Howse's advice to see what could be seen from the [casualty clearing] station in the gully... [Bean spent the rest of the morning moving within the line and talking to officers.]

I went back to D.H.Q. about midday. Blamey told me he had been up to the 3rd Bde. H.Q. [at Bolton's Ridge] — that it was quite safe getting up there and you got a good view. The only thing was to dodge to the right (instead of going straight up the gully) to the back of one of the hills in the valley where it became too exposed.

The 3rd Battalion dressing station in Shrapnel Gully, 26 April, and some of the wounded Bean passed along the way. (AWM neg. no. G920)

I started up the same gully in which the dressing station was except that this time I went up it not down it. The shrapnel was coming down it pretty frequently and yet stretcher bearer parties seemed not to worry — they brought wounded men down, others came and went with water and ammunition. A good many sheltered under the sides of the creek whilst shrapnel was close to them — and by dodging from side to side of the creek you could to some extent keep under cover... I am bound to say I took an occasional rest under a bank whilst going up — but the parties resting under some of the lower reaches of the creek were so numerous as to be of the nature of stragglers — men who had collected there as a comfortable position having nowhere else to go — and no one to see that they went there — that is the straggler's frame of mind. They were collected afterwards by Foster...

I found the telephone line leaving the road to go up a steep gully to the right. The gully was densely covered in scrub and very steep. But one managed to fight a way up it, occasionally meeting someone who was going the same way... I puffed up to a tiny ledge — mostly sand — in which were the signallers; they told me — that one could nip into the trench just above them — H.Q. was there...

The H.Q. was actually in the firing trench and it was a curious trench too. It faced both ways, down the gully and over the ridgetop on to the hillslope in front of it. Bullets were coming over fairly thick but I didn't know enough about them to say how close they were... It was an excellent place to find out what was going on just then... [T]he 9th and 10th [Bns] came over the hill (from White's Valley I should say) in lines making rushes. You didn't notice the men hit — you noticed them limping or rolling back wounded. I saw one man — wounded or unwounded I don't know, for the surface of that hill was very hot — rolling over and over and over through the scrub until he reached a hollow. Most of the men continued straight ahead but some came back or slipped sideways down into the protection of the gullies and crevices of the hillside. There was a machine gun in front, and shrapnel (although we couldn't see it then) was making the hilltop uncomfortable. I saw a most curious sight there — some of the men in the first lines came back fairly fast — others in the lines going up passed them going straight by them as you might pass a man in the street, taking not the slightest notice of them, one going up and the other coming back, almost brushing one another as a steamer might pass another steamer at sea. Evidently the man going forward had enough determination to say to himself — "My job is to go forward and I'm going forward whatever the other chap does." Generally a man who meets another coming back will come back with him...

April 27

This morning the Turks attacked the 3 Bn. They came on pretty thick.[8] Our men pumped lead into them, standing up so that they showed over the crest of the hill and handing their rifles back to be refilled. When the Turks were getting near our men fixed bayonets and the men on the rear slope of the hill prepared to charge but the Turks did not come on. The Turks had all German methods altho' some of the prisoners told us they had seen no German officers with them. They could be heard getting up to the edge of their slope of the hill and then their officers were heard trying to bring them on — there would be an argument just like the arguments we used to have with the Arabs in Cairo about loading a wagon. They seldom came really near our line...

The dug outs were mostly finished by now, and most of the men were in fair shelter. There were great loads and stacks of provisions growing on the beach and they were absolute protection from a shrapnel pellet. Offices — Supply and Ordinance —

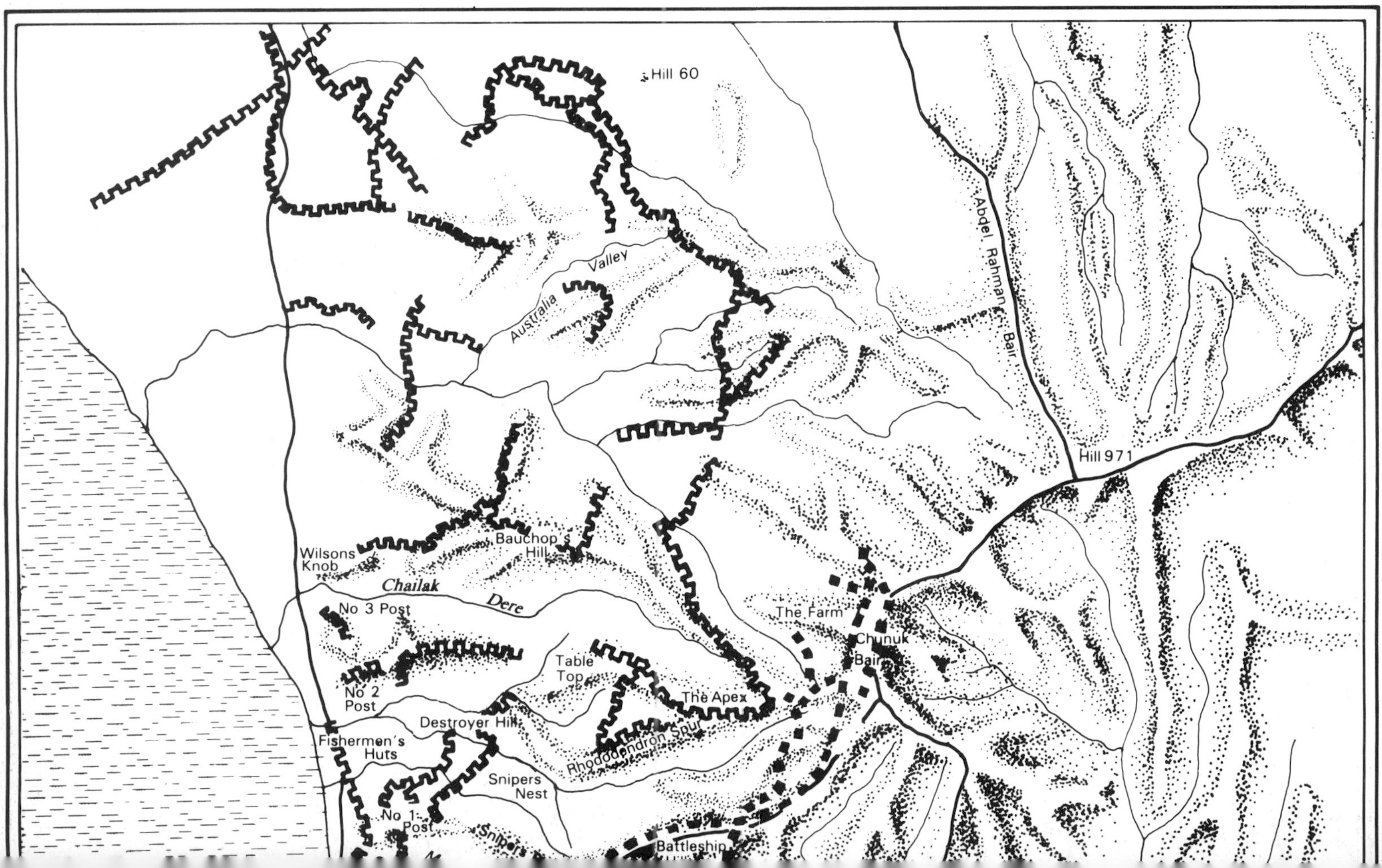

Hill 60
Abdel Rahman Bair
Australia Valley
Hill 971
Wilsons Knob
Bauchop's Hill
Chailak Dere
No 3 Post
The Farm
Chunuk Bair
Table Top
The Apex
No 2 Post
Destroyer Hill
Rhododendron Spur
Fishermen's Huts
Snipers Nest
No 1 Post
Snipers
Battleship

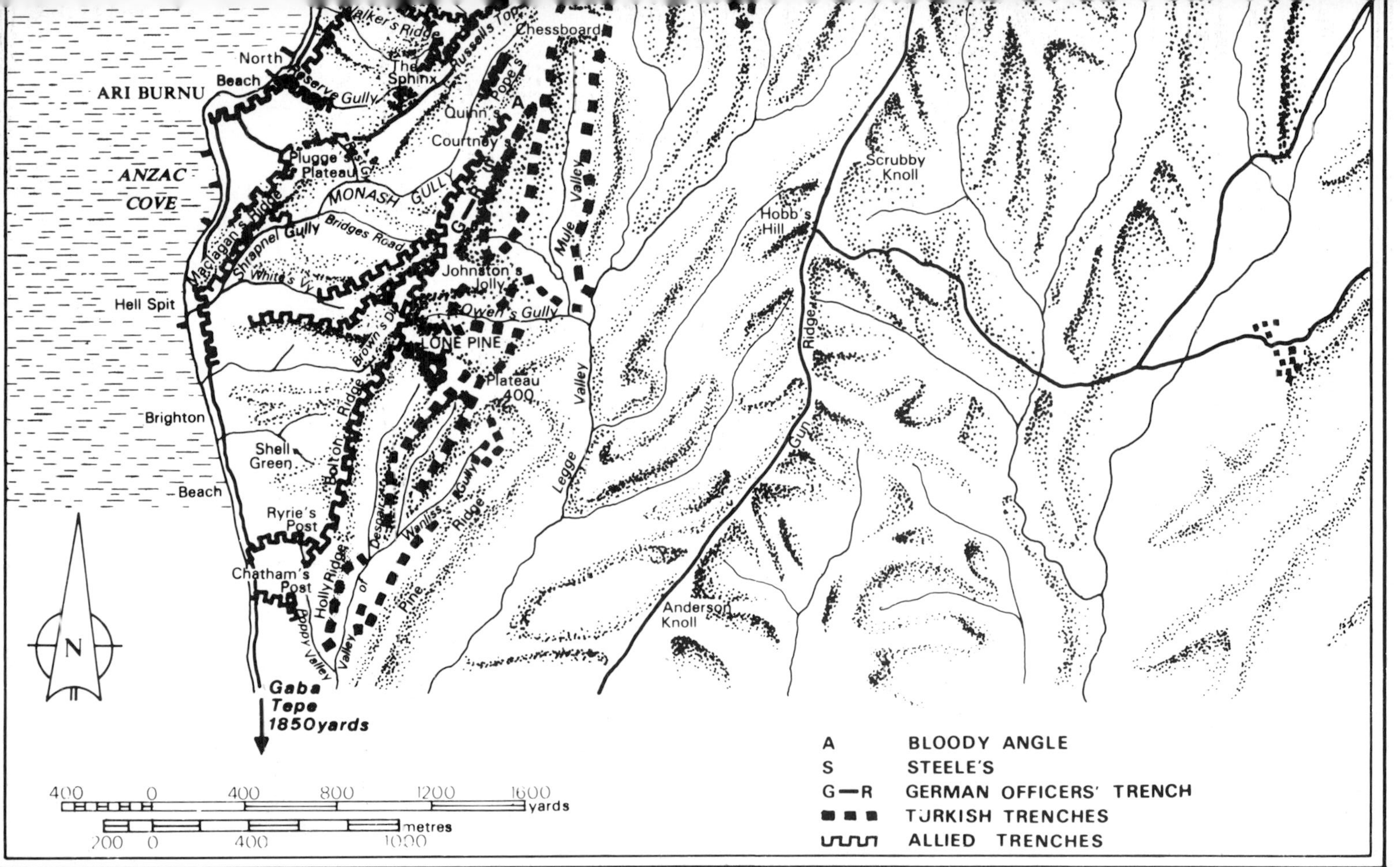

Anzac Cove area

were formed inside these stacks and men and officers of the Corps slept there. The hills themselves being pretty steep formed a fairly good protection from any except distant guns — and you could hear those coming. It was only where the gullies ran back that they could burst a shell low down — and that was the chief danger to Headquarters; especially to our 1st. Australian Division... Consequently a fair number of officers were hit there — fortunately by shrapnel burst so high up the ridge that it often didn't penetrate the clothing. During lunch as we were standing outside Hd. mess dug out Col. White who was inside it was hit ... by a shrapnel pellet pretty hard and laughed as he was hit — fortunately it didn't go through. We couldn't afford to lose him of all men...

I always take up a full water bottle and some cigarettes and the men are very glad of both. The *P. of Wales* is splendid — her men are keeping us alive on cigarettes —cigarettes are <u>the one thing</u> the men in the firing line ask for these days: that and news...

April 28

It is the practice whenever you go about to go with one armed man (generally 2 go together) now, as there are believed to be snipers inside our lines — there almost certainly are one or two or have been, although the state of the men and of many officers is such now that they imagine things that don't exist — just as anyone else would after 4 days tremendous hard work and no sleep. I don't know how many snipers there are — but hundreds are reported...

They have found the cubby hole of a sniper — not I am told the sniper himself — with 1 000 expended rounds of ammunition, 300 unexpended, 3 wks. rations, and a little well of water in it.

The whole camp is seeing snipers. The 9th., I think it was, got leave to go out and look for a sniper who they think has been shooting at them in their rest camp. As I came over the hill we met them out in pairs with their bayonets on guard searching the country like sleuth hounds...

When I got back to camp I found Maj. Brown of the 3rd. Bn. there with his face all over spots from shrapnel or bullets bursting gravel on to him. He had been hit three times, and looked as if he had tumbled down a gravelly hill mostly on his face. He told me a long story. "It was a sniper, I'm sure, that hit me the third time — I think he was beside me in the trench — the bullet seemed to come past from that way — I'll swear they were in the trench on both sides of us — they're brave by cripes, they are, much braver than we are. You could see the German officers in green uniforms with their swords at the carry walking up and down the line prodding the soldiers with them to make them get on." A few minutes later he told me that they saw little or no sign of German officers. That made me think (although old B. was a man whose account one would trust against that of a hundred others), this must be some sort of hallucination. I had just tumbled to it when Blamey as I walked away said quietly "Bean, I suppose you know its not wise to take seriously what a man says when he's in a condition like that... I meant to warn you." I had already grasped it...

April 29

On the beach is everything that is needed for the support of an army, supplies, transport, water, ambulances. There are 4 jetties made by pontoons with floating bridges to the short; laden barges — laden so that they scarcely have any freeboard left — out in the harbour lying at buoys; then a line of trawlers anchored close to one another in a bunch. Then far out the line of the big ships. On the beach are three wireless stations, each two tall masts and a long wire behind them, the masts fenced off by rope over which you trip at night. To the S. is one ambulance jetty. Howse won't have a big Red Cross upon his station — its right in the middle of a lot of stores, ordnance, etc. at which the enemy may perfectly fairly shoot and he says that it is absurd to put a Red Cross up on it. The N.Z. hosp. at the other end of the beach has one but our's ... has only a little Red Cross sufficient to show the men where to go to. There are lines of mules along the middle of the beach both N. & S. of our D.H.Q. gully, huge stacks of biscuit boxes, the kits of men who have thrown them down on their way up to the hills on the first day — and Austin in the middle of his stacks of ammunition. Army Corps H.Q. is in the gully just south of us dug into both banks.

All day long steamers are passing in and out of this busy port. The only sign of accident is the masts and funnel of the sunken trawler on the spit to the south of the beach. All day long there is flash, flash from the warships in the harbour or off it, — the reverberation seems to hit the hill as with a flat hand and shakes it — but you simply don't notice it at all now — either the noise or the earthquake.

All the while from the hills at our back comes the constant rattle of rifle fire — so close it sounds that every newcomer believes it comes from that hill itself. As a matter of fact it is one ridge over. There is the occasional plomp of a bullet into the water. Now and then, especially at meal times . . . shrapnel comes down the gully or over the ridge. Occasionally they fire a few shells during the night. Every now and then some mule starts kicking and once a mule starts that performance it is a very thorough business, it continues to kick either careering down the beach or turning circles, with its nose as the centre and its heels punctuating the circumference, until its load is on the sand, however long it takes to get rid of it. The men go into fits. Beyond the N. and S. end of the beach the concentration of our 3rd. and 1st. Brigades is going on — each battalion finding out what men and officers are here and which are lost. Even now there are many in the trenches, sandwiched in with other battalions, who will turn up in a few days. What happened to the rest — those who are not here and are not known to be killed or wounded — no one knows! They may have gone to Alexandria wounded — because in the first rush it was impossible to keep the names of all who were sent off — many went back wounded in ship's boats as soon as they landed; or they may have been wounded and taken prisoner or killed by the Turks. . .

Over opposite us as the afternoon turns to evening [the nearby islands of] Imbros and Samothrace begin to show up grey against the evening rose — the scene is perfectly exquisite — rose pink on the horizon, the sun's track broad upon the sea, the transports and their smoke haze, the black shapes of the barges, the pinnaces dragging great creases across the yellow satin surface — and all the time that lazy cricket going on at your back. Last night was wet and to-day Samothrace is covered with a cap of snow. . .

Turkish prisoners are brought each day into camp. The Australians certainly look on prisoners with disfavour. They have heard stories of mutilation — some of those who came back from the advanced positions in the fight on Sunday night brought stories of comrades whom they had passed, mutilated. The case almost everyone gives is that of Sergt. Larkin of the 1st. Battalion — a member of Parliament in New South Wales and a fine chap, with a fine influence amongst the men. . . He is supposed to have been left wounded and found later on mutilated. Our men — the Australians — will not (for this reason) if they can help it take prisoners[9]. . .

There is a clear and interesting difference between the N. Zealander and the Australian. The New Zealander regards the Turk much more kindly than our men. "Kind hearted beggars, the N. Zealanders", said one of our chaps the other day; "a Turk snipes them and then they catch the beggar and take him by the hand and lead him down to the beach..." Both New Zealanders and Australians have told me that they had orders from their subordinate officers in some cases to take no prisoners, in the first rush at any rate, and whilst things were bad. I don't believe this either, though it may be true. But undoubtedly the N.Z. fights more with his gloves on than the Australian: the Australian when he fights, fights all in.

And the Turk knows it — he is said to be afraid of us. And the truth is that there is no question (at least for operations such as we have had) that the Australian leaves the N. Zealander behind. There is no doubt on this subject amongst those who have seen them fight here. The N.Z. man is a good trustworthy soldier; but he has not the devil of the Australians in him; the wild, pastoral independent life of Australia, if it makes rather wild men, makes superb soldiers. The N.Z.s are outspoken in their praise of the way the Australians fought. They are proud of any praise given them by the Australians...

The jealousy that existed between N.Z. and Australia in Cairo vanished at one blow on the first day at Anzac — vanished utterly as far as the men were concerned...

[Some months later Bean added the note:] The N.Z. men half consciously came to imitate the Australians, e.g. The Australian language was about 5 times as strong as that of the N.Z.s — but the N.Z.s began to adopt it. The Sydney men followed the Sydney custom of trying to get their backs and skins as brown as possible through sun-baking. The N.Z.s followed them — they were often blacker than Turks and blacker than Indians before the summer was over...

May 2, Sunday

I have received permission to write and have spent all day on one long cable...

The Royal Naval Division which we have here is getting decidedly jumpy. On Friday night Australians of 16th [Bn] had to be put in amongst them to steady them. This morning they caught our Col. McNicoll and one of their own officers coming up a communication trench and fired at them. Luckily they missed them. They then tried to bayonet them but I suppose McNicoll was too tough for the bayonets only went in a little way. I haven't seen enough of these people to judge them; but what I have seen has been rather feeble — in fact hopeless. One man on Friday night started lifting his rifle above the trench with both hands and firing. "That's a good idea" he said. Another fat man like a pork butcher in a night cap came crawling along the trench. I must say it was a very bad trench. An Australian officer asked where he was going. He said the trench had fallen in on him and there was no trench left. He just wanted (he said) to get outside and shake the dust out of his clothes. Our officer — a kid from Tasmania in glasses — sent him back. I was several times mistaken for a spy that night.

This afternoon . . . the Turks made a fierce attack on our right. But they had no chance. Our men are now shooting splendidly — just picking their target. Some Turks got within 50 yards, but none got any further. A m[achine] g[un] opened on them from our left.

May 3

I hear that Monash's Brigade retired in the night — so our first forward move has been a failure. It has been pending for two days but has for some reason been postponed till last night... [A]ccording to one report our own artillery shelled our men out. Col. Hobbs was up before the General this morning. All sorts of rumours as to losses... [The objective had been to capture the high ground, Baby 700, and thereby restrict the Turkish line of fire against Monash Valley and Quinn's Post. Strong defence by the Turks repulsed the attack. Australian and New Zealand casualties were 338 and 262 respectively. The report of Allied artillery shelling its own units was mistaken.]

I got my first two cables away today — handed to Villiers-Stuart, who will transfer it to the *Queen* for sending on to the *Arcadian*. That's the best I can do. Maxwell kindly promised to send it on from there to one of the Greek Government telegraph stations, to which I have now leave to send un-prepaid messages[10]. . .

Monash gave me what he believed to be a full account of the attack on the plateau at the head of the gully made by his men last night.

At 6.35 the 16th Battalion started to move up the valley [towards Quinn's Post].

By 6.40 the positions occupied . . . began rifle fire against the crest to cover the attack, and also beyond the crest of the wooded hill. At 7 p.m. the Naval guns and our own started a tremendous bombardment...

At 7.48 a heavy cheer from the hilltop, and at 8 report reached Monash's H.Q. that the 16th were on top of the gully. There was a hot fire, but the 16th advanced singing "Australia will be there" and "Tipperary". The hill was . . . taken by the 13th and 16th, but without support.

At 8.10 more cheering indicated that the hill had been taken. The Otago Battalion was now moving up slowly. Monash put in 1 Company of the 16th to support it.

They hung on till daybreak 600 yards in advance of the previous position. At about 3 o'clock two battalions of Marine Infantry, which were to support them, arrived. These waited in the valley till 5, when it was too late to put them into the trenches. The Australians, however, had dug in and could probably have held on. They had only 70 shovels to the battalion, and could not get more until 100 arrived at daybreak. The battalions had actually reached the first line of Turkish trenches and bayoneted the Turks, but could not remain because unsupported. They had 4 machine guns against them... We dug in as best we could under fire. At 4 a.m. Colonel Monash was discussing a move ahead as he was getting two battalions of the R.M.L.I. Just then (at 5.15, according to Monash) the whole of our artillery opened on the ridge held by our men. They got in three 18-pounder shells and 5 Mountain gun shells — which burst right in the trenches and blew men into the air... The whole face of the cliff of the nearer hill which yesterday was covered with bushes, is today bare, and along the top of it our dead can be seen lying like ants, shrivelled up or curled up, some still hugging their rifles: about a dozen of them. The face of the further plateau is also edged with our dead...

Blamey and I went up this afternoon. We found Monash's men still hanging on to the part of the ridge to the left which we had won, but not to the plateau... Monash seemed to me a little shaken. He was talking of 'disaster', and said our men would certainly have to retire from the part of the new ground which they still held... I'm sure I can't see why they should. The reason may be that they (our men) have been there since the afternoon of the first Sunday and Monday — seven days, without relief...

Blamey and I on our walk up the gully to the 1st and 4th Brigades, had a very uncomfortable time with Turkish shrapnel. The moment we turned over the neck of the Battery Knoll at the south end of the beach a shrapnel case flew very low over our heads. The way up the gully is along the sandy winding creek bed which runs down it. Water comes down this in driblets, and was most useful the first day; but it is too filthy for words now. In parts the creek bed has been churned into thin flat yellow mud, ankle deep. An Indian battery is camped on the back of the hill in the middle of the lower end of the gully; and dead mules, probably water carriers, lay four or five of them right in the water course. A pipe line leads up the gully to a dam labelled 'Reserve of water'. This holds a muddy yellow liquid. Above this, fair in the stream, is a dead mule. Several dead men lie on the side of the creek — I don't know if they are Turks or our men — possible Turkish snipers who have been bayoneted. They are in our uniform, but it is hard to tell from that of the Turks. The smell of the dead animals in this valley is very bad in parts...

May 4

[At dawn a force of 112 men was sent to reconnoitre Gaba Tepe. It discovered, to its cost, that the point was heavily fortified. Several Navy picket boats dashed in and daringly rescued the survivors of the contingent.]

The Turks let us get our wounded into the boats at K.T. without firing on us at all whilst doing so — although they fired at the boats as they went out.

This afternoon at about 2 o'clock, a naval launch went in under a white cross flag to look for a wounded man — and brought him off (One of our wounded engineers in the morning was being left by the engineers comfortably sheltered and provided; but he begged so to come off that at last they took him). The Turks let our boat come in, get its man, and sail. Later — about 3 o'clock — a Turkish party with a white cross and red crescent came out of a trench near Rosenthal's Battery [on Bolton's Ridge] — on the spur below it or else from the near gun emplacements — and went across to Kaba Tepe. It was of course not fired on by us. It picked up some wounded and retired through K.T...

I went up to Rosenthal's battery again this evening... It is the quietest day we have had — beautifully sunny and warm, with only an occasional sniping shot, exactly like the crack of a cricket ball, on the hills above the beach. As I sat writing with my feet in the sun and my back under the shade of the rug, which now forms the canopy of my dug-out, with the sun turning the sea into satin with little embroidered ships on it, I could scarcely believe that this crack, crack, was not the nets at Clifton College or Rushcutter Bay, when three or four men are practising at once.[11] Our men now only shoot to hit — they spend one shot where last week they spent 5. Tonight, however, the Naval Blokes are in the trenches, I believe, and there is ceaseless firing. Far to the south I can hear the rumble of another bombardment. Our ships are blasting the northern slopes of Kaba Tepe...

May 5

Snipers have now been cleared out of the gullies. Our men got them with bayonets. Shooting within the lines is dangerous, although they sometime do it. The sniper lies low whilst you search for him, and won't generally shoot at two or three men armed because the others would drop and search for him. He simply lies low and is generally bayoneted when found...

They think that the Turks must have heard that we intended to land at Kaba Tepe, for they made the place exceedingly strong — I doubt if we could have landed there...

We now know we have 24 battalions against us — we have placed them. We, ourselves, have 12 of ours, 4 (4th Brigade) and 4 (N.Z.) — 20 from Australasia; and 3 R.M.L.I. and Naval Brigades — I don't think Nelson [Battalion, Royal Naval Division] is here. That makes 23, of whom our Australian troops are good and the Naval people feeble. The Navy is quite different — it is splendid, the best in the world; but these poor R.M.L.I. and Naval Brigade lads seem unfitted to hard fighting. Unfortunately our own fine infantry of the 1st Australian Division has lost 5 000 men — about 40% of its strength. The Division can only be 7 000 strong at present. We know the Turks too have lost heavily. Our missing are probably lying out beyond our lines — one knows indeed that many of them are...

9 p.m. I got leave to come off with the 2nd Brigade, and a New Zealand Brigade, to reinforce at Cape Helles. We were to leave at 9.15 — go down by night; the transfer wouldn't be noticed by the enemy...

[Sir Ian Hamilton had been led to believe, mistakenly as it happened, that the ANZAC attacks of 2–3 May had made the line at Anzac Cove secure. He therefore decided to transfer some units from the Cove south to Cape Helles to help consolidate that position. These battalions would assist in an attack on Achi Baba, the dominant peak of the Peninsula.]

May 6

Well, long before 9.15 the first lot of troops were ready in the boats — but no destroyers to take them off. We waited all night. I waited with the staff in Monash's A.S.C. mess for a bit, and then curled up under some flour bags in my sleeping bag and slept on the beach til 2.30. The first lot of boats was just moving off then. At 3.45, in daylight, we were taken to a trawler in a horse lighter. They were very nice to us — let us have our kits in a cabin where I am writing this. The troops take 2 days' rations. They had been

Coming ashore at Cape Helles on 6 May via the beached collier, *River Clyde*. (AWM neg. no. G957)

very cold all night. The A.S.C. mules were sent away from the beach by our staff in order to make room. Some other staff officers ('beach officers' I think, taken from the Egyptian service) sent them back. This happened three times; three times the mules were sent up the road; three times they were ordered back.

Altogether a rotten piece of staff work. The first thing that happened when we got on the trawler was that her captain asked: "Does anyone know when we sail. Who is to give us orders to sail?" We shall have told the enemy that we have weakened here and strengthened down south — a hopeless thing to do.

Altogether tonight's arrangements are in keeping with the worst days of the British service...

As we came up to the *River Clyde*[12] [at Cape Helles] a geyser went up just on the north side of her, as if a whale had spouted. This fire came from the southern shore. The *Agamemnon* or *Lord Nelson* came steaming up towards the Dardanelles, and turned her guns on to a low ridge or false crest about a mile or two inland from the southern mouth. Presently a second shell landed right beside one of our fleetsweepers moving in under the *River Clyde*. I was wondering what they would do, as these were clearly big shells — probably 6" — and one naturally supposed they would do more harm than the shrapnel we generally got at Anzac. We had had big shells there too, but I had no experience of them... No one took the slightest notice. They just put on their packs and landed from the *River Clyde* across the pontoons connecting her with the shore. There were Greek and French porters working stores off this pier. Near it was an overturned horse boat or landing pontoon. They say this big gun on the Southern shore does marvellously little harm: it hurt one man the day before. Its range was only 10 or 12 foot out.

We came ashore... We drew up on the beach — I was carrying my sleeping bag (I try and get it where I can as a protection against the old Pneumonia) and a heavy kit, and was glad of the rest...

We picked up our packs and marched over the hill crest and found ourselves winding down a road which curved round the hillside between olive and other small trees on the nearer slopes of a very wide vista — almost a valley. The land dipped before us, gently undulating, until it rose many miles away to Achi Baba hill — the same we could see in the far south from Anzac. The scene was exactly like an artist's birdseye view of a battle. Straight ahead of us 6 miles away rose Achi Baba, a tall straight side with sloping shoulders and a knoll or peak in the middle — rather like a man's head and shoulders, except that the head is represented merely by a triangular peak. Between us the land ran in gentle folds, with a sprinkling of elms and other trees, and a great deal of open country, grass covered or cultivated, with patches of heath. Some way in front of Achi Baba, on the foot-slopes to the left, was a town with a row of round mills (rather like silos) beside it, which one knew must be Krithia.

The Achi Baba was the peak which we had watched for days from Anzac — eagerly. The warships often shelled the reverse slope of it — and sometimes we believe we saw — or rather, generally heard that people saw — the British shells bursting on the northern side of it. For days we had watched to see any sign of the British on the hill itself, and now, just as we got to the further edge of the raised land above the beach — not a third of a mile from the beach — we found in the bushes on the left hand side of the road, a French battery... As we got a little further down the road we passed an English battery, also clearly in position, with its horses hidden away in the trees. Further on there seemed to be a third. "Seems to me they've got very little further than we have", said someone. "Just a foothold — no more". It was a change to see horses — officers riding up the road... We marched down into the green fields — wheat fields — with a tiny muddy stream running through them; and turned in on to them to the left. There were the rest of the Brigade, and Colonel M'Cay, who had come on the day before, and Lieut. Hastie, his orderly officer. Colonel

M'Cay gave the order to dig in. "They can see you from Achi Baba", he said "so get dug in just as fast as you can. They'll have their shrapnel on to you in a few minutes." The men at once started. There was water about two feet down or less, so the dug outs had to be shallow...

May 8

[The renewed Allied offensive at Cape Helles had begun on 6 May. After 2½ days of hard fighting not even the first of the planned three phases of the attack had been completed successfully. Consequently, on 8 May it was resolved to make a final effort and launch a general attack against Krithia and Achi Baba.]

This afternoon we got up the second batch of reinforcements who had come straight round after one day at Anzac... The reinforcements had just reported to their battalions, and were being allotted to their Companies. At that moment the Brigadier came back (about 5 p.m.) and at 5.5 p.m. there suddenly arrived an order that the 2nd Australian Brigade was to be in line with the N.Z.s and advancing by 5.30 p.m. Its objective was to be the ridge behind Krithia — which was 2¼ miles away.

Of course it was touch and go whether the order could be carried out. It left 25 minutes for the brigadier to get the order to the battalions; the battalion commanders to get the order to their men; the men to get their packs, rations, and gear on; and four battalions to get into position and move up in fighting formation from ¼ to ½ mile. There was no time for the brigadier to get his battalion commanders together to reconnoitre the position or have any sort of conference. The most that could be done was to rip out an order to the battalions to move out at once in fighting column...

The Brigadier ... moved off at the head of the 6th [Bn], and I moved with him. I didn't take my pack, but I took the telescope and camera case... When we were about 200 or 250 yards on our way, the shrapnel came: and it missed us altogether. It flew well over our heads, and burst over the lines then coming out of the trees...

Our artillery ... had begun shelling the enemy at 4.30 — the regulation hour before the attack. I didn't notice the bombardment becoming heavy on our front until after 5 — I think 5.15. They shelled until 5.30, when there seemed to be a lull. When the enemy started shelling us the guns opened heavily again, and the uproar was tremendous. You could not hear the bullets whizz — it was a bit of a relief to that extent; but I was never in the midst of such an uproar — bang, bang, bang, from the front — bang, bang-a-bang, bang-whang-bang-a-whang — and so on from the rear. It was as if the universe was a tin-lined packing case, and squads of giants with sledge-hammers were banging both ends of it, and we tiny beings were somewhere in between. The echoes were reverberating away to Achi Baba, and back again. We were stumbling over the low gorse, tramping ahead. One boy to the left of me carried his spade, shovel end upwards like a fan in front of his head with his left hand, I wonder if it was a sort of instinct — because I think the greater number of bullets were coming from there... About 400 or 500 yards up the plateau we suddenly found a trench in front of us. It was one of our trenches, filled with Lancashire Fusiliers — but it might have been filled with Turks for all we knew. We came upon it quite unexpectedly — a bank of red earth running across the heath. A quarter of a minute later we were up to it, and found a lot of British soldiers looking up at us... The men all flung themselves down to get breath because we had come fast, especially with packs and haversacks...

There was an accident of which something has been made — an exaggerated account — in the papers. I didn't incur any more danger than any poor private even in this one attack — No! not so much. I have no right to the credit of the lowest simplest soldiers — and I am not as brave as most of them.

Whilst we were in this trench — and the brigadier was still there — I kept my head down most of the time; but when one put it up one could see that men had been knocked out — a good few of them. There was one chap I could see wounded about 20 yards to my right front — he was moving. I thought he would probably be hit again if he stayed out there, but the prospect of getting out and helping him in was not nice. However, I thought, if one gets into these positions in the firing line one must accept the consequences. I waited a bit, and presently the youngster rolled over and began to painfully crawl in. One couldn't stay any longer, so I nipped out of the trench and ran out to him and helped him back — with my help he could get along on both legs. We were back in the trench very quickly. I don't think I did much good, but one's conscience wouldn't let one stay any longer — that was my only reason.[13] As I ran back the brigadier said: "Look here Bean, if you do any more of these dam' fool actions I'll send you straight back to H.Q. I've power to you know." A few minutes later he was doing the 'dam' fool action himself up on the parapet... He jumped up on the parapet his periscope in hand. I don't know what officers were in the trench then, but he said: "Now then Australians — which of you men are Australians? Come on Australians!!" The men jumped up — I suppose about 100 of this lot. "Come along Australians" they called. "Come on Australians!" They picked themselves up, many with their rifles at the charge, and scrambled over the trench, over the Tommies' heads, into a very heavy fire. The fire really was very heavy by now. It was knocking spurts of dust off the parapet into everyone's face, kicking up little spits of dust. I saw it knock a stick four feet into the air as if playing tipcat — but the Australians went on like a whirlwind.

As they got up I felt for my camera. There was the case, but no camera in it. Then I remembered I had left it in the trench at H.Q. So I missed the finest war photographs that have never been taken.

The brigadier stayed in that trench a while watching the troops coming up — and I thought he would place his H.Q. there. A second lot came up with Col. McNicholl... They rested there 3 minutes; then Col. McNicholl asked Col. M'Cay what he wanted them to do. "I think they'd better go on", said the brigadier. "Right, Sir", said McNicholl, and jumped up on the rear side of the trench where he had been resting. The same instant he slid down — collapsed rather — with his back against the tree which rose in the trench. "Are you hit!" said M'Cay anxiously. "Only slightly, I think", he said, nodding, gasping a little for breath as he spoke.

Two men tore open his tunic where he pointed, and found that he had only a flesh wound in the left shoulder. He jumped up at once — though it must have given him a great bang — absolutely collected, his normal self, and bent over the trench, drew his whistle, blew it, waved the men on with an under sweep of his right hand, like that of a bowler bowling lobs, and led them on. They'd have gone anywhere with him. I didn't watch them much; I had my head above the parapet a good bit, and it was risky to do too much of it. The men were dropping very fast now. Many had dropped in front of the trench, and a good number behind. Every now and then a man came running or limping back — in every case the man was wounded. One man ran into the trench quite fast — I wondered he could run so fast if he were wounded; but he was bleeding heavily from the throat. One of the signallers of our little party had been hit in the neck, but not badly. Another man came limping in at a half run — he just managed to get to the trench, and then threw himself on the parapet and was dragged in. He looked very frightened and haggard. He was losing blood from a wound in the upper leg. The men in the trench always bandaged the wound, wherever it was, for the man. A man behind the trench must have made some sign, poor chap, that he wanted help, for a Lancs. Fusilier ran out, sat beside him for quite a long time, lying in front of him so as to partly protect him; and then lifted him on his back and brought him in. A good number of men, of course, lay out there and never moved.

The Companies coming up now were some of them a little slower, and it sometimes looked as if the first line might be unsupported unless the others kept up the pace. The first line was over the edge, out of our view or perhaps lying in the scrub. We could see others half way to them, advancing by long dashes, very fast, occasionally flinging themselves on to the ground for a breather — always going on. Some of them were not as quick throwing themselves down as they have been in practice — not like the 9th and 10th I saw on April 26th. They would calmly pick a place to lie in. As there seemed likely to be a little gap between the supporting Companies and the firing line, owing to the pace being uneven, the Brigadier jumped up and walked along to see that the Companies came up. "Come on", he shouted, waving his periscope, "run". They came on very fast, and they were given three minutes in the trench — and then in every case they went over it with a shout of "Come on Australians!!" If there were no officers to lead them on an N.C.O. would. I heard one chap say: "Come on chaps, we've got to get it sometime. We can't stay here always"; and that was the spirit — that, and the feeling that being Australians they must get on. It was very fine to watch, and it was great to watch them as they went, absolutely unaffected by bullets. I never saw one man whose manner was changed by them, except in that moment when they got up and faced them; and rushed over the trench — then their faces were set, their eyebrows bent, and they looked into it for a moment as men would into a dazzling flame. I never saw so many determined faces at once — Oh! what a photograph I missed.

The brigadier called for someone amongst the Lancs. Fusiliers to volunteer to take on the telephone reel in place of the signaller who was hit. One of them volunteered. This was the first I heard of any idea of taking Brigade H.Q. further forward. You couldn't see anything from where we were, and so I suppose the Brigadier wanted to get to somewhere he could see... The Brigadier went on. As he went he said to me: "I don't think you need come, Bean. You're wiser to stay where you are". I knew I was, and stayed there...

I was sitting in the trench when Hastie dropped in beside me panting. He had had a devil of a time, he said, looking for Bolton. The fire was very hot, and running about searching for a man in those sort of conditions is not an easy job. A French company — or half company — which had come up to the trench (they were little French infantrymen running under heavy packs) had not gone on and seemed to have no idea of doing so. So Hastie and I went along to them and tried to explain in French — Il faut avancer avec les Australiens . . . he said — but they nodded and lay still. I don't think they had an officer there. The main part of the 8th did not seem to have turned up, and so Hastie got up and went off to find them again. A few minutes later a message was passed along the trench for Captain Bean. It was from Hastie: "Shot through both hands. Please inform Brigadier".

I accordingly went along by the trench until I could get the wire leading to Brigade H.Q. Then I kept that in my hands and led myself by it as by a handrail. I had gone about 200 yards when someone in the scrub just to my left said: "Hullo old man — you up here?" It was McNicholl: he was lying sheltering behind two packs which had been put in front of him by some chap going across. Word had reached into the Tommy's trench that he had been hit in the abdomen, and I found this was true. He was awfully plucky and cheerful. I told him I would get some stretcher-bearers, and I got another pack from near a dead man and put it in front of him, making him fairly secure. Then I went on and about 150 yards further I came on quite a reasonable sized dug out crossing the path. It was down about 3 feet, about 9 feet long, and parapet about 2 feet or 18 inches. It was the new Brigade H.Q. As I came up the Brigadier called me a fool. Three or four shots snapped about my ears, and I daresay things were a bit close — they seemed to think so there. I found the Brigadier there with one signaller and a couple of others — only the Brigadier and that signaller had got through of the 7 who started with the Brigade H.Q.

The Brigadier told me it was impossible to reach the ridge behind Krithia. "They set us an impossible task", he said. . .

I waited there some time, and then returned. I had got nearly to the bottom of the hill where we emerged from cover at first, when I saw a party of men on the left. It was nearly dark — could just see them. It turned out to be stretcher-bearers. I asked if some would come with me. They said they were going out to the right — hundreds there. I told them McNicholl was wounded. Two men immediately said they would come, and followed me. It seemed a very great distance. We followed the line in the dark to the Tommy's trench and over (one of them went off for a moment to attend to a man who was crying out 'stretcher-bearer' — and came back after fixing him). We asked at the trench if McNicholl had been carried in — they thought some colonel had been. However, we plugged on. The way along that wire seemed very long, and I didn't like dragging the stretcher-bearers into it, but they never hesitated. I was beginning to think he must have been carried in — but decided to go right on to H.Q. You could only just see. I scanned carefully everyone I passed, and at last found someone lying behind three packs. We carried him in. Somehow we had picked up his batman in the Tommy's trench. He carried part of his kit and I took his pack. It was a very long way back to the dressing station — under some trees down a bank. The place was getting very full — you could just see the two dim lanterns by which they did their work (I had to lend them two candles the next night). The ground was strewn with wounded taking their turn, and the path along the bank of the creek was a constant succession of men limping along with supporter — generally a wounded man also. About 400 yards further up along the bank was Mathison's dressing station, the medical officer of the 5th; he simply took men who were not already treated at all — they were constantly calling across to know the way, and his cheery voice answered across the creek directing them.

On the way back to the Tommy's trench I saw one poor devil — out of the hundreds who were lying there — trying to get back to cover. I asked if I could help him — he was hit through the leg, high up, and was crawling. We went some way together, limping — he in great pain — when he fell saying: "Oh God — Oh Christ — oh it's awful." He had been hit a second time through the same leg, or the other leg. I asked if he could still come on. "Oh, no — no I can't", he said. The plateau was very exposed, so I simply dragged him by both legs — he consented — into the nearest thing to a dimple in the ground that I could find — got hold of two packs and put them round him, and left him. He had torn open his trousers, as they generally do, to see the wound, and was bleeding pretty freely. I don't fancy he can have lived — poor chap.

I made my way back to the old H.Q. in the creek bank — I stumbled up and down the creek a long time before finding it — and into Mathison's place once. It is extraordinary how difficult it is to recognise places by night, which you know by day — looks entirely strange country. I finally got to H.Q., and found Chamberlain — the Brigadier's batman, anxious to start up to H.Q.

with the Brigadier's blanket, etc. I offered to show him the way there, and so trudged over the same hill again. The cries of wounded all round, who thought us stretcher-bearers, were most distressing. We could only tell them the stretcher-bearers will come — there seemed to be none about at all. There were numbers of wounded in the Tommy's trench. For a second time we followed the wire across the heath — it used to get tangled round bush, but we could always find it going on.

When we got to H.Q. we found men there, but the brigadier had gone on to the firing lines. The men at H.Q. were working to deepen it — with two spades and one entrenching tool. They had pulled in around it several wounded men — 4 altogether, I think, certainly 3. One was the signaller — wounded through the leg. He was still helping with signals although his leg was broken — had telephone to his ears lying along the top of the trench, just outside it. When a message came he would transfer the receiver to the ears of the man next to him in the trench — at least that was, as far as I could see, the proceeding. Behind us was lying the poor volunteer from the 8th Battalion, shot through the intestines, in terrible pain — at times crying like a child — incoherently — asking for "Doctor, doctor!" They asked if I had any morphia. I found some J. had given me, and gave him. One lozenge was dropped, so had to give another. He seemed quieter after that, but soon was in pain again, and kept on rolling over on to the broken leg of the signaller. "Oh, can't you keep him quiet — what does he want to roll over on my leg for?", said the signaller. The boys in the trench tried to readjust them — and told the poor chap in pain: "Try to be still, old man. It's the best thing for you. Try and bear up!" It was all they could do. He asked: "Water, water", and they moistened his lips. "You must not have it for your own sake, old chap", they said — as he had a wound in the abdomen. There was a third wounded man lying around the left front of the dug out — absolutely quiet and uncomplaining — he only spoke when the men asked him how he was.

Away to our right — 50 or 60 yards — was a man always crying "Stretcher-bearer! stretcher-bearer!!" — and somewhere out in the dark was another — they cried in a rather dry, quavering voice. You could hear plenty of others further away calling always the same "Stretcher-bearer"; and as one went over the heath that night, on every journey 6 or 8 men or more would call out to you asking if you were a stretcher party — sometimes coherent, sometimes not. One messenger who came up to H.Q. dug out, when the wounded men there called for stretcher-bearer, said:

"You wont see them tonight my boy — they're rarer than gold. You wont get them along here." It was an idiotic thing to say. "You might let us think we will" said one of the wounded men feebly.

The Brigadier came back presently; said the men had dug in and that the right of the line was all safe... A policeman and myself accordingly went back to the old H.Q. leaving Chamberlain at the new H.Q....

I went back with the policeman — i.e. the sixth trip across that heath — but fire was now spasmodic. The brigadier was anxious to get water and stretcher-bearers up and asked me to do what I could about the latter. I went to H.Q. and told them, and then went on to the dressing station. I saw Chambers there, and he said that all the stretcher-bearers were fully at work, but could I get a message to A.D.M.S. asking for waggons or wheeled transport to be sent to take the wounded from the dressing station to the beach as the stretcher-bearers had to be used for this. This explained it all: the awful sounds of the wounded upon that heath. As the brigadier had said — the wounded must be cleared from near the firing line first, as it would be impossible to get at them there once day broke, as no one could cross the heath by day except by bolting like a rabbit and at imminent risk. Yet not one stretcher-bearer seemed yet to have reached the firing line, and it was now past midnight...

I went back to the old H.Q. in the creek, and found Mathison... He had been doing work — going all night wherever wanted. I borrowed a water tin (petroleum tin) got it half full, and was just starting the seventh journey over the battlefield, when news came by messenger "Brigadier hit". He was on his way to H.Q. to see about getting up water, stretcher-bearers and food, when the Turks, I suppose, got one of their firing fits, and he was hit through the leg — sent messenger on for stretcher.

Mathison with another chap and I with water tin at once started out to find him. Goold put us on the wire to the new H.Q., and we followed it up the hill searching carefully. About half way up the first slope Mathison went off to some poor chap who was calling. I left the water tin near the wire and went on for a bit searching along the line. Mathison twice called out if I had any luck, but I could not find the brigadier. I went on — past a patch of scrub — this time passing it on its left hand side, so felt pretty sure I had the wrong line — we had left it and picked up the wrong one. It led to the Tommy's trench. I thought it better to go on and make sure — so went over the plateau apparently endlessly,

The dead lie in no man's land after the 8 May attack by the 2nd Infantry Brigade at Krithia. Photograph by Capt. J.E. Stevens. (AWM neg. no. C1079)

hoping to goodness the Turks wouldn't start firing again in one of their panics. The line finally led to two chaps lying in a shallow dug out, curled under the parapet about a foot deep. They were the signallers of the 8th Battalion, and the line must have been the 8th Battalion wire — but they didn't know where the 8th were, and the wire had been cut, probably by a bullet. They told me that Brigade H.Q. had gone back to the old H.Q. — or to the Tommy's trench, so I went back again (journey eight). The cries of wounded were heartrending. The Tommy's trench was full of them — little Mathison had been up there attending to them. The poor chaps there badly wanted water.

I went back down the hill, struck the wire to the 8th up which I had come, searched for the old water tin, and found it — much to my surprise. I decided to take it right up to the firing line. However, when I got to the wounded in the Tommy's trench one could not help giving the poor chaps a drink. I told them I had very little to spare, and they must be content with a little. We got a mess tin and handed a little down to each one in the trench or under the parapet. They were as good as gold. Each fellow took about two sips and then handed it back — really you could have cried to see how unselfish they were...

It was late — 4 o'clock, nearly — and there was not a great deal of water in the tin — so I decided to leave it at the Tommy's trench with two Lancs Fusiliers who were there, to give the wounded every now and then. I stumbled home through the gorse, falling heavily once or twice. On my way I passed a poor fellow I had spoken to once before. He was groaning so much that I had gone out to speak to him. "Oh, I'm in agony", was all he could say — "I'm in agony". I told him what I had told them all, that the stretcher-bearers would be along soon to take him away. It was most unlikely, but it was the one thing they clung on to; so did the men in the Tommy's trench; so did those around the firing line. It made you mad to think of the dull, stupid, cruel, bungling that was mismanaging the medical arrangements. The men in the firing line would gladly have gone without a days rations if only the carts could have been used in carrying the wounded down from the dressing station to the beach, and the stretcher-bearers left free for taking the men from the firing line. One knew now that there was no earthly chance of many of the men near the firing line being taken in before daylight, and that meant that they must lie unattended, sometimes exposed to heavy fire, for a whole 15 or 16 hours more.

(The Medical arrangements of our division have been first class since the beginning — the work of the stretcher-bearers magnificent, and the wounded quickly cleared; but once the wounded leave our hands there seems to be the same general muddle which is the one thing that impresses you with almost everything this British staff has done as far as we have seen it. Everything is late — nothing up to time — no evidence of brains that I have seen, although I know brains do exist there. Braithwaite, Ward, Ian Hamilton, are undoubtedly good men, but I think there must be an impossible proportion of dugouts.[14] As for the Medical Staff — the arrangements are a sheer scandal. They have foreseen nothing. We from Australia spend thousands of pounds in sending splendid hospitals, and we cannot get even a minimum of attention for our troops. The losses on our landing of course took them completely by surprise. We knew there might be 30% of casualties the first day — which is apparently what there were — but, naturally, nothing of the sort was provided for by the British Staff: the wounded had to be taken on transports. On one of these there were 400 or 500 patients, and not a single bedpan! They had to use paper instead, and shortly ran out of paper — after that they had to perform their natural functions on the deck as they lay. One of our officers in the end managed to borrow for them three bedpans. All this time, and up to the 20th May — when I am writing this from my notes — there was the Hospital Ship *Soudan* with about 10 surgeons and a full staff aboard, and not more than about a dozen slightly wounded men. The 1st Australian Stationary Hospital at Lemnos with all its equipment which was nearest to us was packed off elsewhere, and the Authorities are only now — four weeks after we started — thinking of asking the Government for leave to establish a General Hospital at Imbros, where Turkish prisoners are being sent. Some of our wounded of the first day arrived at Heliopolis without a wound having been redressed for seven days...)

The appearance of a fight at night is quite different from what I expected. The rifle fire ran along the enemy's trench (I suppose it must have been a trench, for I couldn't see the place of course) like the flashes of light along a diamond necklace — rippling all the time. The flashes were quite white — almost like electric sparks — just a pin-point, not a stab like I have seen in other places — I suppose this was either because they were distant or else because they pointed straight at one.

The officers believe we could have gone a lot further after dark — but of course at the Turkish trench machine guns would have to be met and faced...

I got back to the old H.Q. at about 4 o'clock, pretty well done. Mathison was just starting with a party of stretcher-bearers — about 18 or 20 of them. Just afterwards one of the Turkish panics broke out, with heavy firing. That is the only occasion I have seen stretcher-bearers jumpy. Four or five of them came rushing back into the trench where I was, and remained under the shelter of it some time after the firing had ceased — they didn't like to leave it at all, though it was just on daylight, and this was the last chance of getting the poor chaps out. I said something pretty straight, but it didn't seem to affect them — they were youngsters. Presently Mathison came back and got them all away. I lugged out my sleeping bag and slept till 9 o'clock, or later...

May 9, Sunday

This night there was a night attack by the Turks. I decided, as I had no work at all done since arriving, to go right back and camp near the beach, and work for a day or two in quiet. I had tried typing in the trench at H.Q. but it was ruinous to the typewriter. I humped my heavy pack, stationery, valise, and typewriter down the gully. It was awfully heavy... I wandered round ... till I was dead tired of carrying the sleeping bag — and finally threw it down in some abandoned dugouts and slept there. The banging of

Bean, looking tired and drawn after the fierce battle of the previous night, relaxes with men from 2nd Brigade, 9 May. (AWM neg. no. G967B)

the artillery at night over one's head was terrific, but I slept, like a bird almost, through it — it was rather pleasant than otherwise...

I wrote out under a tree all the morning... [He stayed there another week before returning to Anzac Cove.]

May 16, Sunday

It was about 5 in the evening before we got on to the Fleetsweeper, F.S.2, and sailed... We got opposite Kaba Tepe very quickly — after passing up empty steep coast. As we got opposite our old position there was great interest to see how our fellows had progressed. Was the position extended? We had heard all sorts of rumours: they had taken Baby 700. A man had been recommended for the V.C. for taking a trench single-handed (an Australian)... [Neither rumour was correct.]

We anchored almost opposite the beach near a battleship — I think the *Vengeance*. A picket boat came off and we were told that we would stay on board that night. They thought we would be more comfortable there. It was the usual exquisite evening. The fleetsweeper gave us dinner ... and we slept on the floor of the smoking-room, perfectly comfortable. The men slept on deck...

3

Life and Death on Gallipoli

BEAN was now returning to an Anzac Cove where the fighting had bogged down into trench warfare much as it had in France late in 1914. The rugged terrain around the Cove imposed severe restrictions on both sides' ability to effect rapid or decisive advances. On one side, the Anzacs had established a firm toehold on the slopes leading up from the beaches; it seemed that only a massive land assault or the severing of their naval supply lines could dislodge them. Conversely, the Turks still held almost all the vital high ground and thus retained the strategic ascendancy. Neither army was deterred, however, from mounting occasional major attacks (such as the 19 May Turkish offensive). Generally, these attacks suffered massive casualties but produced no worthwhile gains.

For the most part, the fighting had evolved into an unceasing struggle for local supremacy. All along the line, soldiers on both sides relentlessly sniped, sapped, mined and bombed in an effort to strengthen their position. Gradually, patterns of life, and death, emerged in the daily routines along the opposing sets of trenches.

May 17

This morning on getting up I went on deck being rather anxious to see whether the beach was being more shelled than before, or less. They had sent off a signal to us to keep the men under cover whilst landing, and something we heard led us to believe they had had more severe shelling of late. Presently, Colonel Wanliss told us he had heard that General Bridges had been severely wounded, and General Birdwood slightly wounded.[1] That sounded as if our Army Corps had been having a bad time...

Watched shells dropping into water very fiercely as the first boats went in — salvoes of four lashing the water just this side of the pier. They shelled the first lot of boats going in and the second, but became very spasmodic afterwards. The beach was fairly clear but I could see men going about working careless of any fire, in the good old Anzac way...

Got off to the beach about 9 o'clock... The first thing I noticed was that Bazley was leading me off up a path up the hill! Our old H.Q. had had to be shifted. The shells got too bad there and Gellibrand was hit in the arm as he stood there at lunch...

I got up the hill and Ramsay told me the General had been very badly hit — that there was very little hope for him... He said Howse had gone off on the ship with the General and had said that the limb must be amputated, and that no one of the General's age could stand the shock of the amputation. Indeed, they had decided not to attempt it...

Casey and White went off to see the General on the ship... He could just talk — was just conscious. I think he knew he was dying. The wound had become gangrenous through the failure of the blood supply, and the enormous loss of blood also had affected him...

The trenches have got much closer since we left, especially up near Quinn's Post — the crux of our position — the 'jaws' of the gully; where we hold the jaws and the Turks the end. The Turks have been using bombs there quite a lot — and so have we: the engineers have been making them...

Since we have been away Anzac has become a very back show. The only thing they have left us is the troops. It's a funny situation. I can't understand it, and nothing but success will justify it. I know after having seen the other troops in action at Krithia and the Point, that they can't get along there unless they get troops of our class in plenty to do the shove; or unless they adopt some method they havn't tried. If they had troops of the class of our division and the N.Z. & A. they could do it, provided they had enough — but they haven't... There is no way of getting through there except by pushing through; and, therefore, unless very large reinforcements of good troops (not Deals)[2] can be landed, there is nothing for it there but a slow trench warfare. In that case, what is the use of us as a containing force up there? When the Turks try to drive us here into the sea the Allies can't attack down there and take advantage of a withdrawal of troops to fight us. 30 000 of us might do it — but a division of 12 000 would be used up in two days' good fighting; so what is the good of reinforcing by one division per fortnight or per three weeks? Even if they got Achi Baba there's a huge job in front of them in the Kilid Bahr Plateau [south of Maidos, facing the Narrows] —

worse than Achi Baba I should think. Even to pass the two and join hands with us leaves a very big job ahead.

They have taken every aeroplane away from us — they promised, I believe, to send some, but none came. We see the [observation] balloon about once a week — they have left one little balloon instead. The German aeroplane roams over us exactly as it pleases. The Turkish artillery is more troublesome here, by far, than down south; it has us from both sides and we can't alter our gun positions. They have taken our reinforcements — the 29th Indian Infantry Brigade — for the south. They have taken our artillery for the south — they must have 120 guns by now, including 16 Australian and 4 N.Z. They have landed 2 big howitzer here but they are stopping ammunition from coming to them — only 130 rounds, so I hear, for both guns. They cannot shove through with all this because they have not got enough of the class of infantry which is capable of shoving through; so they have taken two of our brigades — who made the one solid fighting advance which has been made there for a week — and sent them back when they had no further use for them, i.e. when ours had lost 40% of its men and N.Z. Brigade 30%...

And what is it all for? Ian Hamilton sends letters to our Army Corps telling them that they are doing magnificent work of the most useful sort in their role of containing force. They can't see every move on the board, he says, but it is all working to the right end, etc. He may be right — we are holding up a big number of Turks here; But the position is that, whilst we are doing so and sending them every help and going short in artillery, aeroplanes, gun ammunition, to help the show which the big guns are raining down there, they are not pushing on apparently because they can't push on. The fact is that, while most of the material for pushing on is down there, most of the personnel which could push on is up here...

May 18

Last night ... our telephone line between K.B. and an extension to an artillery observation station, was tapped. Someone began calling K.A. very badly. We asked "Who are you?" There was no answer, but presently (just after the relieving operator had come on) there was tapped out a message — very badly operated, and badly and slowly spelt — as follows: "We will put you into the sea tomorrow, you Australian bastards. Big guns we will give you; we will give you mines, you Australian bastards." If I havn't got the exact words these were almost the exact ones. It was a question whether this was a half-witted man — possibly one of our men; a German or Egyptian who had learnt the Australian vernacular in Egypt or Australia: or someone who wanted to give us a friendly hint!! It seemed to me probably an Egyptian who hated us pretty badly.

The day was unusually quiet — as quiet as a lazy holiday afternoon in summer. They gave us a shelling on the beach in the morning, but, so quiet was the day — barely a rifle shot — that everyone was asking what it meant. "The Turks are up to some devilment, I suppose," said Watson of the Signal Company. Colonel White answered me when I remarked on it: "Yes, I wonder what it means"...

G.H.Q. sent in to say that the aeroplane had seen a division landing ... just opposite us on the Dardanelles coast this side of the straits. The *Triumph* also saw Turks pushing up from Krithia, and, I believe, movements of troops are reported from the north.

So we shall probably be attacked tonight.

May 19

At 3–20 the Turks attacked. Our men had been ordered to stand to their arms at 3 o'clock. They had been there about a quarter of an hour when the sentries reported (1st and 4th Battalions) that there were men coming out of the Turkish trenches. Fire was immediately opened. The Turks made no noise about their first attack this time. Afterwards they frequently blew bugles to get their men out of the trenches, but the first attack was noiseless. They seem to have come out all along the line at nearly the same moment, except on the right where a battalion probably lost its way and did not work up through the scrub until about 4–30 [a.m.]. The Turks did not seem well-trained. There was no attempt at covering fire, and so our men could sit right out on the traverses of the trench, or even the parapet, and shoot for all they were worth. The Turks would lead out all along the same path, one after another — simply inviting death.

They made two charges in most parts, but opposite Quinn's Post and opposite the 4th Battalion (where the sap[3] from the 4th to the 3rd is not yet quite finished) they made four charges. Indeed, at Quinn's Post they made five or six. We did not realize that this had been a real serious attempt[4] — but today, from there at the saphead of the 4th Battalion, you could see, between the two sapheads, running down the scrub zigzag, just as it had been dropped, a marching tape such as the Germans use in their night attacks. There must have been 20 men still lying along it like this:

Dead Turks lying as they fell in the scrub, 19 May. Photograph by Colonel C.S. Ryan. (AWM neg. no. H3955)

There were a certain number of men lying inside the saps, and right on the parapet of the 2nd Battalion trenches, about 50 yards from the saphead, were 5, one on top of the other. One was a wounded officer; and when we were there they were trying to get him into the trench by throwing a grappling rope over him with a hook at the end. Theodore, a Greek (the 2nd Brigade interpreter) also spoke to him...

Most of the Turks out there were dead... [The Turks had suffered 10 000 casualties in this day of suicidal attacks. The Australians had lost 160 men killed and 468 wounded. Australian rifles and machine guns had fired 948 000 bullets in repulsing the Turks.]

Some of those ... Turks under the parapet had frightful wounds in the head — half the head blown away. I saw one head wound like a star, or pane of broken glass; another more or less circular — you could have put your hand into either. This does away with any conviction in my mind that the wounds sometimes talked of by the doctors in our A.M.C. must necessarily be caused by dum-dum bullets.[5] We know there are dum-dums because I have seen those picked up where the bullet was reversed and hammered in again. But all these terrible wounds are not caused by expansive bullets.

We first went up this morning — Blamey and I — with . . . one of our interpreters. A report had come in that some of the wounded enemy were in a trench close by and were likely to surrender if spoken to, so we gradually inquired our way up into the trench . . . Through the periscope you could see about 20 yards away a Turkish trench running at right-angles to us. After some of their attacks failed the Turks had crept in there for shelter from their own men and ours. Many of them were dead — and some wounded just moving. One or two, quite unwounded, had been seen getting away to the trenches in the rear. (Some of the Turks during the morning, when they tried to retreat to their own trenches, had been kicked out by the men already there).

The interpreter shouted out to these men but they did not answer. We heard after from one who came in that they did hear, but what was the use? If they came in with rifles our men would shoot them; if they came without rifles their own men would shoot them.

At the same time Lt. Hough, an Englishman who was in the Consular Service at Jerusalem, and was sent out as interpreter, went to the 3rd Brigade to do a similar job there. He got into the trench with a periscope and a megaphone had shouted out to the Turks: "Comrades, if you come in you will be treated kindly: we are friends of the Mussulman. We give our prisoners good food" — and so on. One grim old Turk was lying out with a rifle, and every time Hough spoke blazed at his periscope. He shattered it twice. The Turks trickled in one by one — the young officer (a kid still in the Military School) first. He was awfully shaken. He was wounded in the face — he prayed to have himself taken off in a ship at once. The Turks were going to attack us — what they were going to give us would be far worse than anything that had happened so far . . .

As there was a chance that this attack would be renewed after trying hard to catch up with this diary I went up to the 4th Battalion trenches. A flag was being sent up — a big yellow flag which when waved to and fro by the Turks apparently means "Our artillery is shelling our own men": this can be done when they shell us.

The usual mules were coming down all down the path. I got into the 4th Battalion trenches, past a rather suspicious sentry, to Lieut. Osborne, and he (as he was having two hours' duty) — 10 to 12 [p.m.] — kindly let me have his bunk in the trench side. These dug-outs in the trenches are just like bunks of a ship, about 12 inches off the ground. Opposite was a little bastion observation post. This particular trench being a sap, and not meeting the opposite sap has to expect the enemy on both sides. There were two sentries on a low shelf looking out just to my left, and two in the observation post opposite looking out on the other side — all through loopholes. The enemy kept up a constant fire — this continued all night. One man in every three is a sentry — and two sentries stand together. The men seemed perfectly contented and were inclined to tell one of what happened during the morning... They were in splendid form — just what you would want troops to feel like before a big fight; cheerful, contented, willing — only hoping the Turks would come at it. I yarned to an N.C.O. — a capable little chap who was looking after that part of the trench — until nearly 12 p.m. At the hours the different men were awakened and relieved the sentries — and one can see how, when sleep is so precious, an unselfish chap ought to go straight to his job on the exact hour, and not ask the sentry whom he is relieving to wait half a second until he has a drink, etc.

At 12 Osborne turned in, and Captain Simpson took over. As he was to be up for the next two hours he made me take his bunk in the H.Q. of his Company. There was another officer sleeping there, but I crawled in under the blankets and slept with that constant peck! peck! of the mauser, and the swish of bullets about 6 feet overhead. I woke at 3 a.m. — Simpson had promised to wake me at 2 when his watch ended, but he turned in to another dug-out. The men were just about to stand to arms, so I went down into the trench again... Presently Simpson came along and made the men all stand up and face the side from which they expected the enemy — the right. As the ledge was narrow and a squeeze for four, one of the chaps offered me his dug-out opposite. I climbed in there and watched them. I could see under the doubled up waterproof sheet their legs and overcoats, and, by lifting it, their round forage caps. They stood there, occasionally two of them yarning, all with their backs to me like schoolboys standing against a wall, shifting their legs occasionally — two of them yarning in a low voice about Sydney; about their mates; and about the war; absolutely contented. I never heard a suspicion of a grumble from them. They seemed such simple, frank chaps; light-hearted, with all the fascinating freshness of Australians playing their game there just like children. All the time the enemy was firing away over our heads. The only shots on our side were from sentries — occasional bangs like a big heart thump, with a flare at the same time — you could see the haze of the flash over the parapet line. They were allowed to blaze an occasional one at shrubs near them or at a loophole from which sniping came, so as to make the Turks keep their heads down.

In the midst of this there was a scuffle of earth and clothes, and one of the men before me came tumbling backwards — he fell right on to his back in the bottom of the trench. I thought he had been hit — the others only looked over their shoulders at him; but he picked himself up: "That's what happens when one goes to sleep" he mumbled quite contentedly, as he scrambled back on to the shelf.

Presently light began to grow in the sky. Word had come along (from the 3rd Battalion) "Keep a good lookout on the right; the enemy has been seen massing in front of the 3rd Battalion." However nothing happened... The light grew, and I watched the enemy's trench occasionally... As there had been no attack and there was no prospect of one I left the trench at about 5 [a.m.]...

May 20

The N.Z. Infantry Brigade came back [from Cape Helles] today. We were very glad to see it. We are all Australians and N.Z. here now and it is wonderful what this means to the men. They have the utmost confidence now in the people either side of them. They never really felt that confidence whilst the Naval Brigade and so-called marines were here — nor at Krithia...

The Turks today came out under a white flag and began to bury their dead — it was in the afternoon. Gen. Walker ... was up the trenches with Casey, who is his A.D.C. when they noticed a white flag being waved from the Turkish lines... Presently a Red Crescent flag appeared and a Red Cross flag on our own parapet with Capt. Thompson (1st Battalion) standing by it on the parapet. Gen. Walker sent Casey along the trench at once to tell our people that they must tell the Turks that if the ambulance came out it must keep to its own half of the ground whilst we attended to our half; and that it must pick up wounded only, and not touch the dead. Casey went along, and when he got to the trench he found a Red Crescent man already there. He had been right on the parapet of the trench, if not into it. Our people had already got in one wounded Turk — the Red Crescent man was going back to his lines. Casey told them he must be stopped — he had been into our trenches and couldn't be allowed to go back. They said: "Oh, he was only a Red Crescent chap — didn't matter." Casey told them that they musn't think of letting him go — so they called him in and sent him back to the beach.

Several doctors had by this time left the Turkish trenches, and were moving about looking at the dead — men in decent uniforms. There were very few wounded — poor chaps, they had mostly died. The general had given a message, written by an interpreter, to the Turkish Red Crescent people, that they must stay in their own half — the same as he told Casey; but because things looked as if they might get irregular, or because it was becoming late, he decided to go out himself and meet them. He left Casey behind with orders to keep him covered in case of treachery, and went out over the parapet to meet them. There were 3 Turkish doctors and a lieutenant (Turk) who had come out. They stood chatting — our general handing them cigarettes. While they were talking a man came out and began collecting rifles from the dead. The Turks were sitting on their parapets, and our men were, as far as possible, kept down behind our trenches — there seemed to be a great many Turks. Presently the general came back. He had told them — and letters were sent out and handed to them — that any truce must be more formally ratified. If they wanted a truce to bury their dead they must send in a formal flag of truce along the beach from Kaba Tepe. The present truce was ordered to be off in ten minutes, but he gave orders to our men that they must wait until either the Turks fired or it was 7 o'clock. They leisurely got back into their trenches, but no shot was actually fired until about 7–30; the Turks fired a few shots — we fired a few, and gradually the firing became general. There was no underhand work at this point except the collecting of arms by one man — at any rate, so far as our people saw...

Further down, opposite the 3rd Battalion, where one of these informal sectional truces was arranged, a man began collecting rifles — and we fired at him and hit him — quite justly. Later, behind some stretcher-bearers, there came out about 200 men with rifles. We fired on them. The stretcher-bearers somehow were hit — the remainder of the party at once ran for the stretcher, picked it up and carried it in. [Major] Ross said he had no doubt from the look of things that the stretcher contained a machine gun...

It is extraordinary how the men have changed in their attitude to the Turks. They were very savage the first day because they found some of their wounded (or dead) mutilated; but since the slaughter of May 19th, and since they have seen the wounded lying about in front of the trenches they have changed entirely.

They are quite friendly with the Turks; anxious to get in the wounded if they can — give them cigarettes. The Indians with the mules down here also take the prisoners chocolates — they give our men some also. The way the Indian has fraternised with some of our Australians is remarkable...

May 21

Today was fine, but for some unaccountable reason there was a slight swell coming in from the N.W. on to our beach. It was not much, but it made the old lighters and pontoons rock; and it gave one an idea of what extraordinary luck we have had in the matter of weather. We have not had one rough day — not one day even mildly disturbed. Except for one occasion, when there was a wind from off the shore — which of course did not affect us — we have had glassily smooth seas from the day we landed. It only makes one wonder again what I have asked myself again and again since we landed: "What arrangements have been made for water and supplies in case real rough weather sets in?" We have two old water pontoons on the beach — or possibly one — which are filled by water from Alexandria or Malta. But a single storm would finish them — there is no reserve at all on the beach — no provision for condensing, that I know of. A certain number of wells have been sunk at the mouths of gullies and the trenches are partially supplied from these — as far as possible. The few people I have asked about it say — "Oh, we've only got this ships water coming every now and then from Alexandria — its very limited." But in goodness' name why is it limited? They have any quantity of water at the point — you can't sink a dug-out 18 inches in some parts without getting it flooded! Surely it can't be beyond the resources of the Mediterranean Expeditionary Force to safeguard — and safeguard over and over again — our water supply!!...

May 22

This morning in answer to our letters that if the Turks wanted an armistice they must come along the beach from Kaba Tepe with white flag and proper officer, a white flag appeared on Kaba Tepe. It was seen by our men, and hundreds of them could be seen standing on the ridges watching it. A white flag was then to be sent out by us — but we hadn't got one. A signaller waved his flag whilst a scurry was made along the beach to get a bath towel, which was finally sent out on a stick. Some time later you could see the Turkish white flag start marching along the skyline of

Kaba Tepe. Men were walking about there everywhere; I saw some coming out from the ridge between our right flank and Kaba Tepe — one or two. Presently the first horseman I have seen at Anzac came over the ridge and cantered up the neck of the side of Kaba Tepe. The white flag stopped. The horseman came down the hill again and on to the beach, and along towards us. Out with our white flag was an officer from G.H.Q. and an officer from Anzac. Blamey and an interpreter were waiting some way nearer to us with a second white flag. I went down to the sapper post on the beach. The horseman came along to our foremost officers waving a white handkerchief. He got down, talked a minute, left his horse, and started walking back to Kaba Tepe, when three more horsemen appeared coming along the beach. They came up to our officers; there were clearly two officers and two horse-holders. The officers shook hands — took out cigarettes. Presently they signalled up Blamey. It turned out that they wanted an officer of equal rank to stay with their junior officer (a major) whilst their senior officer came in to see us. Our two officers brought their senior officer along the beach. When about a quarter of a mile from our sappers post they blindfolded him very carefully with two handkerchiefs, and then each taking an arm led him between them like a child, chatting volubly — I suppose in English. He had two small wire entanglements to cross before he reached our sandbag wall; a low trip wire maze and a higher one stretching down to the sea. They directed his feet carefully over the first one — like you do in the game where a man is blindfolded and set to step over a lot of books that aren't there — irresistibly like it. They shouted for coats to help him cross the second one; but in the meantime someone had a brainwave. There were several Australians bathing along the beach near by. Someone rushed off for a stretcher — then they called for the bathers. Two of these big Australians — naked as the day they were born — took the stretcher round the larger entanglement. The Turkish colonel got on to it — the two naked men carried him into the water, round the edge, and back to the beach. And I got three photographs!

As he came along the beach a procession gradually formed round him, as it would round a Salvation Army band in Market Street — no officer seemed to think of sending them away. They all took him for a German, as they do every Turkish officer they see, of course. He was rather heavy limbed, and that decided it. "Oh he's a bloody square-head — I'd shoot the beggar" was the sort of remark one heard. Our men have a sort of a kindliness for the Turk, but they've none whatever for the German. Every trick

Bathers carry the blindfolded Turkish envoy round the wire entanglements on Brighton Beach. (AWM neg. no. G989)

of the Turk is attributed to German officers — and our chaps can't stand the way the Germans play the war game...

The officer ... was in the Anzac H.Q. until late in the evening. The officer who was with Blamey began to get very anxious as dark came on... The Turkish major explained that he was not uneasy about our fellows shooting, but about what his own Turkish sentries might do if he went back after dark...

Our own gun fire has been drastically cut down. An order comes from G.H.Q. that, except when we are attacked, each howitzer is only to fire 2 shots a day; each field gun may fire four. I don't know where these instructions come from: I suppose G.H.Q. But batteries now have to watch the Turks digging without being able to fire a shot at them. The Turks are making a big road — almost a railway cutting so they say — in the direction of Baby 700, I believe. Before we used to frighten them off this sort of work — but now we can scarcely interfere with them.

One of our observers ... asked the ships to fire on a good target the other day. The reply was: "Sorry, I've used my 5 shots." It is said this rule would apply even if we saw a battery coming into position — but I think our people would surely fire first, and ask leave afterwards...

The hills behind the beach have long come to look just like

Manly — with little made paths winding all over the hillside. In the gullies at the back you find clustered up under the crests, and on the hollows behind them, hundreds of little booths — dug-outs with waterproof sheets over them — where the supports and reserves, and the cooks and signallers and H.Q. live. Really Walker valley (or whatever it is called, opposite Walker Bay, where the N.Z. position is) looks like a big country fair. I wonder what the old Turk who owned his bit of scrub two months' ago, would think of it now?... Glasfurd tells me that when first he landed — that first morning — there were goat or animal tracks all over the hill face. So it must have been someone's pasture. Far up on the shoulder of [Hill] 971, facing the sea, you notice from the ships quite a large patch of green field and poppy field on the lap of some ridge top, about a mile north of our lines. Otherwise the country is green arbutus and holly scrub with some gorse and beautiful flowers and occasional sand patches amongst them...

May 23, Sunday
As I went up some fellows, who, I suppose, didn't know me — Artillery or A.S.C. — camped in the mouth of a gully, picked me up. "That's Bean", they said as I passed — "Who?" "Bean — War correspondent"... The next thing was the old shout: "How about the bally Australians?" I don't take any notice, it's the first time for a month they have gone back to the matter. The men, since they have seen me in the trenches, and so on — and especially the 2nd Brigade, who knew me down at the Point — have quite changed in their manner. They generally make me very welcome now — good chaps...

We heard yesterday — what we knew must come within a day or two — the news of General Bridges' death. I sent a cable about the manner in which he was wounded — as White had told me the story. Tonight, when I was passing, White called me in. "Bean" he said, "I want you if you will to make an exception to the rule about not mentioning names. It is in the case of the general — General Bridges. I think his work deserves to be understood in Australia, and I don't think many people will understand it"...

I stayed up this night to send a wire to Australia with this appreciation of the general. Tomorrow is the truce, and I am going round the lines with Col. White. The truce begins at 7 ... and ends at 4.30 for burying dead.

May 24
There was considerable gun fire up to 7 o'clock this morning from

Burying the dead during the armistice, 24 May. This photograph, taken by Colonel C.S. Ryan, contravened the terms of armistice. Bean took no photos during the ceasefire. (AWM neg. no. H3954)

the ship opposite Kaba Tepe, and from our batteries. Before 7 it stopped and the truce began. Some of our men walking about were shot dead at 7–40 . . . certainly 2 were shot. The probability is that they were shot by a sniper out by himself, and who either had not heard of the truce or was out in his time. If a Turk had been shot I dare say the firing would have begun at once. We drew their attention to it, and no more men were hit.

The orders to our men were that only stretcher and burial parties were to go out — mostly A.M.C. men; all others were to keep their heads below the parapet. With the enemy the agreement was that there should be no reconnaissance, sketching, photographing; no work done, no digging or moving of troops during the day. The delimitation party, with Col. Skeen as member of it, was to go down through the midst of the lines. We were to cover the ground up to half way to their lines, they were to cover their own half — neither to cross it. We were to give them the rifles from the dead in our half minus the bolts (they said they wanted to bury their dead with their arms. As a matter of fact we knew they wanted their arms; they could collect all the rifles and accoutrements in their half. What we wanted was to have their dead buried so as to improve the life in the trenches. Some of our men were actually sick with the stench; I know it was bad enough on May 19th — it must have been awful by today)...

When Col. White and I got up in to the trenches it must have been about 8–30. The burial parties had long been out. A line of unarmed sentries with white flags was standing on the halfway line through the scrub. Some of them were in bright blue uniforms with black skull caps — most of them in khaki. Here and there was an officer in topboots.

White kept to the strict letter of the agreement — at least as strictly as you could expect anyone to do. We went through the lines of the 11th and 10th [Bns] on Bolton's Ridge — he showed me the ridges on our right and the importance of the ridge with the green field where the two main gullies join, or rather which spreads over the top of a corner of 400... Col. White had a pleasant word for everyone, and they for him. He made everyone keep his head down below the parapet and look through the loopholes — indeed most of the men in this section were obeying the order. One engineer officer was on the parapet walking about. White jumped down his throat — told him what sort of an example he was giving to the men, and told the Brigade H.Q. to send him down to the D.H.Q. later.

The 2nd Battalion sap was very nearly finished — about 3 yards from the 3rd. Officers had stopped men working, and some of the men grumbled a little at it. One man was carefully digging a bit and getting rid of the earth not along the parapet. White let him dig on. The enemy had been digging energetically in parts until they were stopped, and they were making loopholes all day at points here and there along all the line. Their attention was sometimes drawn to this.

In the 2nd Battalion lines Colonel Brown (the one who was so nervy in the 3rd Battalion) — he had a few days rest and has turned out a splendid colonel — showed us Johnston's Jolly very clearly. The dead were very thick indeed opposite there, but thicker still opposite the 4th Battalion — to the right of the break in their line; but thickest opposite Courtney's. Opposite Courtney's, or opposite our 1st Battalion, a ridge runs out a little way. You see it from the 4th Battalion (from the right of the break in their line where you can see to the left) on the one side, and from Quinn's or Courtney's on the other. Here our men were shovelling Turkish dead into a short abandoned Turk trench and the Turks were dragging their men to the edge of the gully opposite Courtney's and shovelling them over — where they lay as we saw them 20 or 30 together in a crevice. So much for 'burying them with their arms'...

At this point we got out of the territory of the 1st Australian Division and into that of the 4th Infantry Brigade. The poor old 4th certainly has the worst bit of country to hold. Our 1st Battalion has a beautiful field of fire of about 50 yards — the 4th near the break has not so much — but on the whole our division's line has a splendid field from left to right. At Courtney's and Quinn's, however, things are different. We are higher than the Turks opposite us and therefore have to get up fairly high to fire at them; but at our left and left rear are Turkish trenches higher still on Baby 700 — and if our men get their heads up there these enfilade them...

The trenches at Courtney's are pretty deep. But in Quinn's, where the Turks come within close range of us, they say they can't make them deep, as we may have to get up on the parapet at any time.

I had never been in Quinn's at all. It is a perfect rabbit warren. It is connected now with Courtney's, but the tunnel connecting Courtney's with Quinn's was blown in by a shell, and they only connect through the support trenches. They couldn't work a bit today, but will open it up as soon as they can... It is easily the worst place in our line. The fire trench is shallow; the parapets very low — and they look very thin; and the tunnels through which you grope your way from one trench to another are simply a rabbit burrow — you can scarcely get through some of them. In one trench there is an archway such as you often find, left to avoid enfilading fire, I suppose. It is not four foot — scarcely three foot — thick; but in it is a dead Turk. His boot and his fingers of one hand stick out from the roof as you squeeze your way under.

When we got to this point all the rules about remaining under the parapet were being so disregarded that it was useless to attempt enforcing them. This was the case the moment we entered the new section occupied by the 4th Brigade. The men were fine breezy chaps, but they were far more amateurish and casual than in any of the lines we had so far gone through. And one of the officers spoken to by Col. White was almost disobedient — had to be told twice to stand below the parapet, and acted then in a way intended to show that he resented the order. I have never seen or heard of anyone behaving like that with Col. White before. However, when we got along a bit to Quinn's there was more reason for the attitude of the men. The trench was shallow and uncomfortable; and even sitting down in it you could see the

Turks crowding up to their half way line. The trenches here run up to within 10 yards of one another: in fact they are at one point joined by a communication trench made by us on the night of one of our attacks when we took the Turkish trenches. When we came back we filled up one end and the Turks filled up the other — but for a time it was open. Our men used to throw out biscuits occasionally, or Bully Beef tins to the Turkish end of the trench, and shout out "Saida." When a Turkish hand appeared reaching for the tin they would blaze at it. On one occasion I believe they threw a hambone over — an abhorrence to the Turks — and caused quite a disturbance...

The men on the half way line between Quinn's and the Turk trench were not more than five or six yards away from Quinn's. The ground was absolutely bare of scrub — it had been cleared. They were burying dead between the trenches, and shovelling some into the communication trench which connected the left of our line with the left of a Turk trench around the plateau, only a few yards distant.

Our men and the Turks were offering each other cigarettes: occasionally there was a squabble as to whether a bit of accoutrement had been found on our side or theirs of the centre line. A Turk would run to point to it. "Mafish" our man would say, gathering it into a little bag.

There must have been a hundred men and officers at this point... They made no pretence of busying themselves with the dead — they simply stood there surveying our lines from the edge of the plateau — chattering in twos and threes. Higher up Baby 700 in the Turk trenches was a group of about 7 of them. It was obvious to myself — as to Col. White — that they were reconnoitring, surveying the gully from as high a position as they could get, and calmly working out their exact attack. "It will be a much better planned one than the last", Col. White said to me. All the dead except about two had been buried at Quinn's and Courtney's — but that crowd of men remained there all day...

We came out of Quinn's (from the back of Quinn's you see the whole Turkish front on Baby 700 clearly, but our fire prevents them from firing there — a good illustration of covering fire) and crossed the steep gully to Pope's, where the Light Horse were — a curious set of trenches, looking up the hill at Turk trenches above their head on Dead Man's Ridge... It was here, as we were climbing up our trench, that we saw General Birdwood, General Godley, Col. Monash, Onslow, and the staff who had been quite frankly walking along the front of our trenches reconnoitring.

They climbed down where we were, and as they did General Birdwood said to White: "White, I want you to have a look at that 400 plateau, and Johnston's Jolly. You get a splendid view of it from up here, and I am sure it can be done — you'll see that it's not enfiladed. Just have a look at it and then I think you might get on with your plans at once"...

After Birdwood's advice we got out on top of the bank and White made a survey of the country. He stood behind me with his glasses, and looked hard at the 400 plateau. One of the Turkish sentries saw us I fancy because he began to make a noise to some other sentry or officer — we climbed down into our own trench, and sitting with our backs to the parapet had a good look...

This quite disillusioned me as to truces. We wanted it to clean the battlefield for our men. The Turks wanted it to get rifles. The Turks made no pretence of burying many of their fellows so far as I could see. We both frankly reconnoitred the other's position — I don't know which got the better of it. Our men got a day's rest, but so did theirs. I though this truce a good thing before it came off — but I don't think I would ever desire a truce again under the same circumstances; better to go on and let them attack again if they wanted to with such knowledge as they have...

May 26

Exceedingly quiet night and day on the beach — as it has been ever since May 19th...

What are we doing all this while? I wish I knew. The Turks are now building us in all round, getting their lines stronger and stronger every day; I doubt if we could move out through the front, even if reinforced, today; they have guns in their firing line at Johnston's Jolly, and our howitzers say they can't get at them, and our 18 pounders have no common shell. They are making grid-iron trenches in places where their trenches were weak — and our job is sitting and looking on. Our artillery ammunition is pretty strictly cut down;[6] we get about one half hour of aeroplane in 3 days. The Navy is now out of it — we can scarcely expect them to come out and be torpedoed day by day,[7] although there are warships visible down south — possibly some of them are sham warships. Sixteen of our guns are off helping in the push down south.

We are a 'containing force' — we are holding up one force of Turks whilst another force of ours somewhere else does something:[8] but what is there any prospect of its doing? We might with a shove have got our main ridge, but no force under 250 000

Support troops from 4th Brigade waiting behind Quinn's Post after it had been recaptured on 29 May. (AWM neg. no. G1011)

will get Achi Baba. As far as I can see the force down there is doing exactly what we are — namely, allowing an army of Turks to make itself each day tremendously stronger in a position already naturally strong...

May 27

Moved into my new dug-out this evening, after being for two days Casey's guest...

May 28

Tonight a party from our 9th Battalion went out on to the ridge S.E. of their lines with the trench overlooking Gaba Tepe; and news came back that they had bayoneted 6 snipers and taken one prisoner. Whilst I was writing this a dark form appeared in front of the dug-out — outlined against the sea. It had a fixed bayonet and carried two rifles. It was part of the guard sent down with the prisoner. They inquired the way, and then passed along in front of my dug-out — the fourth tall form with skull cap being that of the prisoner...

As I write this the hills are echoing behind me like an empty fives court, and the rifle shots sound not unlike the knock of a fives bat. Every now and then I can hear the plunk into the sea of one of the enemy's bullets — sometimes the long whine of a rick first. Then at times all the echo stops and all one can hear is the constant distant plump, plump, into the sea of bullets from rifles which we cannot hear at all. Once or twice there has been the usual outbreak accompanied by the punt of a trench mortar, as when a rather flabby football is punted about the field — and once or twice no report at all, but the mysterious swish, swish, swish, swish, of a flight of machine gun bullets through the air. It is getting late — almost time for our nightly fleetsweeper to start for Lemnos[9]... The mules are stamping in the gully below — occasionally some chain on the picketing rope or on a bridle jingles. From the dug-out beside me comes a solitary snore. I must blow out the candle which is close beside me under the wall (so as not to show the Turkish eyes on Nibrunesi Cape, jutting out 5 miles away to the north). I will drag the sleeping bag out a bit away from the earth wall so as to get out of the way of centipedes, one of which dropped a little while ago, whilst I was writing — down my neck; it seems to be a resort of theirs; I found two in my shaving mug this morning — and so to sleep.

May 29

I was awakened last night by a wild outburst of firing at about 3.20. It seemed to come from Quinn's Post. I had been working late and didn't want to get up — but as it continued I went up the Signal Office and asked if they knew what was on... The signaller told me it was nothing...

This morning on getting up the first thing I heard was Phillip's battery still firing. Then someone said the Turks had taken a trench at Quinn's Post and that we had retaken it. The firing there was still furious: I started off at once.

I found that there had been fierce fighting during the night... I went on to the post and sitting out on the slope behind the post in the support trenches heard the actual story... Whilst I was ... there on the edge of the path talking to Col. Pope about his adventure ... our men were dragging dead Turks out of another part of the trench, down the path and on to a slab of hillside at the back. Two men had just passed pulling a Turk by the leg when there was a general scatter. Men got on to the side of the path or shrank back up the hillside. Somebody said: "What is it — a bomb?"Someone answered: "Yes, a bomb" — and down the path came rolling an innocent black ball, like a cricket ball. It reached the dead Turk, who was about 6 feet from me, and then exploded like a big Chinese cracker. There was a blue smoke and a bit of dust, something hit me on the hip — don't know what — and the dead Turk was lying there with his leg blown off. I expect it would have been mine if it hadn't been his. I was spattered over with bits of dead Turk — fortunately not very thickly...

May 30, Sunday
I stayed in and wrote all day today, except for a short walk to the road up the hill behind the N.Z. headquarters, which overlooks the left of our line...

June 1
I saw General Birdwood last night. He was in his dug-out reading the paper after dinner, with his spectacles on his forehead. He wanted to know if any of my articles had yet appeared. We got yarning about Clifton and about things here. He told me that the Navy had originally thought they could get through without assistance — or else with the mere assistance of landing parties. Kitchener accordingly sent him to get an opinion. He came up in the *Swiftsure* [early in March]... Birdwood saw that the fleet had blown the forts at the entrance to pieces, but had not even begun on the narrows... Birdwood wrote back that it would certainly need a Military Expedition...

Gellibrand thinks, that the episode of our landing here will be very much discounted someday because we are content to hang on here and not push forward — that it will fall in value as much as the siege of Ladysmith did [after the Boer War]. It seems to me that this is a superficial estimate...

Birdwood tells me that Legge is coming to take the place of Bridges. I told him that Legge was a tremendously hard worker, but possibly apt to jump at big conclusions without working out all the little finnicking annoying details in between. I fancy some of the elder officers were rather horrified with the appointment of Legge, and had been talking to Birdwood. His fear was: 'Has Legge the toughness to stick it — in extremis?' I said: "You can't tell until you have seen him tried in action — look at Bridges!"...

Another Turk got right up to the lines either today or yesterday — Birdwood told me he believed this. He appeared suddenly in the wire of the 2nd Battalion with about half a dozen water bottles hanging over his arm. He was caught there with a startled look. Someone shouted: "Hullo, there's a Turk." Everyone looked up. "Where?" By the time he was pointed out and they got their rifles to shoot he was bolting, and they think he was not hit. He may have been returning to his own trenches and missed the way; or he may have been a sniper laying in a store of water and accustomed to get in through that gap; or he may have been a man coming to give himself in. Those who do come to give themselves in run a big risk — creeping up to our trenches even without arms they may have bombs — and some think some have been shot that way. Some prisoners, however, believe our pamphlets, and it is a pity if those who come up to our lines on the strength of those promises of ours (which have been distributed to them) get shot as they are making their bolt. If they are properly covered they ought to be harmless...

June 2
An uneasy night at Quinn's. There was a lot of spasmodic firing. I sit up and write all night these days, and sleep in the morning; but even so find it hard to keep up with my work... Between 2 and 4 o'clock the rifle shots down the gully sound so loud that one could almost swear there was a sniper creeping down it and shooting continually. One bullet struck with a bang outside my dug-out door the other night, so I blew the light out in a hurry; but the Signal Office tells me it is an 'over'...

June 3
Worked last night until 2 o'clock, or a little later. Walker (Murphy's batman) brought me some splendid candles from the Navy — he's a curious chap — wanders round from battleship to destroyer, submarine, trawler, supply ship, and always finds his feet (when sent out to get stuff for the mess). Austin has let me have temporarily some unwanted blankets for the walls, and I have a good big case for the table — biscuit boxes to sit on, and 2 biscuit boxes and 2 ammunition boxes for cupboard — so it makes home life a pleasure...

June 4
I got the tip — dropped very quietly — that there might be something doing at about 11 o'clock tonight. Later I was told that this was to be opposite Quinn's, and also the 1st Battalion — but that it was very secret. I happened to tell Bazley that I would be out part of the night. "Is anything going on in the trenches, Sir?" he asked. I said, not that I knew of. "Oh, its only they're talking down there of an attack tonight — an infantryman told them that they were going to take the trenches opposite Quinn's" — so that is the way secrets are kept. It was just the same in Melbourne. Later on an engineer told me that there was something on in the 1st Battalion.

June 5
I have been working night and day to try and get square with articles and diary. It is almost impossible on account of interrup-

tions — the people that will come in and talk and talk as though I had nothing to do, whereas very few people in the camp have so much. I wanted this night for work. However, as Quinn's is always interesting and there seemed some prospect of a bit of excitement, I decided to go up. It was worth it. I left the beach about 10.30 p.m. and walked up to the 4th Brigade H.Q. now the H.Q. of the 3rd section, under Colonel Chauvel.

The plan, as far as I know, was that as the British and French were attacking down south, we were to create a sensation on a small scale here. The only thing was that the attack down south came first and our movement here afterwards...

I walked up the valley in the pitch dark — the moon was not yet up. There was a rattle and clink and laugh of talking men just in front of me. The Indian provision carts coming back down the white road were almost on top of me before I saw them — about 20 of them — the first carts I had seen working at Anzac. They supply the depot in Monash Gully, from which quartermasters of battalions draw their stores, with Turkish snipers firing from Dead Man's Ridge [opposite Pope's] all the time...

There was a light shining dimly in Col. Chauvel's big dug-out when I got there. It was like a fair sized old fashioned room with broad flat beams laid parallel across the dark ceiling — the planking from some barge that had gone ashore and been broken up. The light was shaded by a big flat wooden biscuit box — the box was set up on end and the lantern placed in it; you could see the light dimly through the grain of the thin wood at the back. They had had the light naked a few minutes before, but a sniper had seen the glare of it on the sandbags of the rear wall which juts beyond the door, and had put half a dozen shots one after the other into the sandbag at the top left hand corner...

At a particular moment the shooting at the valley head seemed to increase a little. There was a shot, then two or three shots together, then a few more.

Col. Chauvel said: "Hullo, I expect that's our job — sounds as if they'd begun." He looked down at a watch which was on the table at his side. "Yes, just eleven o'clock" he said.

So our men must be up there, rushing over that deadly little bit of skyline. There should be half of them across by now, I thought, it's only a few yards. The fire was growing thicker — the crackle of machine guns joined in; the thump of a bomb — then more and more thumps; within half a minute it was a regular roar. We went to the door and looked out. Over the black hill brow opposite us there was a thump. A fizzing red spark like that of a rocket stick rose in the air ever so high and slowly turned and fell. It seemed to go almost straight up and down. There was a momentary pause — then a roar as though some shell as big as a house had plunged into the ocean. You could hear the plunge and then the shoot up of the crater of water all round it — plun — ge. The sky had flushed above the horizon as if with summer lightning. They were firing into some of the trenches opposite them in order to keep those trenches from firing at Quinn's. Up at the valley end where you could see the black outline of the Razor Back [the ridge running between Shrapnel and White's gullies]. . . and Dead Man's Ridge one could see the occasional sparkle of a rifle shot, very faint on the top of the Razor Back; but one very bright flash on Dead Man's Ridge. It was right down the ridge, at least half the way to the bottom of it, one would say. Over the horizon at Quinn's came the constant flash of bombs — no one could say if they were theirs or ours.

Presently our first gun began to fire — a heart satisfying sharp bang down behind our backs. Then another and another — more flashes in the sky behind Quinn's — then a brilliant little rocket flash just this side of the ridge. It lighted the long line of the ridge top — pink bare earth — too instantaneously for one to see anything that was happening there. A Turkish star shell flew out like the star of a Roman candle; then a second and a third, slowly falling towards Courtney's and showing up the whole horizon as though with a very bright moonlight — the shadows lengthening together. All the time our guns were firing up the valley over our heads. You could hear the swish of the shell, and for the first time I noticed that you could see the shell. I had thought that occasionally I saw a pinpoint of light moving deadly fast overhead — didn't know whether it was imagination or not; but then once or twice I saw it most clearly — a faint pinpoint travelling overhead from one horizon to the other with almost sickening swiftness.

There we stood with this uproar going on all around us, overhead, on the ridges, and up the valley — lights, flashes, explosions, twinkling like summer lightning. . .

The firing outside was subsiding — things had settled themselves one way or the other. Only a quarter of a mile away and we had no idea what had happened there. The first message that arrived was from the 1st Infantry Brigade of Australian Division:

> "Inform guns they can fire against German officers' trench; none of our men are out there now. The enterprise failed."

The enterprise — I forgot — was first to send out 8 men and 2 engineers to blow up the machine gun in the German officers' trench...

June 6, Sunday

No papers or letters for nearly a fortnight. We have a ferry service established to Mudros now — times of call here uncertain owing to shell fire, but one packet (fleetsweeper) always leaves for Mudros at 3 o'clock every morning...

June 7

[Harry] Freame [a scout in 1st Battalion] spoke to me of it as being as easy to go [out scouting] unseen as if there were no one about. Provided the back parapet were high, and therefore you didn't appear against the horizon, you could always creep out of a trench or of a hole; but you must go flat like a snake on the inside of your knees, big toes and elbows and not on your kneepads and palms. Then in getting over a rise you shouldn't get up so but go over it like a snake, bending your body over the top of the bank, your chest almost scrubbing it all the way. "I only touch three places when I'm going on hands and knees," he said — and he tapped inside of elbow, inside of knee, inside of knuckle of big toe. "You oughtn't to have a rifle either. Your job is to see, not to shoot unless you are at the closest possible quarters, and a revolver is the weapon for that. A rifle, especially with bayonet fixed, simply shows you up," said Freame...

The place has been full of spy rumours these last few days... Blamey has asked me if I can get out a 'Furfies Gazette', with these furfies [rumours] so exaggerated as to laugh them out of court.

Some cases of Enteric — I believe 13 suspicious ones — have been diagnosed at Lemnos. The flies are getting very bad, and Dysentery has begun to appear amongst the Officers and men at D.H.Q....

June 8

That firing last night was another night attack by us at Quinn's — another pretty little attempt, and another failure. The men are getting pretty sick of these little half-hearted side shows. I suppose Birdwood, if the truth were known, is not allowed by his instructions from down south to attempt anything more...

I went through the trenches from Courtney's to the 4th Battalion [on Johnston's Jolly] with Freame... [Now that the trench fighting was practically deadlocked, each side was tunnell-

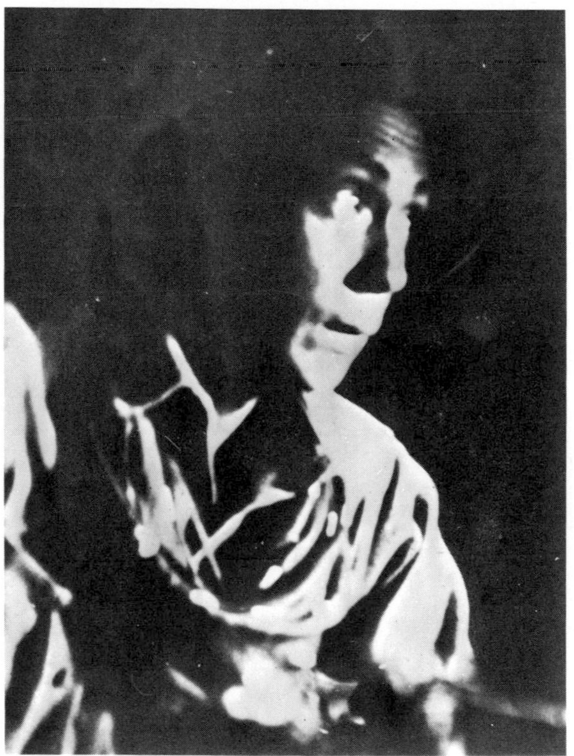

Left:
Looking through the door into Bean's dugout. (AWM neg. no. G1284)
Right:
Sgt Harry Freame peers out from a sniper's hole tunnelled through the side of Wire Gully, 8 June. (AWM neg. no. G1030A)

ing under the other's lines and exploding mines just below the surface, at known enemy strongpoints.] At one place we looked down a shaft and 20 feet below saw a couple of hefty fellows dragging sacks of earth along a gallery as if they were mine ponies... Just north of the 4th Bn. gap ... is a tunnel from the trench with a T. head and three small loopholes on the outer face of the hill each choked with a sandbag, or an old shirt. Freame crawled in there with me. They are snipers' holes looking down the valley to the north of J. Jolly. I took a couple of photos through the loopholes, and two of Freame sitting inside them...

At the 6th Battalion I saw a local topical paper written, illustrated, and issued by Sgt. Mjr. Noonan, formerly in the Victorian State Audit (Spring Street). He had several papers busy going on the *Honorata* and in Egypt; and his present one, *Snipers' Shots*, is really very good indeed. There is a frequent kindly laugh at the reinforcements; e.g. Corporal: "Have you your rifle loaded?" Pte. Jones: "Yes, Sir, I think so; at least there's 9 in the tin box and one in the funnel"... I asked Blamey if I could get Noonan to help me with the proposed newspaper. I showed him

Lt S.H. Watson (right) supervises the construction of what became known as Watson's pier. A Turkish shellcase served as pile driver. (AWM neg. no. G1046)

Snipers' Shots, and he showed it to the General. It is certainly very good indeed...

June 10
Nearly all day writing this Diary. Made one break to go down to photograph Watson, the second in charge of the Divisional H.Q. Signallers, making his pier [in Anzac Cove]. He started (by order) with tressles, but is now pile driving with an 8 inch shell full of shrapnel and sand — weighing 3 cwts. — as a pile driver...

June 11
Sgt. Mjr. Noonan was here this afternoon and composed the first issue of the *Dinkum Oil*. I can't say I ever helped him. All I did was to hold the pen and write clearly. He really has a very remarkable wit — the thing is very good indeed...

June 12
Writing all day.

June 13, Sunday
Morning paper article 8 and evening paper 8 finished... I've got clear of history, and into the nice sketching lighter stuff which one can reel off faster...

June 15
The first tolerably rough days (with one exception), today and yesterday — and they say we are without water on the beach tonight... The pier is unfinished — one shell went very near it, and the tressles are rather knocked about by the tiny waves — not the shell. The waves even so weren't really approaching roughness...

Bazley and I had an experience with flies in here last night, which was rather like delirium tremens. We literally fought them for a quarter of an hour — waving towels, burning Keatings scattering them. We must have killed 1000 or 2000 but only excited them. They swarmed in our faces, crawled all over us (I suppose the Keatings made them silly), dropped off the ceiling on to the floor. The place was filthy with them this morning — nothing but dead flies. We turned it out and swished it down with creasol, and it is comparatively free today; but perhaps the cooler weather accounts for that. The men find the flies at present far worse than the Turks.

I was sniped at twice today whilst looking over parapets.

Diving from the picket boats and pinnaces was the favourite recreation activity of the troops. (AWM neg. no. G1043)

People in Australia, when 50 casualties were published, seem by the latest papers to have been almost shocked. We know that by then the list was really 5 000 for this Division alone, and we can't help wondering what they thought. I am hoping that J's wound was announced to father and mother in a comforting form: My cable may have arrived first saying his wound was not serious.

It is rather cold tonight — 3–25 . . . and it seems to be blowing up for the storm which is overdue, and the Hospital Ship is out there very beautiful with her green stripe and red cross brightly lit — and I am going to turn in. . .

June 17

A little off colour. . .

Some of the *Triumph's* wardroom wine was washed ashore the day before yesterday, and several of the men got away with some of it. Consequence — two men given six months each. . .

June 18

This evening all sorts of furniture, pots, pans, plates, came flying out of the engineers' dugout. There must have been a fight going on in the depths of it. This is the first fight I have heard of. It is extraordinary how our men have come to lean on one another. When they started out they wouldn't share a tin of bully beef, but now they have come to lean on one another and on their officers, almost like a big family. Since the first day I have hardly heard a word except of praise and indeed of affection for any officer that had given them a good lead... I have never seen a more healthy relation than that of these Australian men to a good officer...

June 19
On cornflour diet for a day or two...

June 20, Sunday
The *Peninsula Press*[10] publishes with great scorn an article in the *Berlin Courier* saying that 'our attack as at present conducted, is a fizzle, due to the ineffectual bombardment of March 18th; the insufficient size of the landing forces; and the failure to embroil Bulgaria against Turkey.' As far as the Military operations go it seems to me that this statement is literally and absolutely correct. If these operations have brought Italy in they are worth it at any cost — but otherwise it's a far better summing up of the position than our official reports give. This is the point to which the Censorship has reduced us — that the German Official accounts are far truer than our own...

The Turks are getting very cheeky — actually performing the offices of nature in front of their trenches. Our men should stop this; but the 8th Battalion (which has taken over from the 1st Battalion) is new to the trenches, and is not keeping down snipers in the way the 1st Battalion did. It will learn, I suppose...

Quiet — quite like a Sunday today. Very few shells. I counted 404 men bathing, or sun-bathing on the beach today, and a lot more sitting down there half dressed, browning their backs, or dressing and undressing. Many of these chaps are much darker than Turks. The Turk prisoners' latrines are not far in front of our ridge, on the next ridge, and I have excellent grounds for saying that many Turks are as white as Europeans. That accounts for all officers being put down by our men as German Officers.

June 21
A mail today brought me two letters from Alexandria from Jock — one dated May 12th, the other May 19th. In the second he said he was unsure whether to have the bullet removed — a difficult operation. Of course this made me very anxious; and what I want to know is why cannot the Post Office get a letter from Egypt here in under 5 weeks? We have letters from Australia later than that one of May 12th from Alex.

Everyone who returns from Alexandria says that the base is in a state of miserable disorganisation — that men who want to get back cannot, and men who do not seem anxious to get back are not made to... I hope to goodness Legge can straighten this out...

Received another bunch of cuttings by the mail today from England. The picture agencies ought really to be shown up — they are a disgrace to English journalism. There is never a bundle of these cuttings comes in but it contains a barefaced fraud on the public. A photograph of our men jumping out of boats without packs and with overcoats rolled is given as 'the first Australians on Turkish soil'. The men here take it as obviously a picture of one of our practice landings in Lemnos Harbour. It was far too dark when the first lot landed to take any instantaneous photograph. Photos taken around the camp at Mena or on the old drain along the road, are given as views of Active Service on the Suez Canal. This is the sort of stuff the picture papers are supplied with and dish up to the public — there really ought to be a law against it...

June 22

Our health organization is ... now far better than it was. The latrines are now mostly in brigade areas, one to each area, with sanitary pickets posted, who are fairly particular. The trenches of some battalions are swept three times a day and sprinked in bad places with 'creosol' — a certain amout of creosol is drawn for all purposes daily. Food, if found in the trench (scraps, etc.) is swept into scrap pits in the back of the trench and buried there. The men sometimes will throw scraps over on to the parapet — the swarm of flies at some parts was hard to understand until this was discovered. Now there is a fairly strict check on it.

I suppose from Quinn's we must get the flies from the trenches of the Turks. Six or seven of the men employed on fatigue there, who have their meals there, go sick every day, and this may be the cause. We can hear the Turks there and at Pope's — hear them talking at night, laughing, sometimes smell their tobacco. In spite of any disadvantage it is lucky for us we had the armistice now — if all those dead Turks were out there the place would be horrible with flies — far worse than it is. We occasionally come upon Turkish bodies in our saps. There are about 50 Enteric cases from amongst the N.Z., and about 6 or 7 from amongst our men reported from Mudros.

The divisional health arrangements are good, and the stretcher bearers splendid; but when you leave here the arrangements seem one hopeless muddle. For example: a man here had broken his plate, and as we have no dental corps or equipment — although

A typical scene on Anzac Beach in June. Watson's pier (left foreground) is under construction. Swimmers can be seen dotted in the water. (AWM neg. no. G1038)

we have now to accept men with imperfect teeth — he had to be sent away. He was sent to Lemnos or Imbros to be treated by a dentist there. At Lemnos — after being there some days — he found that the dentist had gone, or couldn't fix him, and was sent on to Egypt and was told to return in ten days. He came back in ten days and was told the dentist had gone, so he was sent back to Lemnos. He found nothing could be done at Lemnos, and so was sent back here arriving just four weeks after he left, without having the trouble attended to...

Two of our water barges have been sunk during the last two days... I wonder what provisions have been made for replacing these barges! The Australian Division is now pretty well independent of the imported water, both for men and mules. Up the gully they are allowed one water bottle per day — though Arthur [Bazley] tells me they are allowed to wash in a well unfit for drinking. Many of the men, however, now manage to bathe occasionally...

June 23

Two shells got into the ammunition depot at the southern end of the beach today. One got into a lot of rifles and smashed up about

50. The other got into the ammunition and set fire to two boxes. Some men immediately dumped them into the water and put the fire out. The Turks have been singularly unenterprising with all this ammunition and stores about, because there is a very great amount on the beach now — oil, food, fodder, carts, ammunition. They don't even try to sink the barges — they reserve their shots for trawlers, destroyers, and, sometimes, tugs... One of their shells today hit a man in the water and took off his arm — at least it was hanging by a thread, and he came out of the water holding it. It didn't stop the bathing. I heard there were 8 casualties on the beach in all, but bathing went on as usual, except for a few minutes. Some men didn't, I think, even get out... When some Australian (or will it be a Greek) starts a hotel here after the war, bathing will be one of the chief recreations — you'll have to walk nearly to Kaba Tepe for your golf...

June 24

Major General J.G. Legge arrived this morning from Mudros... Many of the senior officers objected to Legge's appointment, and several wanted to resign, but Birdwood told them resignation could not be thought of in a war like this. They must stand loyally be their Commander; and if he was as weak as they made out, there was all the more necessity to stand by him and help him through...

June 26

My first reports in papers from Australia arrived today. I see that they didn't all take the first cable — the *Argus* didn't — considered it late, I suppose[11]...

Bazley ... handed me a letter which gave me something of a shock. It was from Major Ward at Army H.Q. and told me that it had been decided to establish a camp for War Correspondents at K. Beach, Imbros, and ordered me to present myself there as soon as possible.

For the European Correspondents who want general news of how the campaign is getting on this may be all very well. For me — it would be just as good to be in Australia. I put the letter before Blamey and White, who saw the General, who saw Birdwood. Our general, so Col. White told me afterwards, would like me to make a memorandum in writing, attach it to the letter and send it in. I did so — and my memo. is attached...

C.S.O.
1st Australian Division.

Headquarters
1st Australian Division

June 27th, 1915.

With reference to the instruction from General Headquarters that I should move to Imbros, I would submit that, while, of course, I must take any course that is laid down for me, it is quite impossible for me to do at Imbros the work for which my Government appointed me.

1. The Australian Government in the instructions given me during my interviews with the Minister for Defence attached importance to two points: (a) to having with this distant force a representative who could satisfy the poignant anxiety of Australians for news of their own men — their daily life, behaviour in action, their peculiar Australian interest which could only be given by an Australian, and (b) to be special instructions given to me to write after the war the history of the Australian part in the war, as a permanent record for libraries, schools, and the nation generally. In their speeches at the dinner given to me in Melbourne before I left, the Minister for Defence, and other ministers laid special stress upon the latter point.

2. The category of news which my duties require me to obtain has no relation to that required by correspondents responsible to newspapers. I am paid and employed by my Government for the above duties. I have not attempted to sum up the general trend of the campaign, except in one, or possibly two small references to events already long since published in England. I do not know, I do not want to know, and, needless to say, have not attempted even remotely to touch on any future plans.

3. The only news obtainable at Imbros would be of the general movements of the whole force which interests most correspondents, but which I do not need, and cannot obtain at Anzac.

4. The news which I cannot obtain at Imbros is the details as to the life, scenes, bearing of men, scenes that will stir Australian pride (there are plenty of such details told to the British people of their soldiers) — which is what the nation I represent wants to hear.

5. News from Anzac will get into the papers — from letters, returned soldiers, third hand exaggerations from Cairo — only it will be as it has already been, false news as to imaginary

atrocities, etc., often distressing, sometimes alarming. My duty to my Government has been to steadily correct these, distinguishing most carefully falsehood from truth.

6. If I make reference to general events the Censor has every word I write addressed straight to him, and sees it before he forwards it. I have no competitor, and the possibility of my thinking of sending news otherwise than through the censor, would not, I imagine, be considered any more than in the case of any other official appointed by the Government.

7. For the purpose of the Australian History of the Australian expedition, I might as well be in Australia as in Imbros.

8. The British have plenty of constant news from their homes. Our nation has not one observer with its army, 8 000 miles from home, to see and record similar things of its men, except myself, and if I had not been present a feat such as the Helles charge of the Second Brigade (which deserves to live as long as the nation exists) would have gone almost unrecorded.

I would submit that my case is really quite distinct from that of private correspondents or of British correspondents, and trust the authorities will see their way to let me remain with the Australian Force.

(signed) C.E.W. Bean.

June 29

The night was stormy. Coming along the beach I looked in at the Casualty Clearing Hospital to see how they were. They had the sea washing almost up to the doors of their tents, and any amount of seaweed on the beach — so what will happen when it really does get rough and blows a S. or S.W. gale I don't know. I rather dread to think — the wounded would have to be kept here until the weather was calm — and if any big attack took place the Casualty Clearing Hospital would be insufficient — you might have 2 000 or 3 000 wounded on the beach unable to clear them...

June 30

This evening another fierce thunderstorm came up. It was dark before I got home... When I reached the beach it was pitch dark, and I was wet through. I couldn't for some time find Anzac Gully, and on one occasion I walked into the soft hairy nose of a mule. An occasional lightning flash was all that one got at all. I scrambled up the gully eventually; got to the dugout — and heard from Murphy (just returned) that old Jock was on the fleetsweeper just off the pier, and would land this night. I finished a cup of tea and some pears and went down... Old Jock came off presently with a lot of medical stores for his battalion — looking very well... Jock came up to my dugout and slept there. It was wet, so Bazley had a corner in it also...

July 4, Sunday
The H.Q. has sent its answer to my request to be allowed to stay at Anzac... [It had been decided that no exception could be made; all correspondents would be based on Imbros. GHQ did agree, however, to grant Bean one concession: he could visit Anzac Cove as often as he wished and extend each visit to three or four days.]

This, of course, means that I shall have to go to Imbros a day or two in the week. It is probable we shall be able to carry on — the only drawback being waste of time and the moral certainty of being shelled almost every time we come in and out — which is quite unnecessary seeing our business gets no benefit and the State no security...

July 5
The other day a shell landed in the dentists' dugout, and covered the hillside with false teeth. We want dentists badly, now that they let through men whose teeth aren't perfect. The N.Z. people have a corps of them, but we haven't. A man who breaks his teeth is no use on biscuits, and has to get back to Alexandria to get some more...

We are now losing about 100 men a day — today in both Divisions it was about 150 — almost entirely by sickness. Yesterday it was 55 by sickness and 7 by wounds in the N.Z.: about the same in our division. If they could be got back in three or four days — as ought to happen — it would be all right; but as things are it means a month...

[Yesterday] I sailed for Imbros — a huge waste of time. Wasted all the morning trying to catch the ferry (trawler) which I was eventually told by the seamen had started. Went back to my dugout, and half an hour later saw the trawler start. Eventually got the torpedo boat at about 4.15 p.m.... The torpedo boat landed us at G.H.Q., Imbros. There I met Col. Ward. He was very nice. He said to me: "You can see we can't have you all scattered — we must have you together" — but I can't see, all the same. So long as all my stuff goes straight to the censor and only to the censor I can't see how it makes it simpler or safer, or in any way better for me to live at Imbros... It was too late to get out to the Correspondents' Camp (Ross[12] had gone there earlier), so I camped at the Assistant Camp Commandant's Camp... There was something flat about the air — it was like lemonade without the tingle (as one officer said 'beer out of a cup'). It really was as if part of the background — the grit in it — were missing; it was the stillness. The bugles in the camp were new, and a dog barked that night!

July 6

Went down for a bathe — no shrapnel. Our 1st Battalion enjoying itself — no work — the men very quiet (had a concert last night) but very happy...

I found the Correspondents' Camp under some elm trees with the camp of the officers of a Manchester Battalion. Ashmead Bartlett's tent was there with his kit — but no tent for me. Accordingly I walked over to G.H.Q., and there in the first tent I enquired in — the H.Q. Mess — I found Capt. Maxwell. He was exceedingly nice and gave me a glass of beer — I don't often drink beer, but I did enjoy that one — and had a very long yarn. He said he had hardly had to censor my work at all; that it was much the most complete that had been done here. The reason for rounding the rest of us up was in order to round up Ashmead Bartlett. They weren't at all satisfied with his proceedings, and wanted to have him thoroughly under control — and so made the rule to apply to the lot of us. I must say it's an infernal waste of time. Maxwell told me that Ian Hamilton wanted my despatches published in London (or he himself suggested it, and I.H. agreed subject to my approving). I had done far more work than anyone else he said, and he had never had a correspondent who had given him such little trouble — all of which was very good hearing. He had altered one or two small points in my despatches where they were not correct — which was a good job.

I walked back to the Correspondents' Camp and found Ross there outside the batmen's tent. A. Bartlett was over at Helles...

July 7

Breakfast with Ross after a bathe. A. Bartlett told us how he had seen this campaign going all wrong, and had been home [in June][13] to tell people he knew there (I forgot whether he said in the War Office or Parliament) exactly how things were going. It seemed to be typically and exactly the thing that a War Correspondent ought not to do; but I am bound to say I think he's a competent man, though certainly inaccurate...

I caught the torpedo boat . . . at 10 a.m. — by the skin of my teeth, getting a warship's steamboat to take me across. . . It was a scorching hot day, and I was fit for very little after getting to Anzac. Old J. came down and had some dinner with me.

July 8
I was extraordinarily limp today — I don't know why. It was very hot and relaxing. . .

July 10
It is curious how men get back to simpler habits during a time like this. I have found one or two officers starting to read the Bible — and one told me he found it extraordinarily interesting. I wish I had the time, but I haven't. . .

July 18, Sunday
Yesterday I took Nevinson up to Quinn's, and Malcolm Ross also. Quinn's was absolutely transformed since my last visit. It is laid out in terraces, each with a shed on them with an iron roof, well sandbagged, under which the supports sleep. We had tea with Col. Malone . . . on a little terrace in front of his dugout. "The art of warfare," he said, "is the cultivation of the domestic virtues." If he had reason he would plant them there. The trenches are well bomb proofed — our fellows (the bomb throwers) can throw the bombs from behind the wire. We have steel loopholes, and two m[achine] g[un] emplacements — one of which was blown down, but is up again — and the loopholes are level with the ground. They don't get much bombardment by now.

We have already exploded 16 mines in front of Quinn's. We have a series of tunnels going in from the hill front, and then a gallery connecting them, and further tunnels dipping down, and branch tunnels with listeners in them. Our system is a defence against the enemy's mines. The Turks exploded 1 mine under our trench.

Eleswhere we have exploded, I think, at J. Jolly 3 mines, as against the Turks 2, and at Lone Pine 2 against their 3. The 3 they last exploded were hopeless failures — right away from ours. But the 2 before that, opposite Lone Pine, were a success. The one we exploded opposite J. Jolly today at 3, flung 2 Turk bodies into the air and made a big crater — the Turk trench must have been above it. 2 others were exploded yesterday, one opposite Quinn's with a small charge, and one opposite Courtney's. All this work is planned by the engineers. Our front is pretty well protected, though we couldn't guarantee the front trenches everywhere. The mistake was that we didn't begin with a regular plan — we only woke up to that necessity later.

The Turks used to find our tunnels by crawling over the ground at night and listening. We have put a sudden end to this — we have our own patrols out now waiting for the Turks. Last night one of them met a Turk, shot him with a revolver. The wounded Turk ran down between the trenches shouting "Ahmed! Ahmed!!" until he was shot from our trenches. When we used to allow them out of a night, by not firing a shot, they placed two of our tunnels and dug towards them straight away, and exploded mines under two of them near Lone Pine...

July 20

Peter Schuler arrived today and is staying with me. I'm afraid all my hospitality really is Bazley's hospitality — all the work falls on him. We had four to dinner as old J. came down and stayed, and had a bathe afterwards. I do hope we all get through this all right — it will be something to talk and think of afterwards between us...

July 22

Nevinson and A. Bartlett came over from Imbros today having heard of the chance of an attack, and A.B. being anxious to get the cinema pictures which Ernest Brooks had been going to take.[14] As he wanted to see Quinn's we went up there first. For the first time I went into one of the tunnels at Quinn's — it seemed to be near the extreme left. We entered fairly low down in the hillside and worked up — presently downwards, lit candles, and then past a second? gallery down a steep slope into a squarish chamber in which was sitting a man in a felt hat. A heap of fallen earth was in the left hand corner. Our party and the men around then were making a good deal of noise, but when they got silence, Gibbs (the infantry officer in charge) said: "There they are" and you could hear the faint pick, pick, pick very rapid — as if someone were tapping on wood. It was the Turks picking about 8 feet away. They were above us, and I think our people had ceased working. You could stand up straight in one chamber, though the tunnel was only 3' or 3'6" in height...

July 26

Went out with P. Schuler to the left flank today to the N.Z. No. 2 Post. It was like a walk in the country. The Post was taken up about three weeks after we came here. At that time there wasn't a trench outside of it — now the whole place is fortified and entrenched... We saw one Turk with his black head and shoulders over the trench top. Paddon of Otago M.R. ... had three shots at this Turk at a mile, and made him move his head at the second shot... Paddon asked me if I would like a shot any time — but my job is not to shoot — I am not a combatant — and I will not do so...

I can't go to Imbros — things here are too much touch and go...

July 27

About 250 men left Anzac yesterday — most of them men seriously sick with diarrhoea, but some influenza cases which may be typhoid. Our whole Division is living on an area much less than half a square mile, and this illness is bound to come with the heat, dust and overwork. It would not be very serious if the men could get back in a week as they ought to, but they cannot. They are taken to Mudros and sent on from there to Alexandria, and men who ought to be back in a fortnight, who are practically well by the time they reach the port, are asked whether they prefer to go to England or elsewhere. The consequence is that men who ought to be back in 6 days are not back in 6 weeks. The Division is just keeping its present strength, and this is all — with all the reinforcements coming forward.

This had been placed before the generals again and again. Each one says: "It is not my business, it is the L[ines] of C[ommunication]". Really Gen. Woodward ought to lay before Gen. Hamilton the state of affairs and get him to represent it — I have had it said to me: "Isn't it your business?" — but it is not. It is strictly against the regulations for me to criticise and I have not been asked by the Authorities to do so. My job is to tell the people of Australia all I can about their troops here and I should be sent back if I tried to do anything else — that I know only too well. Besides, even if I were free to criticise L. of C., I'm not on the spot — I'm at the front and not the base. The unofficial correspondents in Cairo and Alex. will take it up and it will be righted through a Press agitation and not the official channels — I have no doubt...

July 29

Spent the whole of this day going round the 1st, 2nd and 10th Bns. getting stories of the first day...

July 30

Have pretty well finished my enquiries into the 1st day's fighting... One thing I can't understand about our Australian officers; they're mostly very brave, but they won't credit their brother officer with any bravery. They often, without actually saying it, hint that so-and-so was in his dugout all the time, or was not in the firing line (when in some cases it is not his business to be). There's sometimes absolutely no grounds whatever for this insinuation...

July 31

Spent all day getting particulars of work of 4th Brigade on 1st day...

4

A Losing Battle

THREE months of continual Allied hammering at Cape Helles had produced no worthwhile gains. Hamilton fully appreciated that the time available for achieving a break out was fast disappearing. Accordingly, he resolved to launch one more offensive; this time not at Cape Helles but north of Anzac Cove. The British War Council provided 25 000 fresh reinforcements to assist in the operation.

The attack was set for 6 August. The British launched a feint from Cape Helles at 2.30 p.m. A second feint was made at 5.30 p.m. by Australians against the strong Turkish trenches on Lone Pine. The real attack commenced after dark on this moonless night when, in a three-pronged operation, the New Zealand Mounted Rifles cleared Turkish outposts around the foothills of Chunuk Bair; the New Zealand Brigade advanced up the extremely rugged Rhododendron Ridge to attack Chunuk Bair; while on the extreme left the 4th Australian Brigade, led by Brig-Gen John Monash, and a contingent of Gurkhas advanced through similarly inhospitable terrain to attack Hill 971. While these night marches were underway, two British divisions were to disembark further north at Suvla Bay. Next day they would sweep around to link up with the ANZAC units. If the plan had succeeded and control of the major high points (Hill 971, Chunuk Bair, Baby 700) were gained, the Allies would be poised to push the Turkish army back across the Peninsula.

Monash had briefed Bean fully on the plan during the evening of 5 August. The two met again next day early in the afternoon, each aware of the importance of what lay ahead in the next few hours.

August 6
Left Monash and went to see Jack... He and I had previously been along to see where the fight could best be seen from. I thought I would get near where he started from. We went along to see — it was S. of Brown's Dip — but tunnel was crowded...

About 5.25 as I reached convenient point in trench S. of Brown's Dip, after having tried a good many, I arrived at recess near No. 9 (?5) Tunnel. It was crowded with 3rd Bn. Men were chaffing one another — seemed to be quite eager to go out and do something. About five were on the fire step — a little officer crouched in corner — and about five or six in trench below. I saw not the slightest trace of nervousness. Men all had packs with some sort of tucker or knick-knacks in. Presently order came: pull down top bags in recess — so as to make it easier to get over. Whole trench looked suspiciously ragged. Officer took whistle from wrist "Prepare to jump out," he said. Put whistle between his teeth. I didn't hear mines go — presently he blew whistle...

5.33 rush — men crowded under parapet of T's trench. Some bayonets in the trench. About a quarter of an hour afterwards many men started to hop into enemy's trench. Seemed busy over something — thought I saw rifle butts come up. [The Turkish trenches were covered by heavy pine logs so the Australians recklessly stood above, firing through the gaps, or jumping in at any available opening.] Colonel went with second rush. Turkish shrapnel got on to our trench and afterwards on to space between trenches but wonderfully few men were hit. Some got into second trench. 1st Battalion now filing into fire trench...

1st Bn. began to go over and reinforce. It looked as if this was unnecessary on the right because numbers of men were lying there — they were dead men. Enemy's machine guns always told when our men were going forward. Not a man came back. Attempts to signal — telephone carried by two men came rushing back. Dropped into a hole. They took one line over, another line back. It got cut by shrapnel. Then messenger came. Left weak. Turks massing for attack on left.

Col. Smyth, V.C. ..., Col. Bennett by me in trench. There arrives a message presently from Col. Brown. Left safe. Centre wants a few men. 70 Turkish prisoners. Will send them in as soon as possible...

Telephone line again broken. Hear we had about three trenches... Things seemed settled here by 7.30 o'clock so I came back and had dinner... As I came out of trench saw some of J's men. Heard J. had been wounded in the hand and gone down to beach. On beach I heard about 10 p.m. that he had been sent on to the *Sicilia*. On Aug. 9 I heard from him that it was a nasty wrist wound — shrapnel and was found to be septic and drained under chloroform. He was going to England...

At 9.30 there was a tremendous fire in centre — N.Z. had gone

4 p.m. August 6: men of the 3rd Battalion wait around before the assault on Lone Pine. They wore white arm bands and patches on their backs to distinguish them when darkness fell. (AWM neg. no. G1124)

in... Fighting also down South. 10.30 more heavy firing on left...

11.15 I heard at A.C. Headquarters ... that N.Z.M.R. were held up on Table Top and were late. But Monash and Ghurkas were starting out in spite of this (some small risk perhaps if [NZ] M.R. could not clear ridges — might make Monash's retreat difficult — but worth taking. Gen. Birdwood clearly thought so).

Bazley sewed white patches on to my coat [as were being worn by all our troops this night for purposes of identification] and I took field glasses. I somehow missed the sap in N.Z. lines. [On] coming [upon the] bank of it I jumped in. The jump was much bigger than I expected and I got a rather nasty shake. Went on; then, 10 minutes later, found I had lost my pince nez. A couple of hours later found I had lost my field glasses. No chance of seeing them again...

N.Z. were not clear of the sap when I got to Godley's H.Q. [beneath Table Top] but fortunately Monash and Ghurkas were ahead. Monash had gone along beach. Indians a little further inland parallel. I walked down through dark and struck Ghurkas and later Sikhs marching in fours about 100 yards below the N.Z. Post...

It was clear the attack was getting much behind time. Godley said to Pinwill: "Can I tell Army Corps that both the Brigades have cleared this place?" P. didn't seem to know, but said he'd find out. Presently he reported Monash's stretcher bearers just passing. "Then I can say both Brigades are past here?" said Godley. "No, no, Sir, the Indian Brigade is only arriving." "What, are they behind Monash? Good God!" "But that was the order they were told to go in, Sir."

It seemed to me rather an elementary part of the attack for the General to have forgotten...

Godley gave me a whisky and then I went out to see if I could see anything of the British landing. I thought I had seen lights out there. I looked for my glasses and found they had gone...

Bullets were whipping into the sand in front of Godley's H.Q. at No. 2 Outpost. I decided to stroll along and see if I could get some news of Monash before daybreak, which if it overtook me might make if difficult to get back. So I strolled along by the Indian Column which had been passing for about 2 hours, and was still passing just inland on the sand hills. It would halt — shuffle on a few paces — halt again.

Just before I went I heard Godley sending messages. Col. Hughes (?) N.Z. Inf. had reported that he had gone forward; had sent on his guides and was only waiting for the guides to come back — would move as soon as they did.

Godley sent back: Do not wait for guides, move on at once to your objective.

He sent to Gen. Cox commanding the 29th Indian Brigade: Push on at once to your objective, and I think he sent same to Monash. At any rate when I told him I was going to Monash he gave me the message "Tell him to hurry up" he said.

I went off past our old boundary out along the fields — the Indian Column beside me. Moon just getting up; the troops were wandering, slower than a funeral, along a bank with a path running along it. By the side were several Australians and an Englishman — wounded by strays or shrapnel. A few strays were lisping into the ground... The column turned in towards the dark hills on the right. Occasionally some shots came from there. I thought Monash was further to the left, and was just starting to stroll off towards the left when I heard some very distant firing ahead of me. It must be the landing of the British, I thought. I was moving on again when something gave me a whack (like a stone thrown hard) in the upper part of the right leg. I could feel it whack the right side of the leg and bruise the inner part of the left side. I was pretty sure I had been hit by a stray which had gone in on the right and not come out, but I couldn't feel any blood, and so thought it might not have penetrated at all. Some of the stones from shell bursts had hit me quite as hard earlier this day — but presently I felt my hand greasy [with blood] in my pants — so I knew I [was wounded and] must go back. I could limp along pretty well. As I went a good deal of fire burst out in one of the gullies to the N. of me —either Indians or Monash clearing out opposition. Monash's men had orders only to use bayonet till daylight, so shots were probably enemy's.

I looked in to see Godley and he was very kind and gave me a whisky and sent me to dressing station. They looked after me well. I walked slowly home along the sap. As I got opposite the Sphinx a tremendous bombardment broke out... The dawn was just growing and the shell shaped cliff around the Sphinx fairly bellowed with sound. Tails of black earth were being flung up from Walker's Nek against the sky. It stopped at 4.30. I believe the 3rd L.H. Brigade was a bit slow in getting out[1] — didn't start for a minute or so after the finish [of the naval bombardment] (One hardly wonders — they didn't want a shell in their backs by starting early) and the Turks had time to get up again and get out their rifles. Few men reached the Nek...

[Bean hobbled back to his dugout and went to bed without waking Bazley. Later that morning, after Bazley had made himself breakfast, he decided to wake Bean who, he felt, was sleeping rather late. "I've been hit, Baz", Bean groaned. Colonel Howse, the senior medical officer, was summoned. He strongly recommended that the patient be evacuated to guard against the danger of tetanus infection but Bean refused to leave. For the next three days he rested in the dugout. Peter Schuler frequently called by to keep him up to date on the fighting.]

What happened to Monash I believe was: He was held up by finding opposition (he was rather anxious about this because his track led him past or near their reserves) but opposition cannot have been great for his losses were small. He didn't get to Abdel Rahman ridge — he waited till his left was in touch with the British — apparently not on forward spur to left but one behind it. The valley was very narrow; troops had to file singly in parts; progress was slow; day came rapidly on. There were difficulties ahead — some risk of losing touch and being quite in air. Shrapnel was pouring on them going up valley — men were deadly tired, and so Monash did not push on but dug in on the ridge nearer this way than [Hill] 971...

It seems to me a decision which many weak commanders would make but utterly unjustifiable. That is to say — instead of pushing on in spite of fatigue till he was actually stopped by the enemy, he stopped short of his objective without being stopped. Our whole plan had been to try and ensure that there were very few men in front of him for 12 hours or so. In order to give Turks the impression that we were going to push through down S. end of our positions, we attacked one of the most difficult positions in Gallipoli — a trench the Turks had put a tremendous amount of work into. It cost us 2 000 men to create this diversion which was splendidly done. The 6th failed . . . at German Officers' Trench — but at any rate a very splendid effort was made to keep the Turks here. The whole essence of the attack was that it should issue suddenly from our N. and whilst the Turks were staggered by the heaviness of the first blow and thinking only of that — the blow was heavy enough to make them do so. Naturally the northern attack was a little late — but there is every sign that it was unexpected. The Turks on Bauchop's and Big Table Top were broken and fleeing in small parties which our columns often stumbled across and some of whom they captured. There is no evidence that the main ridge northwards was strongly held at this time — there is every reason to conjecture that it was weakly held, but it certainly would be strongly held by next night. Yet we allowed ourselves to be held up — not by enemy for we never threw ourselves against him — but by apprehension that he might be too strong if we attacked by daylight and by fatigue of our men — If he might have had machine guns then it was certain he would have them next day. If he might be in numbers, and digging trenches, then it was certain that he would be next day. Our men might be fatigued then, but it is nothing to the fatigue and strain which a superior enemy would inflict on them if they went on and did their job next day. They might lose heavily or might not but it was dead certain that somebody would lose heavily by their stopping if he had to attack the same ridge after the enemy had arrived there in force. The whole chance lay in avoiding the risk of this battle crystallising again into a trench battle and that could only be done by sacrificing everything to speed. We might not have succeeded even then. The point is which some of these Brigade commanders seem to me grievously to have failed was that they did not on the first advance find out whether they could have succeeded — they stopped before the enemy stopped them. I don't believe General Walker, or [Sinclair-]MacLagan, or McLaurin, or M'Cay would have stopped[2]. . .

Face to face with the enemy: Anzacs stare at Turkish prisoners in the POW compound. (AWM neg. no. G1188)

August 8, Sunday

Today is Sunday, August 8th, fifteen weeks after we landed . . .

I have just seen as caddish an act as I ever saw in my life. About 100 Turkish prisoners and two Germans were sitting in the pen built by the Australian Division opposite my dug out. There is an incinerator within a few yards. Some chap had poured out a tin of kerosene on the ground in front of it and laid a trail of kerosene . . . Some chap put a light to the trail, it flared along and when it reached the kerosene there was a huge flare of fire very uncomfortably close — if not dangerously — to the Turks. The wretched prisoners rushed to the far corner of the pen like a flock of sheep rounded up by a dog, and the fellows looking on laughed. There were both Australians and Britishers there amongst the onlookers. I wondered someone hadn't the decency to hit the man who did it straight in the face. The same thing exactly was done yesterday.

The treatment of these prisoners makes you blush for your own side. They are under the control of the Army Corps Police and A.P.M. . . They have put Indian sentries over them, who are about as capable of keeping off the Australians who crowd around to stare at them as an old woman with a stick would be. Three Turkish officers are among the lot. So far as we know they have treated our captured men and officers excellently. These three officers were sent off under an Indian sentry to a vacant shell of a dug out in Australian Divisional lines. They went sent there in the morning and absolutely forgotten. No food or water was sent to them. Our Divisional interpreter happened to be passing in the afternoon, when these Turks told him. He went to the A.P.M. of Army Corps, whose business it was. A.P.M. said he was too busy — would the interpreter get some other officer to do it.

The interpreter saw another officer who said he would have bully beef and biscuits sent up. Interpreter said he wouldn't take bully beef and biscuits up — the Turks wouldn't give our officers bully and biscuits if their own officers were feeding better. The officer saw things in this light and sent up a decent meal. The Turks had some tea but no one provided them with any water. Interpreter had to go round for that and couldn't find any. They are there now in a bare dug out, no blankets, no water proof sheet, no comforts of any sort...

August 11
Woke up to find everything pefectly quiet. Sea glassily smooth. One Hospital ship here (there were two and several fleet sweepers last night) and two Hospital ships off Suvla Bay... Evidently our big battle has come to its standstill... [The offensive had been a costly failure. Apart from the small gain at Lone Pine, all the attacks had been repulsed. The British had been landed successfully at Suvla Bay, but their inability to exploit this landing meant that their presence only lengthened the now over-extended Allied lines. Much of the failure can be attributed to the extremely cautious approach adopted by the British commander at Suvla, Lt-Gen Sir Frederick Stopford.]

I went down to see General Birdwood after dinner. He was just looking over the list of officers killed. He was particularly sorry to lose Col. Brown, he told me. He was writing to his mother to say what a splendid officer he was. Other Colonels sometimes pulled a long face and said: "We've all these reinforcements, Sir, and they can't shoot at all." Brown would say "Can't shoot, my lad? Well, come along to this loop-hole and I'll teach you. Now then..."...

B. tole me he had two grave anxieties — water, and the left of the line. As to the first, the pumps had broken down for three hours and if they did not go the 1st Australian Division would be in a parlous way. Luckily we had found water on the left and he had given instructions to dig wells...

Secondly, as to the line. The Turks were massed pretty thick at

Left:
Australian troops relax in a captured Turkish trench at Lone Pine, 10 August. Note the heavy head cover of pine logs. This was the first day since his wounding that Bean felt strong enough to go up to the line. (AWM neg. no. G1126)
Right:
Bean (in front) and Ellis Ashmead Bartlett enjoy a donkey ride on Imbros. (AWM neg. no. A5382)

Rhododendron and might attack to-night. We held now no part of the main crest, but we had got to get there somehow. He had asked Godley and the Commander of the XIII but they said their men were too worn out for it to be thought of to-night. Besides, we were just a little short of howitzer ammunition, which was absolutely necessary — I do not know that it would last for another bombardment. There was more coming in ten days.

We had obtained a foothold on the crest. The [New Zealanders,] Ghurkas and the British had looked down on to the Dardanelles — they could see the water in the Straits and motor cars going along the road. And then the shells of our own naval guns got on to them and blew them off the ridge... It was in the dull light of morning — and — these things will happen in war![13]... [In five days of ferocious combat the Allies and Turks had each lost approximately 18 000 men.]

August 12
Quiet. Came up to Lone Pine trenches. Counter attack now over except for an occasional bomb. Went through trench. Turkish headcover extraordinarily good — rough pine logs — not much

knocked about by artillery — slightly broken here and there. Gave for first time splendid view over Turkish communications. All the stables for mules and dug outs at back of [Johnston's] Jolly were deserted and there was a beer cask under a lean-to roof where they used to draw water. The Turks in the Jolly don't know which trenches we have got and which we haven't. I saw a man rather like old Abraham looking over some sand bricks at the side. He spotted us and was quite excited — three of them put their heads up... The place was terribly thick with dead bodies — and those of Australians couldn't be told from those of Turks because the faces go so black...

August 14
Sounds of fairly heavy fighting down south. We here are having a peaceful time again. They have a few new guns against us... We have finished burying the Turkish dead in the Lone Pine. There seems to be less smell today. They say we can still look right over the Turks behind Jolly, but Turks are digging fast...

August 20
Still practically no change in situation. De Lisle has been given command of 9th Army Corps vice Stopford, stellenbosched. (I hope if any one ever edits this diary they'll tone those things down — the expressions are often forcible for the sake of brevity)...

I said good-bye to Schuler and Smith[4]...

August 21
No voice owing to laryngitis...

August 25
Today was to be the beginning of the rainy season and the weather has clearly changed. It was very muggy — I was in bed with laryngitis, and most uncomfortably hot — but a little rain fell. August 23rd was the first noticeable change — hazy with a strong east wind. August 24th thundery with some rain. I am having my dugout bagged in for the winter — Bazley built quite a nice looking front wall...

Cass was in yesterday. He tells me the 1st Australian Division is to be relieved at last — the 2nd Division will take its place — battalions to be moved out at three days' intervals, one after the other, and taken to Imbros for a month. Good canteen to be there and the men allowed 2 good beers a day... Well, they deserve it if ever men did. Brig.-Gen. [Sinclair-]MacLagen, Col. White, and

Col. Braund are all ill, and on hospital ships, so it's about time we went...

The fighting at Lone Pine has been very interesting. Things are so close there that we actually have a peephole through into a Turk trench (which peephole is kept carefully covered up). It only shows the opposite wall, and so far no one (as far as is known) has walked along it.

The Turks have tried to mine, but we blew down their tunnel and are now counter-mining, or sapping at any rate...

The Turk for about the first time did not play the game in the last scrap. That is to say he shot some of our men who were obviously wounded and were rolling down to try and get out of the way. I don't think we can complain about [stretcher] bearers being fired on, because stretchers of a sort not unlike medical stretchers are regularly used to carry food; but shooting wounded is over the odds. At the same time we all know that if men sham wounded it may be justifiable. Our men certainly were not shamming wounded, but the Ts. have done so on various occasions and we have shot all bodies within sight to make sure. The Turks were steadily shooting everybody within sight — putting a m[achine] g[un] on to them if they continued to move...

August 26

Raining tonight; I think our hardships will really begin with the winter — though I must say that, by the way in which the Tommies, who come here from elsewhere compare their previous lot as enviable, I am not sure that we haven't been greater heroes than we were inclined to think ourselves. I suppose you can't honestly claim to be a hero if you have been unconscious of your heroism, and your hardship didn't seem to you so outrageously hard as it did to others...

August 29

Our men have a tremendous admiration for the little Gurkhas — they say they don't mind getting up against N.Z.s. or Gurkhas — but they (and the N.Z. men too) do not trust the Tommy — they all except the regular army, but they have not the slightest confidence in K[itchener's] army — nor have our officers — nor have I. The truth is that after 100 years of breeding in slums, the British race is not the same, and can't be expected to be the same, as in the days of Waterloo. It is breeding one fine class at the expense of all the rest. The only hope is that those puny

narrow-chested little men may, if they come out to Australia or N.Z. or Canada, within 2 generations breed men again. England herself, unless she does something heroic, cannot hope to...

September 2
I have to go slow with laryngitis, and now that is over I have the beginning of an attack of diarrhoea which is running through the whole camp. We had very little enteric — but any amount of dysentery...

September 3
Keith Murdoch arrived today. He is going to London for the Sydney *Sun* and Melbourne *Herald* to manage their cable service from the *Times* office [and had been commissioned by the Australian Government to stop off in Egypt to investigate alleged irregularities in the mail service to the troops]... I had to lie up, but took Murdoch up to the top of this hill to see the view.

September 4
In bed. Murdoch went up to see General Walker and Lone Pine.

September 5, Sunday
Hoped to take M. out to the left, but wasn't fit. He went out himself...

September 6
Took M. up to Quinn's. He had an interview with little Walker yesterday. Walker was really expansive — told him how he had come to believe in and love his men, and how he would not change his command for the world. The men like little 'Hooky' too — he's a man we owe something to. Nevinson tells me that 'Hooky' was his name at school. M. left at midday...

September 7
1st Aust. Bde. will begin to be relieved today. They have been putting the 5th and 6th Bdes. gradually into the trenches and now the 5th is fairly well blooded. Our men are a little cynical and jealous of these new troops because the papers have always said: "The last contingent was the finest that has left Australia". "So you've come at last, have you?" said one man as the new battalion filed past into Lone Pine. The new men didn't say anything in reply; it may have been meant for a joke, but it was a little bitter. The new lot are fine men, but the officers don't impress one at all

— and some battalions have not the remotest idea of sanitation...

Tummy still very sore. Bazley in same way...

September 9

I am going off to Imbros in a day or two, and probably to Athens.

September 10

Breakfast — a cup of weak tea without milk or sugar; a plate of porridge; a piece of toast — better than all the condensed milk of the past few days...

Well, the problem of Gallipoli reduces itself to — why can't the British fight? Take one of these slum kids and turn him into a different man by 9 or 10 years hard training, or even less — and put in a set of N.C.O.'s over him who have will enough to make the stickers of the army — the percentage who go into action with their minds made up to stick, and who really make up the minds of the other 90% who are simply going in to do what somebody else does; give him that training and those N.C.O.'s and he can fight like the 29th Division did. But in a year's training he can't be turned into a soldier because to tell the truth he's a very poor feeble specimen of a man — and it seems to be the British social formula to make sure that he sticks there. In a nation with only one class, it's in nobody's interest to keep anyone else in "his place" — and his place is, from his birth, the best place he can get and keep. To my mind this war, as far as I have seen it, is just Britain's tomahawks coming home to roost... They have neither the nerve, the physique, nor the spirit and self-control to fit them for soldiers...

Had an interesting talk with Monash. He is an able C.O. but never knows the facts about his command...

September 11

Got some money from Major Griffiths and decided to clear out on my holiday trip... Bazley and I [left for] Imbros (via Suvla Bay) by the 2.30 trawler ... after giving the cook and some of the clerks what eggs, fruit, etc., we had in the larder...

Reached camp and had a jolly good dinner. Nevinson insisted on my drinking some champagne and so did Bartlett, who is rather seedy himself. Ross and I are thinking of going to Athens to get out winter clothes, etc., but Maxwell has a trip to [the Greek island of] Mitylene for the whole lot of us on the boards first...

September 12, Sunday
We arranged with Maxwell to leave to-morrow morning for Mitylene. Grey day all day — the first as far as I remember... [The correspondents spent the next ten days relaxing on Mitylene. They broke the return voyage by calling at Lemnos for a day.]

September 24
Started at 8 by a very slow trawler for Imbros and arrived at about 4... I hear things have been dead quiet at Anzac and rest of front, except for aeroplanes...

September 26, Sunday
Nevinson and I went to [the village of] Panagia [on Imbros] to-day... Had an astonishing talk with W's nice servant X ... on the way over... He was in the Munster Fusiliers and he told me he had been in many bayonet charges — 7 altogether...

On Sunday, May 2, the Turks during the night broke the Munsters' line. The most of the line did not know it but a body of Turks got through and cut up the Headquarters Coy. of the Munsters. The line heard men behind them and thought it was their own men coming up to reinforce. However, there was some doubt so a Sergeant told some of them to fire a shot. Immediately there arose a babel of "Allah! Allah!" The front line immediately opened fire and killed or wounded 15 including the German officer who had led them and who was trying to get them further. "We took his life next morning", X said. I could hardly believe my ears — this is a kindly, capable, mild-mannered Kentish man — ignorant and ill-educated, but a good man and a willing chap... I was too utterly sick to say anything. The man clearly didn't understand in the remotest degree the wicked horridness of the thing he had done — he was rather proud of it. Good God — if this is the way some of our ignorant English Tommies fight — Well, Australians have boasted of killing the wounded too. But that was in the heat of action. I don't think there are many who would kill a wounded man — even a German — in cold blood the next morning.

But what wretched cant it all is that they talk in the newspapers...

But that is why I can't write about bayonet charges like some of the correspondents do. Ashmead Bartlett makes it a little difficult for one by his exaggerations, and yet he's a lover of the truth. He gives the spirit of the thing: but if he were asked: "Did a shout really go up from a thousand throats that the hill was ours?" he'd have to say "No, it didn't". Or if they said "Did the New Zealanders really club their rifles and kill three men at once?" or "Did the first battle of Anzac really end with the flash of bayonets all along the line, a charge, and the rolling back of the Turkish attack," he'd have to say "Well — no, as a matter of fact that didn't occur". Well, I can't write that it occurred if I know it did not, even if by painting it that way I could rouse the blood and make the pulse beat faster — and undoubtedly these men here deserve that people's pulses shall beat for them. But War Correspondents have so habitually exaggerated the heroism of battles that people don't realise that the real actions are heroic. If you say "The line went forward and not one man came back" — that is really a thing that can very seldom be said of any but the most magnificent troops — but people say "No, of course they didn't — they were British soldiers and British soldiers don't run away." As a matter of fact everyone who has seen a battle knows that soldiers do very often run away; soldiers, even Australian soldiers, have sometimes to be threatened with a revolver to make them go on — in individual cases. I have seen it happen once to an Australian N.C.O. whom Col. M'Cay threatened to shoot — and I know MacNaghten of the 4th. Battalion on April 26th, and Howell-Price of the 3rd. Battalion on August 8th, and others have done the same, and it has done what they wanted it to do. The Turks have to be threatened with machine guns from behind — I have seen it in their divisional orders. There is the case of two of the finest fighters in the world, the Australian (possibly the very best in the world) and the Turk — (certainly one of the best).

Then there is the nonsense about wounded soldiers wanting to get back from hospital to the front. I have asked the nurses, I have asked the men, I have heard them discussing it — and everyone says — what everyone here knows — that it is not one soldier in fifty that wants to go back to the front. They dread it. Not very many will actually shoot their fingers off to escape from the front, but even this is not uncommon even among Australians, and it is probably less common with them than with most. There are men who want to get back to the front, great stalwart, true Australians — but there are not many like them in any army.

There is plenty of heroism in war — it teems with it. But it has been so overwritten that if you write that a man did his job people say: Oh, but there's nothing heroic in that! Isn't there? You come here and see the job and understand it and get out of your head the nonsense that is written about it. There is horror and beastliness and cowardice and treachery, over all of which the writer, anxious to please the public, has to throw his cloak — but the man who does his job is a hero. And the actual truth is that though not all Australians, by any means, do their job, there is a bigger proportion of men in the Australian Army that try to do it cheerfully and without the least show of fear, than in any force or army that I have seen in Gallipoli. The man who knows war knows that this is magnificent praise. The public can never know it.

The war correspondent is responsible for most of the ideas of battle which the public possesses. For example —- the public thinks in black and white and nothing between — the public thinks a retreat or a rout is a matter of simple cowardice; whereas if ever there was a case of mixed motives the ordinary retreat is one. A hundred men go forward of whom, in the best of cases, perhaps twenty per cent wish they were not going forward at all when they start — and 80 per cent before they get there. The remaining 20 per cent are going to do the job or die simply because they are the sort of men to whom life is not worth living except on those terms.

As the enemy's trench is reached, and some of the 20 per cent are killed, the enemy's machine guns (say) find them out, or perhaps they merely notice that not a quarter of their number are there; or it may be they take the trench or the ground and hang on to it and the enemy's shrapnel find them out. A moment comes when the weaker men are ready to turn at all costs — there are wounded men running back all the time. One man starts to run back — perhaps 2 or 3 on either side start to run with him. The others coming up see them running back — and have not the remotest idea why they are running back. Perhaps (it enters their heads) they are running away. Perhaps the trench has been found impossible to take. Perhaps they've been ordered to retire. One man coming up, or hanging on, shouts to the man who is getting up to run: "What's up, Bill?" Bill may answer: "That is too bloody 'ot for me" — or he may and often does answer "Word passed along to retire!" The order to retire is sometimes, no doubt, attributed to an officer who has been killed. "Captain Smith give the order to retire." It goes along the line — "Word passed to retire at once." Every weakspirited man — and there is always a sprinkling of them — taking it up with especial vehemence. It needs a lot of grit in a man to say (especially if his officer has been killed) "Retire be damned! Who says we're to retire! Pass along and ask who gave the order!" And yet strong men do that. They know the "order to retire" is sometimes an invention and they are not going to be cheated out of doing their job by any weak spirited being in the force. The success of an army like ours chiefly depends on what proportion of these strong independent minded men there is in it. And in the Australian force the proportion is unquestionably undoubtedly high — may amount to 50 per cent or more. I have seen them going up against a rain of fire and the weaker ones retiring through them at the very same time — the two streams going in opposite directions and not taking the faintest notice of one another.

Well, this is the true side of war — but I wonder if anyone would believe me outside the army. I've never written higher praise of Australians than is on this page, but the probability is that if I were to put it into print to-morrow the tender Australian public, which only tolerates flattery and that in its cheapest form, would howl me out of existence.

One has some satisfaction in sticking to the truth in spite of the prejudice against it — the satisfaction of putting up a sort of fight. But I have a suspicion that I've spoilt my chances for ever of being some day tolerably well off.

September 27
Stayed in camp and wrote all day... Bazley still at Anzac.

September 28
To Anzac by the torpedo boat...

September 29
To-night two officers came back from G.H.Q. with Bartlett. I was writing in the Mess tent when they told me Bartlett was going home. "Lucky beggar," I said — and presently some mention came up of his return. "Well, as a matter of fact, he's not returning," they said. "He's got the sack!"

Bartlett was in Nevinson's tent when I went in and told me to stay. It was true. About a month ago he got Murdoch, the Australian *Sun* Correspondent, who was going to London, to take home with him a letter to the [British] Prime Minister putting the state of things here in a somewhat crude light. It was a brilliantly written letter — rather overstating the case as Bartlett always does, but a great deal of it is absolutely unanswerable and badly needs understanding... Bartlett's letter was worth the consideration of any man, and I've no doubt it will be considered in time. Several members of the Cabinet asked him to write to them privately — which was not a very loyal thing of them to do, but then politicians are not loyal.

He made one mistake — I think. He ought to have taken the letter home himself after he had written all he wanted to about the battles of August. It was difficult. It would have been scarcely loyal to his employers to go home and leave the work here, and I don't know if he would have been allowed to return; unless he went I don't think the letter could have been got through — the censors would not have passed it. So he decided that the object was worth any means. The little worm of a Press Officer who I think keeps a spy in our camp in the shape of one of the servants seems to have found out that Murdoch was carrying the letter. A wire was sent home and M. was either searched or forced to give the letter up.[5] Hamilton received a wire from the War Office telling him that Bartlett must be recalled.

It is unfortunate that this Major had in this case at any rate the formal right upon his side for he is a most objectionable person. Sir Ian Hamilton has seen Nevinson (who is a writer of British reputation and quite as big a man in his own line as Sir Ian H. is in his) about an article written by Nevinson, in which the facts had been queried by [Delmé] Radcliffe [the press officer] who suggested that some of them were invented. I think Col. Tyrrell (who is a more or less able man and chief of intelligence) backs this little whippersnapper up, because he was angry with some protest or other of Bartlett against Radcliffe censoring our letters (which he has been told is not his duty). Tyrrell said he had to pass it on to him because he had no time, and added that he "considered the censorship of War Correspondents' reports the least important of his duties" — which just typifies the attitude of an obsolete class of British Military officer towards the democracy which pays for such expensive luxuries as the Delmé Radcliffe sort of staff officer and pours out £3 000 000 daily on a war supposed by itself to be engaged in its own interest.

I have been so loyal as I could possibly be — have brought myself into constant trouble in Australia by being loyal to military rules; my own Australian staff knows that it can trust me to the uttermost — but this little whippersnapper the British War Office has put over us is trying to put every difficulty he can in my way along with that of the others: sends us orders by the private soldier from whom he gets 2 reports every week about our camp and who is almost certainly acting as his spy; suggests there will be difficulties in getting leave to go to Athens for the purpose of buying winter things; is going to try and force me to send the photo (which I have never taken for publication and have never let out of my hands) to the War Office which I strongly desire to avoid; there is no question that having been turned out of our camp owing to a quarrel with Bartlett making it too unpleasant, and out of his censorship because it was not his right to censor — by us, he is now trying deliberately to make difficulties for us.

Well — it is worthy of a big part of the obsolete brains of the British Army, this sort of thing. The War Office puts this sort of difficulty in the way of men who are doing their work as carefully, loyally and scrupulously as Nevinson and I (for example); and yet allows any swindler, or at any rate rule-breaker, of an officer, who gets a film or photo. smuggled home past the censor, to have it published in the London Press — which has perfect impunity in publishing it, in advertising requesting officers in flat defiance of orders to send similar photos in, and in booming £1 000 prizes for them. It censors rigorously all the names of officers and regiments out of my letters — written by one who actually saw them; and allows them to be picked and forwarded second-hand in a bundle of exaggerations and untruths quite uncensored from Cairo.

We don't deserve to win wars. When this happens in my department, what happens in others! Ye gods, don't we know too well!

September 30

Went to Helles by 7 a.m. trawler with Nevinson. We spent most of the day trying to find the Headquarters of the 1st Australian Artillery Bde. — no one seemed to have the least idea where it was. . . There is all sorts of rumour in the air about a French and Italian landing at Bulair — and a naval push in ten days' time from now — but you can't believe a word of it. What is almost certain is that the French, Italians and British are going to send an expedition to Servia to occupy Macedonia and also that we shall not be here. Goodness knows what this means, but we have it from two sources — Ross's son has written to him on the subject and he got the tip from Colonel Swinton that his father would be in London in two months' time.[6]

I have just had a letter from the Acting Secretary of Defence in Melbourne telling me that the *Argus* and *Age* proprietors had decided to discontinue my letters because they are of insufficient interest to them, and asking me for any remarks that I cared to make on the subject. It's rather a curious request. If they wanted remarks on the subject they could get them from the *Argus* and the *Age*; or they know for themselves whether my letters are interesting or not. I suppose the *Age* and *Argus* think them uninteresting because they have their own correspondents in Cairo who can send them stuff which is bound to arrive weeks before mine and is not subject to censorship. They are Victorian and therefore what the *Age* and *Argus* want, and it doesn't make them any the less interesting that about ⅓ of what they say is not true — it's not the fault of the correspondents, either; they are doing very well. The *Age* and *Argus*, as the Government knows well, did not like the Government service from the first and I believe that the *Argus* people in London expressed a preference for having their news from Reuter's Agency in Cairo and said they did not desire to have a man with the Australian forces at all. The Empire Press Union which represents them is said to have put that view, anyway; and that was the main reason why there was a delay in authorising me to write letters or cables at all and why the Australian people went without any letter or cable from me at the time when we landed. The *Argus* is getting this special stuff from Reuter's Agency or Cairo and beautiful stuff it is. Not one event in every five of those which he relates are true and most are wild, sensational inventions like the famous one about Germans enlisted in Australia shooting officers here from behind. This stuff has plenty of "interest" for the *Argus*. Mine has merely the interest that I risk my life hundreds of times over on the spot itself in order that they may know that every word is as true as it can be.

October 1

Went over to G.H.Q. to-day and saw Tyrrell, Chief of Intelligence. He asked me if I wished to see the C. in C. I knew quite well why he asked. He had heard what I said about the absence of censorship in Cairo . . . I said that I thought it over and it was no affair of mine. The men there were my rivals and were doing their work well and I was not going to try and prevent them doing it. If there was any objection it would be a military one and that had nothing to do with me. He said they had tried to get some censorship established in Egypt and had failed to get anything sufficient done.

He then gave me his point of view about "War Correspondents". "Your's is a dying profession," he said. "On the contrary, I think I am the beginning of a new profession," I answered. "I can see that the old sort of correspondent is dying — but you have got to give the people news of their troops. They can't send away an expedition overseas and then put up with absolute silence about it. Even Napoleon had to tell the nation something. Well, if you've got to keep the people informed is it not better to have somebody to do it who can tell them the sort of things they want to know (as far as the censorship permits — that is, as far as military secrecy properly allows) than to leave it to some officer who only sees the military importance of events and not the public interest in them. It does no harm to any conceivable military interest to tell the people how their sons and brothers live, how they fight, what a battle looks like — and that can be done a thousand times better by a journalist than a staff officer. The little important news — the outline which is permissible — the journalist can make interesting. The Staff Officer makes it stodgy. Where is the benefit in the staff officer? In the next war every important staff will have one trusted journalist attached — as a staff officer, if you like."

Tyrrell could not understand this in the least — at any rate he didn't seem to. His point of view was: "if the people is properly organized the authorities need not tell them anything at all" — which I don't believe possible in any conceivable condition of a nation; secondly, he had a different ground: "In a properly organized nation the Government does not need war correspondents — it simply tells the people what it thinks will conduce towards winning the war. If truth is good for the war it tells them truth; if a lie is likely to win the war it tells them lies. At the present moment I believe that the truth would do good — I myself would like to send through every word that men like Nevinson and yourself write. But the regulations tie my hands — you see I can't help myself. In any case the one aim the Government and people possesses in war time is to win the war and if telling lies to the people will win the war then the authorities should tell lies to them". I must say I shift my ground also on hearing that argument. If the winning of a war were the end of all things (as no doubt it is the end of all a soldier's duties) it would be sound. But it isn't the end of a nation's existence. There are ways in plenty in which a war may be won which conceivably do far more harm to a nation than defeat. I think, for example, of the enormous damage that you do to a nation's powers in peace if you destroy all the confidence the public has in the Government's official statements; (that damage has been done in this war to the credit of the British Government). You may destroy the belief of all the small nations in your nation's honesty, or humanity — and do more damage than 20 successful wars could repair.

Therefore I think the nation <u>must</u> have as true an account of the war as military necessity can possibly permit. I quite agree you can't have the war correspondent running a modern war; but I do think the people of any modern state worth living in will require some sort of information at least partly independent of their generals and general staffs as to what is happening; and they are not getting that in this war. I can't see any way out except for the correspondent to be allowed to be an independent pressman, and free to see what he likes — instruction to censors and C.Os. to that effect. And then let the correspondent, if he doesn't think the truth gets a fair show, do what others do — resign and give the authorities the responsibility of muzzling him.

"He thinks we're dyin', does he?" said Bartlett tonight. "Well, I'm glad we're dyin' game!"...

October 2

Ashmead Bartlett left this morning by the Mudros trawler for England. He himself thinks that his career as a war correspondent is ended — certainly for this war. He will probably lecture in England and Australia and America.[7]

He had an extraordinary send off on the *Cornwallis* the other day. The crew sent up a deputation to thank him for the way in which he had written... The feeling in the Navy against General Headquarters is extraordinarily bitter. The relation of the two staffs is utterly impossible. The Navy is now intensely bitter with Ian H. for having said in some publication to correspondents that the Gurkhas were driven off Chunuk Bair [on August 9] by the navy's fire. Commodore Keyes is furious at this charge. They say Hamilton made it in a report to the Russians and in his communique to the correspondents. It was certainly in some reports...

So Bartlett has gone... He's a strange chap — very much like Byron, Nevinson always says. He's extraordinarily brilliant in conversation. I never heard anyone who could approach him in unexpected retort — in turning every sentence he speaks into a brilliant paradox to point some very incisive argument. He thinks very straight and his written dispatches are full of life and colour, hit hard, and give a brilliant idea which is remarkably true. He exaggerates a bit to make his points but the general result is a pretty accurate description of what has happened, and always vivid. He's perhaps not quite so accurate in detail as the English papers think him, but he is most honest in giving the real outline and trend of events...

Nevinson is a man of 58 and a more accurate writer than Bartlett; more restrained and with a better style and pretty vivid. He is a fairly clever talker but without Bartlett's extraordinary sparkle. He is a man who has had all the advantages of Shrewsbury and Oxford... He began his press career by fighting for the Greeks when they ran away from the Turks in 1897. He is the friend of lost causes... He was really ... a rebel against the exaggerations of the populace and the stupidity of the foreign office...

He was sent to the Boer War, the War in Morocco, and the Balkan War. He is anti-imperialist and thinks that Britain would probably gain almost more good out of a defeat in this war than out of a victory. Yet he was one of the first to go to the War Office and offer his services for any purpose they wished and he is desperately anxious that we should win... Both (like myself) are at heart thorough rebels...

The other correspondents here are Lawrence and Ross. Lawrence is for Reuters (Nevinson — Provincial Press, Bartlett — London Dailies). He was their correspondent at Berlin and is an exceedingly well read and intelligent little chap whose first experience of war this is... He is a companion who will carry on a friendly argument — and a most illuminating one in which he is obviously interested — for hours any day you wish.

Malcolm Ross is a kindly chap but I can't quite make him out. He has been an outspoken admirer of Bartlett's from the day B. arrived here, almost to the point Toadyism — but B. is so brilliant that I think it may be just real honest admiration. At the same time I have heard him give away B. behind his back in a manner which completely staggered me. I don't really think Ross can be quite genuine but, after all, which of us are? He has got some very lovable and excellent points, and his son seems to be a pretty brilliant journalist — I haven't seen much of Ross's copy itself, but what I have seen seemed interesting.

Nevinson is very game — [on 21 August he] was hit on the head at Chocolate Hill by a bit of shell and covered with blood, but was back within 1 hour. Lawrence is a game little chap too. A good deal has been made out of Nevinson's wound. I wondered to-day whether I should mention mine to Alston Rivers. They would use it to advertise my book of which they are publishing a new cheap edition.[8] In the end I couldn't do it. After all I can't advertise — I haven't done it and I won't do it...

Capt. W. Maxwell — the Press Censor here — is an old War Correspondent who began his career in the Soudan campaign of Lord Kitchener. He is a little man, squarely built, with a great row of ribbons the outcome of his various wars — though I fancy Bartlett has been to quite as many... He has been an excellent

Fellow correspondents (left to right): Henry Nevinson, Malcolm Ross and Lester Lawrence pose for Bean on the pier at Imbros. (AWM neg. no. G1411)

The press correspondents' winter cottage. 'It was the most imposing building in Kephalos', Bean noted on the photo. The men pictured are probably servants attached to the correspondents. Photograph by M. Ross. (AWM neg. no. A5406)

censor — not one word has passed which worried the authorities — Lord Kitchener himself told Col. Hankey this before he came out here — and we have all been perfectly satisfied with his censorship...

October 3, Sunday

I closed with the proprietor of a house in the village to-day — for winter quarters. It is a moderately new house and we shall turn the sanitary picket into it first... Rent — I was prepared to give £5 a month. Owner asked £2; so we closed for 30/- which he was delighted to get.

October 4

Arranged for some timber for a porch for our new house. We have got rid of Pte. Murray [the servant suspected of spying for the staff officers] and Delmé Radcliffe is, I think, going to withdraw himself. I could be reconciled to him personally if he hadn't called Nevinson a liar...

October 5

Went to Anzac with Lawrence. Found my dugout in the process of being rebuilt for the winter — where it was it stopped a drain...

October 8
Beginning our move into the Correspondents' Cottage at Panagia. A heavy storm tonight — heaviest weather since we reached the Peninsula...

October 9
Moved into new Cottage. Hear old Jack is promoted to Major!...

October 11–14
Came over to Anzac by torpedo boat and spent most of the next three days getting information about April 25th/28th, and about Leane's trench [a position on Holly Ridge captured from the Turks on 31 July]...

October 15
Nicholson thinks there are more Turks in front of us than since August 6th.

The news has come that the Russians have landed in force at Varna... Wagstaffe thinks the Turks, who have only 8 000 troops of poor type at Adrianople, have already sent some men away from here. Tonight we have a demonstration (planned 3 or 4 days ago at least) to find out how many Turks there are in front of the whole line...

October 16
The demonstration woke me up at about 4.10 a.m. — our guns on the hill at the back of the destroyers and larger warships firing intensely. There was a fairly thin crackle of Turkish rifles going on all the time — evidently a few touchy gentlemen whom they couldn't stop; but no machine guns, and the ruse seemed to fail to draw.

I went up to the 3rd Brigade and 2nd Light Horse Brigade to see Bert Lowing, and ask after some soldiers whose parents had written to me...

October 17, Sunday
Back in Imbros last night. We had a staggerer in the Correspondents' Camp today. About 10 this morning a telegram arrived from Maxwell at G.H.Q. across the Bay: "Sir Ian Hamilton is going across to K. Beach to say good-bye to the Correspondents too. Don't know what time he is coming." That was the first he had heard of it. (Bartlett had bet Lawrence £10 that Hamilton would leave before the end of September, and he was to have a

week's grace — so that Lawrence only won his bet by a week). It came as a bolt from the blue.

About a quarter to one ... an orderly arrived to say that the Commander-in-Chief was on his way to our camp... We jumped up and went out and found him just turning the corner from the transport camp, riding up through the scrub with about 7 of his staff with him. He rode ahead to us (the others held back a bit) and said: "I wanted to come and say good-bye to you — is that your new cottage? Quite architectural pretentions hasn't it?" We said something about it and told him how really sorry we were to part with him. He gave us a copy of a wire he had received from Anzac and of his reply. He said something about his successor. "We haven't heard who he is, Sir," we said. "General Monro," he replied. "He comes from France. You mayn't have heard much of him, but he's a damned good man."

"I want you to send that about the Anzac men," he said "They're splendid fellows — they'll hold out against anything that can be brought against them in the way of men. I have seen enough and heard enough to know that the Turk though heroic in defence is not going to succeed in attack. The one thing I'm afraid of is if the Germans bring down their heavy artillery. If they had enough big guns and ammunition they might blow us off the beaches... I am not afraid of the men; they would make it unpleasant for the men, but they would hold on somehow. But they could make the beaches so difficult that it would be a very serious matter for us. However, if they only give my successor plenty of guns and ammunition and sufficient reinforcements (which you know I have never had) I think they will pull through — and that would be the greatest consolation I could have."

The poor old chap looked to me very haggard — almost broken up; so were some of the staff. They told us privately that the message had only come the day before in a cypher telegram — that was the first they had heard of it, and, I believe, the first Hamilton himself knew of it. Fancy having to get that cypher translated by some clerk!

I am honestly very sorry to see Hamilton go. He is a gentleman, and has always been courteous and considerate to us. The British Army has never believed in him, but he is a good friend to civilians, and has breadth of mind which the Army does not in general possess.

It is rather fault of character than of intellect that has caused him to fail. He has not strength to command his staff — they command him; especially Braithwaite; his chief of staff, with whom he is on the worst of terms, I believe, has commanded this expedition. Braithwaite is a snob — only a snob could support this lazy G.H.Q., and so far as I know he has only been to Anzac once. He is certainly utterly disloyal to his chief. If Hamilton had had a loyal, agreeable, capable Chief of Staff his success might have been very different; but he is not capable of standing up to any of them.

Hamilton has not the strength to give those with whom he is surrounded a straight out blow from the shoulder — however much the situation demands it. To mix the metaphor — he has an unlucky ability for gilding the pill. He can't administer a pill unless it is golden...

Here, when things were at their worst — after the 6th, 7th and 8th [of May] — when the plan of going straight ahead over Achi Baba was clearly proved impossible, or possible only to a very much greater force, he had not the strength either to give that plan up, or to tell the War Office that the plan must be given up. At least so far as I know he hadn't the strength to say so. The British public certainly was utterly deceived as to the difficulties and the obvious failure. Hamilton was all this time, I believe, influenced by the precious Hunter-Weston whose plan this was supposed to be. Hamilton was said to be on the worst of terms with his Chief of Staff, but not a word of this appears in his despatches — only fulsome flattery of a man whom the Army looks on — in spite of his staff college education — as chiefly notable for an egregious snobbishness...

It is part of the same weakness of character — and perhaps partly the British hatred of anything like a scandal — and shocking — that has caused men in this expedition to be removed by being kicked up stairs, not down. To remove a Colonel from G.H.Q. you find some job in the fighting force for him, and promote him to Brigadier General, and send him pleasantly away. It is a most fatal aptitude this gilding the pill, and Hamilton, with his beautiful style in literature and kind gentlemanly manners, is hopelessly weakened by it — poor old chap.

For it is tragedy!! He, an old man and an old soldier, about the end of his career, to be suddenly removed from command after a long bitter campaign...

October 22

Would have gone to Helles, but a northerly gale is blowing so fierce that Lawrence and I decided to put it off. The day, has been wet and cold — a thin driving rain... The men in all the trenches are going wet for the want of a single sheet of galvanised iron.

G.H.Q. is putting about 20 sheets of galvanised iron into each of the latrines for itself and its batmen.

October 23
Came to Anzac after a wild passage in a trawler through a half gale — the deck swilling with water all the time...

October 24, Sunday
Wet morning. Curious how this stops all firing. When our ships' guns start you feel as if they were breaking a pact.

Spent the day up in the lines of 10th Battalion getting details of April 25 & 26...

October 25
Six months to-day since we landed and a year and four days since we left Melbourne. A beautiful day, clear and cold...

[Birdwood has] issued an order that as soon as the weather justifies it sheepskin jackets are to be issued to Australian & N.Z. troops, and cardigans, mits, 2 shirts, pants, etc. to all troops.

The 2nd. Australian Divn. has mostly now been issued with woollen clothing. It left Egypt in Khaki *drill*. What person was responsible for this goodness knows. The khaki drill was used because someone thought it would be hot in September...

October 28
They have brought in an old steamer (the *Milo*, I think) and sunk her off Walker's Pier [at North Beach] — with great success. There is a hot southerly half-gale blowing. The beach is rough to the south of her, but the water inside her is quite passable. She doesn't fill in the whole gap. I suggested they might bring in and sink the *Aragon* to fill the gap. Howse says it would be worth it for the enthusiasm that would arise on shore when the fat brigadiers and languid D.A.Q.M.G.s were being chased from one end of the deck to the other with the Turkish shells[9]...

October 29
Received a parcel from mother — towel! soap! 3 prs. of socks! sweets! writing paper — just the right things...

November 2
Had a yarn with White last night over matters in general. He was charming as usual. We both notice that the Australians here can be picked out on the instant by their faces — a little hard, but the

Lt-Col C.B.B. White (left) and Col N.R. Howse relax for a moment outside 1st Division HQ in White Gully. (AWM neg. no. G1329)

strong, lined, individual faces which men get who stand and think by themselves. The Australian discipline is for orderliness — to get an operation through in an organised manner. The British discipline has a different reason — to make men go forward because they are told to do so. Our men we have to send forward trusting to quite a different principle — we rely on the strong, independent willed men carrying on the weak one...

White evidently wanted to give me the benefit of an idea which had been strongly impressed on him. "What I had seen since Suvla", I had said, "is making a Socialist of me."

"It's not making me that," he said, "but I'll tell you what I should like to tell the people of Australia — what, if I get the chance, I shall tell them some day — and that is that they are right in the main thing: they may be wrong in the details — I'm no politician, as you know, but I'm sure they're right in this — in giving every man a chance, a good, equal chance"...

5

Evacuation

AFTER the failure of the August offensive and the ill-fated Allied attempt to assist Serbia, it was increasingly apparent that the Allied armies were achieving little in the Balkan theatre other than the steady sapping of their own strength. By November, disgruntled British politicians were publicly admitting this. More and more of the nation's leaders, military and political, were becoming convinced that the war would be decided on the Western Front and that it made little sense to divert forces elsewhere. Some members of the British Government had long been dissatisfied with the Gallipoli strategy, and sought to bring an end to the fruitless and costly campaign. Kitchener opposed evacuation but early in November agreed to visit the Peninsula to assess the situation.

On the Peninsula itself, morale had been dented by the events of August and the steady deterioration in the weather as winter set in. Bean, like many others, was no longer an admirer of all things British. Most soldiers felt it a matter of national and personal honour that they hold out, but an increasing number were coming to accept that persevering might not make good military sense.

November 7, Sunday
Came over to Imbros again yesterday and got newspapers up to October 15 — Imbros is always a week, if not two, ahead of us at Anzac.

By the papers it appears that they have been taking the Balkan muddle very much to heart in England. Milner in the House of Lords asked whether this was not our opportunity of getting out of the Dardanelles 'with dignity' — (I wish he could see us try!) . . . Kitchener has, we hear, left London on duty; and Monro has gone to Egypt. Putting one and one together it looks very certain where Kitchener has gone. That is what Maxwell thinks anyway.

I believe B[irdwood] is strongly opposed to any idea of moving off; and certainly we are making preparations for staying. 40

bootmakers, for example, are due here; and the Authorities after deciding to make Imbros a Rest Camp, then deciding against it and moving all the men and gear away, are now deciding upon making it a rest camp again.

As for the Peninsula — it is all talk of deep digging at present. I have only seen one deep [bomb-proof] position finished — that was in the 2nd Light Horse Brigade line...

November 8
For the first time I am beginning to feel it a little difficult to keep up a supply of really good articles on the matter available — it isn't that the matter's not there, but I am getting a little tired, I expect. Finished to-day the 56th letter since the landing — and the 45th wire yesterday...

November 9
One year since the *Emden*. Lord Kitchener is in Mudros to-day...

November 11
There has been a good deal of communication with Turks of late. We threw over some letters from prisoners saying they were well treated and some pictures of nice fat happy looking prisoners from Cairo (our men don't much like doing this but I daresay the authorities are right). Anyway we got the following answer: "A man who lives by charity is a swine. We have plenty in our stomachs and something besides plenty. We have our hands on our bodies and our bayonets in our hands. The English may have plenty of munitions of war, but we have our bayonets and our thoughts. If you are the great nation that you are supposed to be, why don't you act up to high principles and not descend to trying to suborn others from their loyalty to their sovereign."

A most dignified answer. We can easily overdo these attempts to make Turks desert. Still — they — or the Germans — have tried the same thing on us.

Three weeks ago Turks had festival for three days. They threw over two packets of cigarettes with this inscription:

Prenez
Femez avec plesir
Notre herox ennemis

Scrawled in indelible pencil.

Another: Notre cher ennemi envoyez milk

We sent over bully beef. They threw back a message on a stick and stone "Bully beef non." We threw some biscuits (good biscuits) and jam. This was all about 8–30 to 9–15. They called out "fini" and waved down with their hands — (all had heads up). Next morning same proceedings. Interpreter spoke to them from our lines. They were allowed to go over and get a pocket knife we had thrown over. Third morning we had orders not to carry on...

November 13
Yesterday morning White gave me the tip (knows he's perfectly safe in doing so — I wouldn't breathe it to anyone) that Kitchener was probably landing here that day. It was put off till to-day. To-day I was up Shrapnel Gully when I saw Brigadiers gathering from all quarters coming up the valley with their best red gorget patches, and the little gold curly leaf, and their belts on! Belts at Anzac! There was a meeting at 11, Holmes told me — to be at Walker's Top. Did I think that Monro was coming? (I have an idea he guessed who it really was.) I went round to the beach again and found the Army staff gathering at their new H.Q. (they have just entered it and I have asked to be attached as we are losing our H.Q. on the old terrace). Went down to the beach where we found the men working as usual — no idea of anything out of the ordinary...

K. didn't arrive till the afternoon — we got word presently that it would be 1–15. At about 1–30 a destroyer arrived (from Helles, I think) and off he came, with a staff of about ten, including a Frenchman — and little Birdwood, in a grey woollen jacket, by his side. The tall man walked up the pier (with the brilliant red band on his staff cap towering over everyone else) and shook hands with Godley, White, Howse, and the others. He had scarcely reached the end of the pier when the men tumbled to it — and down they came to the edge of the beach and on to the beach itself. Men began to run from the dug outs above, hopping over the intermediate scrub and the holes and heaps of relics of old dug-outs — some one of the men on the beach called for a cheer and the sound of the cheering brought every Australian on the hill side out of his burrow and scuttling down like rabbits. The tall red cap was rapidly closed in amongst them — but they kept a path and as the red cheeks turned and spoke to one man and another, they cheered him — they, the soldiers — no officers leading off or anything of that sort. It was a purely soldiers' welcome. He said to them, "The King asked me to tell you how splendidly he thinks you have done — you have done splendidly, better, even, than I thought you would."

Kitchener (left, leading column) and senior Anzac officers coming down Walker's Ridge during his tour of inspection, 13 November. Photograph by Major S.S. Butler. (AWM neg. no. G1442M)

The men would not have cheered many men — they would never have cheered Ian Hamilton like it, for all his kindness and gentle manners. K. is the sort of man every Australian admires — not a polished man but a determined one, an uncompromising worker. These men honestly admire him far more than the British do; the British really admire a man who has more display about him, but these men honestly and quite sincerely like the absence of display — they have thought it all out for themselves, and when he comes along nothing will prevent them from each paying their honest tribute of admiration. K. received a welcome which I doubt whether he knows the value. There are not many men that Australians would honour in that way.

He pushed straight up on Walker's Ridge, with Sir John Maxwell and General Birdwood, Owen, White, Col. Howse and so on. I could see the party climbing the awfully steep path, the little grey uniforms always beside the tall red hat band — and I was astonished to see that they didn't stop for a breather. Poor old Maxwell, I believe, was blowing like a grampus and several of the Anzac people were a bit puffed. But within ten minutes the little figures could be seen right away up on top of the bare cliff. The Brigadiers of the 1st Division and Legge's Division were there to meet him — he spoke to them at once without stopping for breath — "Oh yes, I met you in Australia, didn't I?"[1] and so on. He really was in wonderfully good condition, which gives the lie to the talk about his self indulgence. After a long sea voyage a self indulgent liver could not have climbed that hill at all without danger of actual heart failure...

The men noticed that he seemed older than his pictures — of course a man always does. And his red cheeks — brilliant red and full, though his girth is spare — brought one or two comments. "Looks as if 'e did himself well, doesn't he?" I heard one say, "Don't blame him if he did," was the answer. "No, nor I either" — and so on. "He lives amongst the beer, don't 'e?" said one man — but of course K. like the King and most British leading men has not touched beer wine or spirits since the beginning of the war...

He looked at the position from the observation station up there — saw Lone Pine, and showed a quick grasp of the details of the country. He went through the trenches, (held by the newest Brigade, the 7th — where, unfortunately, every man he spoke to had only been here a few weeks) went through the firing line to Bully Beef Sap [the trench linking Russell's Top and Pope's Hill], which is not by any means a safe place. His tall red cap going along awkward corners of the trenches was dangerously obvious and our staff had its heart in its mouth — indeed, they didn't breathe freely till they got K. off the beach and away from the crowd there, which might possibly have brought a Turkish shell if seen from Sniper's Ridge. Birdwood and White were almost too nervous to speak, I am told — they were worrying about this all the time. The men in the trenches — not more than 20 yards away from the Turks in some places, could scarcely be restrained from cheering. He went down Rest Gully to 2nd Division, and there saw the Y.M.C.A. canteen — a splendid Sydney concern, which against great difficulties does manage to do something for the men here and at Imbros.

"Hallo! — Y.M.C.A.," he said. Then, turning to a man, "What can you get in there?" he asked.

"Nuts," said the man promptly.

"Oh yes, but I mean, generally — what have they got in there?"

"Nothing," said the man. Thank goodness these Australians generally keep their heads. The need of a canteen was one of the things we wanted impressed on him...

K. left the beach at 3.30 or 3.15 — two hours, or at most, 2½ hours after landing. In that time he had seen almost every important officer and taken a good grasp of the position.

Yesterday, Butler, of the Intelligence, came up to me and told me that he and Woods had been thinking that we ought to get out an Anzac Annual. There was enough talent in the Army Corps to turn out something really first class... It might be a really valuable memento in future years.

In the afternoon we had a committee meeting — White, Butler, Woods, and myself. All who have been spoken to approve. We decided to have a certain number of competitions for cover design, best story, and so on — about £24 in all; and to invite all contributions by December and have it printed in Athens. It will have to be New Year and will probably be late at that — which can't be helped...

The name 'Anzac Annual' was discarded as too suggestive. It is to be the 'Anzac Magazine'.[2]

Received mother's and father's parcels — will open them on my birthday...

November 17

[Today] there was a fairly strong wind rising in the hills. You could see the breakers rolling in, white, three deep, all along the beach... The seas were breaking over the whole length of the *Milo*, our breakwater ship, flinging themselves against the stern, and then throwing their foam over the whole length of pier. Williams' pier [on North Beach] was fairly right. But the little Walker's Ridge Pier north of it was gone, all except the piles. The water was over the beach right up to the Naval Transport Officer's door.

I went along the beach where natives and big fatigue parties of Australians and the old Navy's Corps ... were lined up and helping to haul occasional relics out of the water... Dead mules were being washed up. Further north, near Fisherman's Hut, several bodies buried shallow in the sand had been half uncovered. Around in Anzac Cove the beach was simply a litter of the trestle of old piers, old barges half broken up sawing and bumping about like elephants dancing some slow side step on the water's edge. The beach was littered with the big debris of the piers over which the waves were bursting in mass after mass of foam. One man was very nearly carried out by the waves — fatigue parties here, too, were carting the stores to higher levels but lots of ammunition boxes were still half in the water; and the shell cases (now worth 10/- each) about 10 000 of them, were in imminent danger of being buried altogether. Further on the A.M.C. dug-outs had been protected against the sea by piles of boxes, but every seventh wave washed in and threatened to carry them out to sea altogether...

After dinner the storm broke into torrents of rain. I went out again to see the worst of it. Our little gully — 300 yards long, was a rushing stream three inches deep. Things had settled on the beach — there were still lights in the A.M.C. dug-outs there. I looked in and found some A.M.C. men sitting round a brazier with holes in it — glowing with an Indian. They were snug and said they thought the place would last out the night now. Anyway if it didn't they could clear as soon as the waves began to break in... I... tramped on round the point. The seas were still roaring in... The mud was over my ankles — I stumbled along the tramway — half of it further on was in the sea. A driver was dragging the harness from two mules that had just been shot — one dead the other wounded. A man had been shot too. I plunged along the mud — "Up here's better, mate." said a friendly Australian — so I got up on the sandy bank below the cemetery — and at last reached Williams' Pier. A light was in the dug-out of the Naval Transport Officer.

The *Gaby* — the tug with the mails on, he said, had sunk, crew aboard, but all saved. She was towing out two lighters, but both her lighters were sunk... The *Milo* had broken her back in two places and was breaking fore and aft... The *Gaby* sank with most of our Christmas mail on board — the outward mail. (I had written 20 letters)...

The Naval Transport Officer said this storm gave no warning. We had not one word from outside — no meteorological warning of any sort. At 7.30 [a.m.] he noticed a swell along the beach (about that time I thought it was so fine that I had decided to go to Imbros and Cape Helles). He sent along to say that he thought there would be no shipping that day. By 9.30 although the sky

The *Milo* (left and *Gaby* flounder close inshore after the 17 November storm. (AWM neg. no. G1248)

looked fairly clear the blue and white flag with the red pennant below was replaced by the red pennant alone. The barometer had dropped then and so they knew the storm was on them, I suppose...

November 18

My 36th birthday — opened mother's and father's two delightful parcels.

The storm has made a clearance of our beach — one pier, Williams', only standing and the end bay of that gone... No sign of Anzac pier (No. 2) and only the stumps of Walker's Pier standing. All the lighters here sunk, and two water lighters. Commander Gipps said to me that we had only 40 hrs water at Anzac. "How do you think we're going to get on in the winter?" I asked — "The winter!" he said, "I think we're within two days of a disaster."

But I think we could use the old Anzac wells after this rain. However, we haven't enough wood to boil it for long: we haven't enough fodder for the mules. We have only miserable reserves of food compared with what we might have had. Our lighters will be sunk by every gale that blows from the south west, and we have no reserves of them or of small boats — we never have had enough, and no pier for them to shelter behind. Why didn't G.H.Q. resign if it couldn't get these things, and force the Government to get them...

The result of all this will be — probably — a sort of Crimea. I think we can hang on, in a sort of a way, but at the cost of the utmost suffering to which our past trials have not been a flea-bite by comparison. Gellibrand and I have been talking this over and we are in absolute agreement as to that. The fault happens in this case to be purely and simply the hopeless weakness, want of imagination, and above all want of moral courage of the British staff. They haven't an idea beyond the present, (many of them say so) — "We can't think of reserves — we've all we can to keep up present supplies" — and those that do haven't the courage to let the people know. The British troops here and the Australian and New Zealand Army Corps are sacrificed to that pure British incompetence; it will cause the utmost bitterness, and worst of all — the bitterness is absolutely and entirely and up to the hilt justified...

The Turks shelled the beach intermittently all day and are shelling it to-night — they know quite well that we are in difficulties and are trying to prevent us working there. It is cold — but not so cold as it will be. A German aeroplane was here to-day and had a very good look at the whole position. I've no doubt it spotted all our new stores.

The summing up of all this is that the British nation has not the brains to make war. It is much better at manufacturing socks. By the same token our winter clothing is not landed yet...

I must write something to give people some idea at least of what is the condition. The Turks clearly know. Beachy [Bill] is throwing about one shell a minute or more, all night. They know this is our one working night.

With one pier of course we couldn't evacuate at present if we wanted to...

November 20

Had a walk — but feeling a little seedy. Must be what Milner had — a sort of epidemic jaundice...

November 22

In bed with jaundice. Heavy strafe on Olive Grove [a Turkish position behind Gaba Tape]. Read *Jaffery*.

November 23

In bed, reading *Brigadier Gerard*. Anzac Magazine articles beginning to come in...

November 24

Still in bed with catarrhal jaundice — (Well's disease). Have been enjoying a glorious read ... and any amount of *Times* and *Arguses*. I fancy Peter Schuler is a more truthful war correspondent than Charlie Smith, i.e. he does see the things. I don't fancy Charlie always does...

November 25
Last night we fired not a shot from our trenches, except at absolutely certain targets. The 1st F.A. Brigade is moving, I think to Salonica, and the idea is to give the Turks the impression that we are evacuating. None of our guns have fired all day to-day or to-night. The wagons are being sent away, too. I suppose the [small] Turkish attack on the Apex [on 22 November] was with the idea that we may be evacuating — to find our strength. It shows which they consider the easiest place to attack at. There was a bit of firing on the left about 7 o'clock this evening. Warships blazing for 10 minutes and some rifle fire with flares. [Unbeknown to Bean, the artillery brigade was indeed being evacuated. Kitchener had concurred with General Monro's assessment that no worthwhile purpose could be achieved by their continuing to hold Suvla and Anzac Cove. Consequently, evacuation plans were completed on 22 November. Only very senior officers were told of the decision. (Bean was not let into the secret until 14 December.) Brig-Gen White was ordered to draft the detailed evacuation programme for the Anzac area. He believed that the withdrawal could succeed only if the Turks were given no sign of such operations. Many ruses were adopted to hide the evacuation. The 'silent stunt', for example, was intended to familiarise the Turks with extended periods of apparent inactivity within the Allies' lines.]

9.30 p.m. Moon is up so there won't be any attack to-night. The Turks have been bombarding the beach all day — desultory firing...

Turks sent a patrol into Quinn's last night to see if it were held — three men crept up to the trench — one was bayoneted and two got away...

November 27
Went up to Quinn's to-day and got some further details of the Silent Battle. It began at 6 p.m. on November 25th. After a night of it, at about 7 on the morning of the 26th (yesterday) 40 Turks got out of their Quinn's trenches (by some hidden means they have behind the broken heaps of earth, which now lie in front of Quinn's, owing to the mines exploded there). Four of them came on very boldly and they got right up to our bombproof wire. At Steele's our machine gunner was watching them with his hands

itching on the grip handles of his gun — but he had orders not to shoot. The four Turks took hold of our bombproof and dragged it back and cleared two lengths of it. They plastered in bombs and then the leading Turk jumped in. Our fellows — 17th Battalion — were really splendid. Although bombed, they didn't bomb back — their orders were not to do so. There were four of them wounded — the Turk pushed by these four and thrust his way into the dark passage of one of our bombproofs — as firmly as any Australian could have done. There a sergeant met him and lunged at him with the bayonet. The Turk grasped the bayonet but the sergeant pulled it away from him and killed him. A corporal coming up — I think from behind — also shot twice into him, and he was very certainly killed. The other three had, I think, a bomb thrown into them and were frightened off. The remaining Turks had gone a little further south, but they were scattered by some bombs being thrown into them, and ran back to their trench. 4 or 5 were hit...

November 28, Sunday

Awoke this morning to find the whole country covered with snow... Still a bit jaundiced, but the only way of keeping warm was to walk round the trenches, so tramped round. After all what does it matter so long as you can move, but climbing some hills was next to impossible to get on; to get to White Gully was a struggle that left me almost exhausted half way up...

The authorities have a new plan. They haven't prepared against the winter; they haven't made a harbour; they now find they can't expect to land water and stores as they would have wished — and the condenser is holed: so they are to take off troops. Imbros will be a sort of camping place for the reserves. What use it will be having reserves in Imbros if the weather is like it has proved to be 3 days out of 5, is a puzzle. But I suppose they realise now that the troops can't be kept here, because they haven't prepared for them so something had to be done...

"Silent battle" ended midnight last night. It was a bit of a strain on the men and officers — but it kept the Turks jumpy... Our snipers were turned on today...

It's bitter tonight... [The thermometer had not risen above freezing point during the day, and showed 7°F of frost during the night.]

November 29

Freezing hard last night, and most of this day, and again

Arthur Bazley, Bean's assistant, stands in the snow outside Bean's dugout, 29 November. (AWM neg. no. G1264)

tonight... I had to walk round to keep warm. Most of the men seem to have little fires — I have at present none. A man of the 11th A.S.C. [Pte R.G. Nash] offered to make me one. He was an unlettered chap — left school at 11 — who came in with a surprisingly exquisite piece of prose and verse on the grey outlook of everything — extraordinarily beautiful in spite of crude faults in the metre... I gave him a bit of a lecture on rhythm and scansion, and he — as a return — offered to make me a stove.

Still a bit jaundiced...

The torpedo boat didn't run today — will get to Imbros tomorrow probably. I can't work here — only walk; it's far too cold. An issue of rum to all troops tonight — poor beggars, the novelty of the snow will soon wear off, but it's worse for the Turks than for us. They get this in their backs — right into their dugouts. Two Turks deserted this morning — came in along the beach with one kitbag about daylight — 6 in the last three days.

Another change in plans, I hear — or perhaps this is the change of yesterday. Up to yesterday the garrison was to be thinned: today they are to stand fast. Our General Staff here doesn't know what it means — unless White does. My appetite is much better this weather, and so long as I'm walking I'm not really uncomfortable; but the poor chaps in the trenches can't walk...

November 30

I moved into Army Corps H.Q. today as I was coming to Imbros and wanted to leave my things safe, and the last of the 1st Div. H.Q. is leaving the Gully. It was fairly calm last night, and perfectly smooth today; but not one bit of work has been done because the last steamboat had been sunk (the man in charge left her stern on to the sea, and she was driven ashore and sunk by the pier; Officer in charge was warned that this would happen, but he wouldn't moor her the other way). The last horse boat was also ashore, so there was literally nothing to work this Army's communications with ... except one dinghy. This morning we expected to find the sea simply covered with the small craft trooping back as usual like ants from Imbros, but hour after hour nothing happened...

I went down about 2, and there were Milner and Pain. They said that the dinghy was only to do one trip and to take three men and no luggage. They weren't going to leave their luggage — naturally; and so they decided not to go. I was the 3rd man — and the M.L.O. threw in Bazley with me — but we left our kitbag for Milner to bring, if he would — I'm sure he will if possible...

The trawler captain let me travel in his cabin — where I was warm... If this happens after our first storm, and blocks us from doing any work at all now that we have a perfectly smooth day, what is going to happen later when we have two months of intermittent gale?...

There was a light in the window of our little Imbros cottage — it looked so snug — when Bazley and I got there. I was very beat — with my heavy overcoat, and I suppose the jaundice has pulled me down a bit. I found the lower room dark, but a light in the upper, and there was poor old Ross in bed with an overcoat over him, and very much in the middle of an attack of jaundice — worse than mine was. Lawrence is in Alexandria buying winter clothes.

I am writing this over a warm wood fire, simply hugging the hearth — after a nice dinner; appetite, thank goodness, means the jaundice has pretty well gone. It is better than last night, though when I turn my front to the fire my back gets very cold, and when I turn my back my knees begin to freeze. One's breath make clouds of steam, even over this fire.

However, it's better than last night. Last night — after walking about all day in order to keep warm — I had a hurried dinner and got into bed as quick as I could — but not before my feet were getting frozen. (I wrote a few pages of diary and you can't do that with impunity). Bazley boiled me a mess tin full of salt water — and warmed my water bottle before the kitchen fire, and then poured the water quickly in (it is a fine big stretcher-bearer's bottle, made in Australia with a little pannikin over the big bung, and covered with khaki felt). He put this in my sleeping bag and then I crept in. I was determined to sleep warmly for once, so I took off my coats and boots — wet of course — and gaiters, and put on my pyjamas over the rest of my clothes. I took off my socks — 2 pairs — they were wet, of course, and hung them over my hurricane lantern to dry; the nearest thing to a fire one has is this reading lamp. I put on two pairs of dry socks instead, and a leather balaclava (it's really an airman's cap) over my head and ears — and crawled in. The hot water bottle was beautiful. I pulled up the biscuit box — which makes my chair, to the bedside, stood it on end with the lamp on it just by my head; pulled the great head cover flap of my sleeping bag right down over my shoulders and head, leaving just space enough to see my book and nothing else; pulled the blanket (which covered the sleeping bag) right over my hands so that there was only one thumb exposed — and then settled down to read the life and voyages of poor old Captain Cook. At last, for the first time in three days, I was able to read without being frozen — I was just decently warm. I had a leather overcoat-lining (a detachable one for motor car journeys) over my pyjamas; a piece of flannel (in which mother wrapped my birthday billy) round my shoulders; then the sleeping bag — kangaroo skin and fur inside; tarpaulin outside, of a sort; then a rug doubled over my feet to my waist; then a blanket — a big one, singly; then my thickest coat and Jack's overcoat over my legs and feet — all this plus 2 vests, warm shirt, cardigan, mittens, pair of underpants, riding breeches, and 2 socks — well-wrapped up so like an arctic explorer, I managed to keep up my wretched circulation (which is about the worst on the peninsula); and for once I was really warm without a fire. Far down below me I could hear the pick, pick, pick, of the men excavating 15 feet below a chamber for bombs. There are 48 000 bombs underneath my dugout, and if they went up they'd alter the whole shape of the hill — but thank heavens they've got them there and not (as for the last 6 months) about 30 yards across the gully under a few feet of loose soil heaped on the roof. And so I read of the fate of the poor old Yorkshire seaman, the matter of fact Cook, who found the most important part of my country, and I scarcely think realised what he had found. If he had been told that 127 years later his barren discovery would be sending to the Mediterranean 300 000 of the best troops the British nation possesses, he might have been a little more astonished at himself for discovering it...

They say that the Indians on the Suvla plain were standing partly in water yesterday. They seem to bear up pretty well — but the Egyptians are cracking up...

It's all very well for the troops in Flanders. They get 4 days of this sort, and then they go back for 4 days to sleep in a house; to warm baths and dry clothes. Once <u>our</u> men are wet they can never properly get dry again — I doubt even in their monthly or two monthly visits to Imbros if they can. They have to be cold and wet all the time. They're clever at making the best of things; making fires in a hole in the trench wall 6″ × 8″ with a few sticks of broken biscuit box: but they have no houses or baths. A man can't wash this weather in the <u>sea</u>, and there is no other water... I boiled some water over two candles in a cake tin, which is my washing basin this morning — it was yesterday's washing water, but I shaved in it again today and washed my feet. But that was all that one could do — it was too cold to strip; and if that is so with me, how about those poor chaps with only a waterproof sheet over them. They have been far far cleaner than the Kitchener soldiers — out of all comparison cleaner than the terriers — all the summer; but even they can't get clean now.

A big part of their life is the fight against the fleas. The contributions to the Anzac Magazine are full of it. The flea is quiescent during the day — their movement keeps him quiet — but he comes at them after dark. They try to fight him, but they aren't used to him yet.

By-the-by, an Anzac Medical Association has been formed; 2

papers have now been discussed: 1st meeting "Lice" — 2nd meeting "Catarrhal Jaundice" (the same that I've had). The first meeting was held about three weeks ago during a fairly constant bombardment, but though there was only the tent roof of the Casualty Clearing Station overhead, it didn't seem to make any difference. Some told me that they were anxious for the speeches not to be cut too long, others told me that they hadn't noticed the bombardment at all. When the meeting broke up they stood outside for some time discussing it, just as they would on the steps of the Town Hall — with the shells flying over them all the time...

December 1
Godley came over here yesterday, and, after his interview with Birdwood, the Imbros Rest Camp scheme is said to have been definitely abandoned; and, as those who are more responsible than I quite rightly say, the thing is now to sit down and think what can best be done. If these troops could get off with the loss of a third and half the guns, and nearly all stores, is that the best? Staying on here we should be fighting the winter, which is playing Germany's game. At the same time Helles is some use. Can we stay? I think that with sufficient energy on the part of the authorities in making harbours, sinking ships full of cement, etc., we could. But then I don't know (and the authorities do) how far the Germans have come, and how many there are. Besides, I doubt if we could evacuate from one pier, and in this weather. If it were going to be done I have no doubt the right thing you could do would be to consult all the officers under the strictest secrecy, and get every possible question from them and suggestion — leave guns as late as could be, and then work one gun from three embrasures, etc: leave machine guns until almost the end; have sham camp fires going; sham transport; not overdo it, but have the nearest thing to normal kept up till the very last night; all evacuation done at night at all costs; the light not to be risked; big heaps of empty boxes; hollow inside — landed. Finally try every device practicable to keep up the appearance of men about the place; reliefs marched in and round and out again like stage soldiers — all men camped where enemy sees our camps, e.g. Shrapnel Gully, Ari Burnu Point, and special officers to see that the men are as active at these points as normally.

Some say that before this we should have one gigantic effort... I believe the right thing for us to do, if we can, is to hold Helles. It can be done, I believe, by a national effort, i.e. by making certain at once of providing every facility. About Anzac and Suvla I don't know. Probably the best thing is, if possible, evacuation; if not — hold on. . .

Is the nation equal to the effort? If they would let us War Correspondents tell the truth in full as to the position and its seriousness, the nation would make the effort. The Germans know — there's nothing in the position to hide from them. But do the British people know? If we decided to stay on without a superhuman effort to back us, the result will be disaster.

December 2

Wrote one article. Censor asked me in to qualify an article I had written about the storms. The alteration was justifiable — to let the people know that the men had warm clothes and blankets. . .

December 5, Sunday

Drawing and painting for the Anzac Magazine[3]. . .

December 6

I have been painting and drawing all day — and eating: one's appetite here is enormous, and one will have to look out or one will become a regular gourmand. . .

Got up at 5.30, and came over to Anzac by trawler. . .

December 7

Spent the day arranging matter which has come in. . .

December 8

There are some very polished bits of verse in from some English Officers on the left; and a great deal of strong vivid rather crude stuff from Australians — far more than from New Zealanders. In one or two cases I have picked out a single verse from a long tedious poem, and with the least bit of polish it is excellent. One little gem on "The silence" had its origin in this way. . .

A definite decision come to — we are to take every one off the peninsula except those needed to definitely defend it, as the only method of keeping our supply of food and water. . .

December 10

No time — hard at work with the Anzac Magazine. I went to White, discovered whether we were to go over to Imbros together. I knew he had been at Imbros during the day. He was with Gen. Godley for a long time that night, and when he came out I asked him. "I am sorry, Bean," he said. "I meant to have told you before, but I am afraid I shall be very busy during the next few days — much too busy to undertake the work in connection with the magazine, as I should like to do. I am afraid I shall be able to do very little in connection with it, and that you will have to manage without me." He was very nice about it...

December 11

The Turks were curiously quiet all today. The ships fired 700 shells of 6-inch and over into the Olive Grove. Today the engineers are making a pair of floating piers this side of Snipers' Nest. I left for Imbros by the destroyer which brought over Gen. Birdwood to Anzac for the day. I showed him the Anzac Magazine, and he said to me as we were talking afterwards: "It's going to be a very anxious time, Bean. I should not at all wonder if we finished the winter in Egypt. They are taking this invasion of Egypt very seriously, and if they think we are not holding up enough Turks here, and they are merely leaving a small army to face us, and we cannot do enough to justify our standing, I suspect they will send us all off to defend Egypt.[4] It will be a very anxious time." So possibly he is in the dark as to what is really going to happen...

December 14

Came to Suvla by early trawler. Went on board the *Cornwallis*... In the ward room they told me they had heard that we were evacuating at Anzac as well as at Suvla... The idea is that on Friday night the trenches will be held by the smallest number of troops that can hold them — the rest will march off to the beach about nightfall. Whilst they are embarking the others will leave the trenches. They have put up barbed wire along three lines. They have landed Tommy guns by day, but they have also taken off quite a lot of stores, guns, and other things by day. Of course Anzac cannot be held if Suvla goes. It was all very well before they had the trenches dug, but now the Turks would have a beautiful set of communication trenches on our left, and the ships would never be able to shell them out of them...

I found that White had given leave to my three [Anzac Magazine] artists to come over to Imbros with me. I shall send them and Bazley away tomorrow... I can't go with them or I may never get back, and I want to see the end of Anzac. I don't want actually to be in the last lot to leave the beach, because the risk of being killed or cut off is too great, and because I want to be here the next morning if possible...

And so one is on an adventure again — like the landing... It is an adventure — no one can foretell the ending. It depends largely on the weather. Tonight we have ideal conditions — a cloudy sky covering the half moon; but a very smooth sea. There are three more nights to go. The moon will be brighter each night, and the wind of course may rise. Beachy is firing tonight at intervals — clearly they can see Snipers' Nest men busy on the piers opposite Walker's [Ridge]. 4 guns have just fired — 3 bursts, and one into the sea. The gun isn't firing as if they knew there was an embarkation going on, but more as if it saw that there was some activity on the North Beach, and didn't know what. Troops are being cleverly withdrawn — guides to keep them in the saps; but the idiots actually cheered last night as they were going off — it was explained that they thought they were for Salonika (they are for Egypt). Even Australians are too foolish for words when you take them in a crowd...

Except for Beachy the night is very usual. The ordinary fitful rifle fire — a 30 shot a minute night. We have built a number of long and short piers from North Beach, and the Turks can, of course see these. But they may think that they are meant for the landing of troops, not their embarkation...

Well, I must to bed. Thank God old Jack is out of this. I can every now and then hear fellows hurrying towards the North Beach — footsteps and voices. The hillsides are getting very empty — all the tents are left standing, and they are building hospital huts at Suvla as hard as they can. The men were allowed to take what they wanted from Ordnance for a couple of days, and had a fine time: our mess stores have been sold to them.

Beachy has just put four shells on to Ari Burnu Point (two into the water); they are quite harmless there. I don't know if they will wonder at our guns not replying; but of course in the "silent battle" the same thing happened, so they may be mystified. I think they must suspect something, as they did in August — but are not sure what...

I noticed today, crossing the flats, how very clearly one can tell when a rifle is pointed at one. There is a full crack — like that of a cricket bat driving towards you with plenty of wood behind it. As sure as you hear that crack the bullet sings somewhere near you. If it is very close you probably don't hear the crack first, but if it is 30 or 40 feet above you at a range of 1 500 yards you do — I should say. I didn't hear the crack of the rifle which got me in August, and I didn't notice, I think, the zipp of the bullet...

December 16
I went to bed at about 12.30 last night... About a quarter of an hour after I turned in, I felt a cold breath of air on the top of my head (in spite of its being well covered with good red hair). That breath brought a vague misgiving. Were we going to have a storm? We have had a fortnight of perfect weather, and a storm is about due.

The breeze rapidly increased. The waterproof sheet at the door of my dugout began to fidget to and fro in the gusts. I could hear the constant whistle of the wind in the few scanty shrubs which are left.

I had to jump up and look out. The clouds were moving only slowly, and the sea seemed fairly calm as far as I could see. This backwater of a gully was full of gusts. After I got back to bed the wind gradually rose, and the waterproof roof of the dugout flapped ominously. I jumped up again — still the same gusty gully; the incinerator fires burning rather brighter than usual — I have noticed that everywhere...

I couldn't sleep. I tossed and turned — my hands and the soles of my feet tingling just as they have done before I went into bat in an important cricket match. Here we were committed, and this rising gale seemed likely to stop everything for a week!, for two weeks!! It would perhaps make a shambles of our piers like that other gale did. They would take weeks to rebuild, and would the Turks with their great new howitzers let us do it?...

I don't know when I got to sleep. When the morning came I asked Bazley what it was like. "Blowing up," he said. "What's the beach like?" "Oh, the beach is quite smooth, it's a north wind." Thank goodness. I can't say what a load that took off my mind... The water was covered with white horses at a little distance, but was perfectly smooth in shore...

I packed Bazley and my three artists off today with all my baggage for Imbros. I am only keeping Jack's sleeping bag and overcoat, and my washing things — the 1st Divisional staff moves out today, all except a few of the chiefs up at White's Gully — in our old home here I am the last left...

Anzac looks extraordinarily empty — the beach quite deserted. We have burnt our papers, and there will be very little left to the Turks to interest them. The aeroplane was over the New Zealand

H.Q. yesterday; I don't suppose an aeroplane would notice much of this...

[Today w[as to have been the first day] of the evacuation] — I don't know why it was put back. The night is a beautiful one...

The men aren't sorry to leave — not most of them. They regret leaving all their comrades buried here, and the number of demands for timber for graves has been enormous. I see solid looking crosses going up everywhere over the old biscuit box ones...

The men aren't frightened, and there have been lots of volunteers for the last lot — the Die Hards, though the method is not to call for volunteers but to choose the best men. It is the suspense that the men don't like. The suspense from the beginning of that 1st night onwards will be enormous...

As I had my dugout burgled yesterday (someone, as soon as Divisional H.Q. moved, went through the dugouts and searched my things and took my camera) I have brought everything across to Army Corps and borrowed a dugout there for a night or two — or rather a wooden house; a very fine one. I don't so much mind losing the camera (my second one) as Blamey has lent me his, and I have a small one from Embelton... There will always be these prowlers — they are mostly men who would do just the same in peace time...

I stow this confidential diary in my sleeping bag at Army Corps H.Q. — and leave it there during the day. If the Turks got so far it would tell them nothing they didn't know; whereas if they rushed the firing line when I was there, it would tell them too much, perhaps. I did chance taking a couple of confidential maps in my pocket up Bully Beef Sap and to the Apex — but, after all, I should have had time to burn them; and if the Turks got so far, it would almost be all up with our plans...

December 17

Woke up to find a grey sky with heavy thunderclouds — and through the gauze of the window I could see the scud moving from the south west. Just the wrong direction for us. However, the wind was not heavy, and though there was a slight swell there was not enough to disturb the piers...

There has been produced — as one was sure there would be — a device for firing a rifle off automatically after we have left; with two bully beef tins full of water and a bit of string. It will pull the trigger as late as 20 minutes after it has been left. They would use damaged rifles.

I saw the engineers 5th Coy. yesterday burning their rifles, picks, shovels, tubing, breaking the pumps. I smashed my home made furniture myself and put a knife through the waterproof sheets when I left my dugout. Somehow I don't like to think of that furniture as a curiosity in some Turkish Officer's home...

The evacuation was originally to have been finished to-night Dec. 17/18, but has been postponed till to-morrow and next night — Dec. 18/19 and 19/20... About 200 men go off to-night. Ross, Maj. [?] Anderson, Col. Johnson [?] and myself go off to the *Grafton* (Blister Cruiser) at 10 a.m. to-morrow...

I took some final photos. to-day and made some final calls on 2nd. L.H.Bde., and Cass (2nd Bn.). Cass had a "smoking fatigue" on. A party of men were detailed to smoke and lounge about Artillery Road corner where Gaba Tepe can see it — and to carry water like stage soldiers round the road and then thro' a sap and back again. It is the most extraordinary fatigue we have had at Anzac. K. Tepe saw them alright for Beach began shelling and put in 3 shells right on to the road where they were — there were the marks on the road. The smoking fatigue retired but presently came out again and manfully smoked like heroes — and Beachy started again.

A little further on I found the Light Horse playing cricket on Shell Green (Maj. Onslow batting) while the shells were flying far overhead...

A beautiful night but misty — exactly what we want... A lighter has just come in to Watson's Pier. It is just typical of the Naval Staff work. The fellow in charge first started by bawling "ahoy" for about 5 minutes — 5 or 6 times "Is this where you want this lighter?" he roared twice...

2.35: I had sat up to about 1 a.m. working out a timetable of to-morrow's events and the next days, when I heard a sound of provincial English voices past my door. "Coom along an' help General Lesslie, boys", it said "an' doan' tarry now!" Beachy was shelling vigourously — 8 or 12 shells one after the other. I looked out — and the whole sky to the North was a great red glow. There was clearly some great fire in our lines.

I went across with my (or rather Embelton's) camera — something or someone had set fire to our store — a huge dump of MacConochie's rations and biscuits and a little oil. There was some oil lying about. "It started with someone who knew a thing or two!' said one of the men.

(All the time I am writing this I can hear those damned naval fools bawling at the top of their English voices on the beach —

Above:
'Good shot, sir!' The 17 December cricket match on Shell Green is played with apparent disregard for the shells flying overhead. (AWM neg. no. G1289)
Right:
The smoking fatigue, 17 December. An impromptu game of 'two-up' was organized: 'Heads for Constantinople; tails for Cairo!' (AWM neg. no. G1288)

God has blessed the British navy with much courage and little brains.)

The Army Corps Signal Coy. and as many Australians as were handy were working round the fire might and main, watering the next stack to keep it clear and trying to dam with sandbags the oil which spread along the tram rails. In the midst of them in his shirt sleeves was General Lesslie — spade in hand, sleeves rolled back, wrist watch flashing in the glare, right in the thick of it all the time, as he has been in every awkward strenuous dangerous business I have seen him take up. They had got the fire under within an hour — working very hard... [Bean was evacuated to the *Grafton* during the night. The ship was to remain off Anzac until the evacuation had been completed.]

December 18

Fire still burning — but quite safe now. It was the one topic at breakfast but no two people have the same theory...

So I have left old Anzac. In a way I was really fond of the place. I have certainly had some quite enjoyable times there in my old dugout — yarning to friends; or going round the lines. I can't pretend that I ever liked shells or attacks — but one came to put up with them much as one does with the toothache...

The contrast of the civilised life of this hospitable navy is very pleasant... We had a warm bath first thing — I sat in mine for 20 minutes — and some clean clothes. I only had my one uniform and I have been lent clothes by everybody. The Navy can't do too much for our chaps... By jove, these naval chaps are a sterling lot... The Captain is Grace — son of W.G. — whose brother just beat me for the X1 at Clifton...

The greater part of the 3rd [Bn] and last batch of to-night's troops is on board ship by now, so I am turning in. No sign of offensive from enemy...

December 19, Sunday

The last day. I was not waked last night — so knew that nothing had happened since 3 o'clock. All the troops for the night were clear by 4 a.m.

And there is Anzac today, looking exactly the same as it always has done — with incinerator fires going dreamily and the big fire still smoking. There was a 5 minutes' 'strafe' on Hill 60 after daylight and at 10 a.m. the Turks burst a few fairly heavy shell on Plateau 400 — either after the anti-aircraft gun or the 18 pounder on Phillips' Top [north of Brown's Dip] which was shelling the Chessboard. One of our old 5-inch howitzers was manfully shelling the Chessboard and Battleship Hill...

5.45 [p.m.]: The sun has set — moon is one night off the full — sky a good deal brighter than last night, but not brilliantly clear — a low mist seems to be gathering on the beach...

8.10: *Mars* a dim shape going off through the darkness to the south — only 8000 men left — splendid. Firing quite normal. Moon so bright that I can easily see to read what I write. Moon perfect...

10.05: At this moment there are two motor lighters coming out — probably all 10 motor lighters on the sea full of 4000 soldiers, and only 2360 soldiers in the whole Anzac position. Firing sounds to be quite normal. There are after all about as many men actually observing in the firing line as there are on any night — when 2 are observing, 4 resting in trench, and 6 in support...

11.15: Going very quiet indeed — scarcely a shot at Anzac or at Suvla. The Turks may be listening to the constant shooting at Helles — rifle firing still continuous there.

11.40: Picket Boat opposite Brighton Beach — flares from her funnel. A good deal more firing in the centre — bomb on Russell's Top. Bomb at the Apex. Fair amount of firing about Monash [Valley]. *Picton* moving off to a place between us and 971...

11.45: Several bombs at Russell's Top. Men there are particularly anxious to keep it well up. Firing quite normal...

December 20

2.30 a.m.: Cocoa with the Captain — Chatham's Post must be deserted by now — and the last lot is all that is left in Quinn's and Lone Pine. A thick mist has gone over the moon...

3.05: Last lot now alone left all along the line. Destroyer fired. Can still hear a solitary rifle or two on the right as well as in the centre. Men must be hurrying down Chailak Dere down paths amongst the hills I know so well — can hear them on the left also — just one or two; mostly in centre. Moon too dark to see by. Possibly the isolated rifle shots are from patent rifles to fire after we have gone...

3.15: Left Lone Pine — poor old 1st Brigade. Gun or bomb on right. Bomb at Walker's. A shot at Suvla. Very little firing now — and almost all in centre. Just before Lone Pine was left there was more firing. A shot at Suvla — ship's, I think. Helles pretty quiet. Quite normal firing.

3.20: Quinn's and Pope's let — well, it's an extraordinary end to a fine history. The Turks at last have got it — the place they never could take — by our quietly leaving it in the night. And, in the end perhaps, the greatest success we have achieved there is quietly giving it to them without their knowing it. Light still burning on little Table Top. Two or three rapid shots from machine gun at Quinn's.

3.23: Beachy [Bill]

3.25: Walker's Nek left. The old Anzac line is now open to the Turks. A desultory fire still continues...

3.26: The mines at the Nek have been blown up. Tremendous firing — two huge red clouds. Turks firing for all they are worth all along the line. Message: "Left flank party all embarked." — Great finale...

5.0: Turks still firing — no one ashore. Machine gun going every now and then.

5.15: Turks still sending an occasional sniping shot at our trenches. Little Table Top light still burning. Heliotrope [signal] — Anzac to Suvla, 9 Corps: "Operations completed" — 3.57

5.40: All Suvla stores burning. We had at least one man wounded. Turks still firing at Anzac. Red glow in sky. Every now and then a cask of oil gives up a whirl of flame... Dark shape of ships against red glare reflected in water. We have to stand by to see what can be done in the way of destroying Anzac stores tomorrow. At present I don't suppose we know what men are left ashore...

7.5: Signal to *Grafton*. All ships to be prepared to open on mule carts and stores; as all wounded have been evacuated can be made without danger. Bombardment still going on — all very high.

7.15: Shelling stopped and crowds of Turks could be seen running across our trenches. Attack from Lone Pine and German Officers' trench. We are going to fire on the stores on the beach... [The firing continued until 7.37 a.m.]

Went down to breakfast, and then transferred to the *Beagle* and steamed fast into Imbros. In harbour was a wonderful collection of warships of all sorts and sizes — transports full of troops — cruisers, destroyers alongside them — battleships, old and new — all busy talking to one another, just like the crowd that foregathers at a club, after the break up of some meeting. They seemed to stay long enough for a meal and a yarn as it were — and then off to Mudros, Salonika, Helles: I don't know where. The harbour quickly emptied down to its normal again...

I heard [at the press correspondents' cottage] that we lost three wounded at Suvla, and two wounded at Anzac. We all agree that the thing to do is to get our account of this to the world before the Germans can do so . . .

December 21
We have to make our articles refer only to the last day — in case we abandoned Helles. They didn't want the Turks to know how many days it took us to get off the troops and stores and guns, or how many lighters there were and how many got off in each lighter . . .

December 23
The whole of this cottage worked all yesterday till dinner time, and even midnight, getting its various despatches away. Ward Price is clearly especially keen on making this story a magnificent one — a chef d'oeuvre — and he couldn't have a finer subject. The only thing is that few people in England will realize what an extremely dangerous operation it was. Ward Price, in a sort of humourous way (but sincerely for all that) envies me for having seen the Turks come over. "The thing that spoils it, from the journalistic point of view," he said, "is that there wasn't a battle — a rearguard action by the West Yorks on the beach would have made the story one of the finest possible."

I say that battle stories are almost commonplace nowadays; and the spectacle of our whole position gradually left bare to the Turks; with all lights burning, as on every other night; and the Turkish rifles popping off occasionally all along the line; and the Turks in the morning bombarding; and finally charging our now long deserted trenches — whilst we, after a night of intense anxiety, waited and looked on — is as good as any battle story.

But I am afraid that it shows the Turk is a most unenterprising fighter — and yet, in patrolling and sniping, he is energetic and bold in the extreme, more so than our Suvla troops, so one of their staff officers told me. It is his vigilance that is so imperfect . . .

December 26, Sunday
Working all day at the Anzac Magazine — a great deal of which really is excellent. On arriving home last night I found a note from Butler enclosing a wire from the Censor. It regretted that Major Delmé Radcliffe and correspondents had not been informed that no details whatever could be despatched, from which a hint as to the methods by which the troops had been withdrawn from Anzac or Suvla; and that our messages had been carefully read and seriously curtailed.

Exhausted Anzac Book staff members catch some sleep on the trawler from Imbros, 29 December. (AWM neg. no. G1312)

This was like an unexpected shrapnel shell in the pit of the stomach. The despatch on which I had poured out more care than anything of which I have written here — the only chance one has had of even attempting to rival Bartlett's work (which no man ever censored in this degree). However, the authorities are quite right. They know what they mean to do about Helles, and I don't. The only thing I could wish is that they could have told us this before we wrote and not after. We had a long conference with Aspinall (Chief of the Staff, Dardanelles Army) and the Press Officer before we wrote, at which the lines within which we were allowed to write were carefully laid down — all to appear as if done in one night — and I had kept strictly within this, and Radcliffe had scarcely had to alter a word of my article. If we had known that it was to be written within still narrower lines, we would have written it so. As it was, of course the best article of the campaign goes to the wall. However, the important thing is the other place, and one can't expect the authorities to have everything cut and dried for us on the instant, and never to change their minds at any moment. If Colonel Tyrrell had been a little quicker he would have saved us a lot of trouble — that's all . . . Very little harm done anyway — and that, such as it is, only to us and none at all to the Empire . . . [On 27 December the British Cabinet decided to end the Cape Helles campaign. The evacuation of 35 268 officers and men, together with large quantities of stores, guns, horses and mules, was successfully completed by 9 January.]

December 31

Packed last night. The 1st Division are taking almost all my gear to Alexandria, and I am travelling light with the magazine and my note books to London — with Bazley. He can develop my films on board the *Wahine* (the fast packet by which we travel) and look after the Magazine and the diaries. I have now 25 diaries full and a dozen notebooks besides, large and small and dealing with the battles of Gallipoli. They are in many cases the only records available. A few are in shorthand but nearly all could be understood by anyone if I were to peg out.

These diaries have been a weight on my mind — and so have my photos — I shan't be happy till I get them to a safe place, the diaries duplicated and the photos printed. A single shell or a submarine could destroy 9 months hard work and the best records we have of the Gallipoli campaign.

By mid-January Bean had visited the Western Front and sent off an article comparing the two theatres. He continued his work as Australia's official war correspondent during the next three years in France. Throughout this time, he also took a keen interest in the collection of war relics for a proposed Australian war museum. Yet not until 1918 was an assistant correspondent appointed to lighten his burden.

But Gallipoli still haunted his mind. How close had success been? What went wrong on the night of 6–7 August? Where was Beachy Bill located? A thousand such questions puzzled him still. So, when the armistice was declared, he quickly arranged that he and a small, official Australian delegation revisit the Peninsula. The party reached Anzac Cove on 15 February 1919. It spent four weeks retracing key points of the campaign, collecting relics, and investigating arrangements for Australian cemeteries and memorials. Once back in Australia, Bean sat down with his diaries and countless other records to assist him in what became his life's mission, the writing of the incomparable twelve-volume *Official history of Australia in the war of 1914–1918.*

them) ws horrible. At last a message ws passed along by ~~the Harrington~~ Col. Macla[illegible]: "The N.Z. howitzer battery is landing & will shortly be supporting you." Up to then no reply whatever seemed to have been made to these horrible guns up to the north. It was simply ~~~~ Bang ~~~~ Bang ~~~~ Bang ~~~~ Bang; then half a minute. Then the same Wheeeooooo Bang Bang Bang Bang again — & so on. Not a gun of ours seemed able to answer them at all — It was getting on towards evening so I decided to go on & find the 3rd Bn, if I could, myself. I went along the trench to near the mouth, jumped out, & ran across ~~[illegible]~~ the top & at once found myself in a little dip in the front side of the hill. There were a few men there, all lying down under the brow of the slope. On the edge of the slope was standing — I think he came up at the moment — Evans, the machine gun officer of the 3rd Bn. I thought he was Carter (who I heard had been wounded) & always confuse the two, — I told him I was glad to see he wasn't hit. I lay down under the cover of the edge of the ridge — it was slight cover — but he sat up on the edge of it alerting himself, treating the bullets as if they didn't exist, & they were pretty thick. The men were lying down pretty closely & I did the same. He didn't know where Jacks dressing station was & the men of the 3rd Bn with him didn't either. [I think it must have been in the very place to start off with]. As I lay there a lot of New Zealanders came up the hill behind this ridge, to left & right: The firing seemed to be ~~[illegible]~~ heavy away on our left all the time & I couldn't help thinking that the Turks were getting round our left flank — I thought I was looking at the left of their position (I could see the across the valley with men entrenched on the rear slope of the hill the other side as well as the ~~[illegible]~~ top of it. You could see them hanging on to the edge of the hill → and you could see them farther to the right entrenched on both faces, several tiers of dugouts facing our way. It looked as though they were preparing for fire from their left rear.

I thought I was looking ~~&~~ ~~the~~ & that the Turks were getting in here

As we were lying there ~~[illegible]~~ six guns just behind us somewhere opened over our heads with a delicious salvo. It was like a soothing draught of water to hear those guns blaze at the Turks. I don't know what they were firing at — I guessed they were the Howitzer Battery spoken of in the message — It was good to hear the men appreciate those guns. ~~Presently~~ They had their effect. The enemy suddenly switched off the big ridge to our ~~left~~ right & four shells went over us ~~[illegible]~~ not at all far down the slope behind us. Presently four more shells came along & burst almost over us. Then four just in front of us — sweeping down the slope. One of them hit the ~~[illegible]~~ edge of the ridge not more than a few yards in front of where I was lying. There was a flash & bits of mud & broken bush were thrown into the air. I thought ~~[illegible]~~ what sort of a hole was this I had let myself into. The chap next me said it was common shell,

Notes

Introduction

1 ED Millen to CEW Bean, 13 Aug 1914. Bean Papers, AWM, folder 896.
2 KS Inglis in *ADB*, Vol 7 (Melbourne 1979) pp. 226–9. Most of the background and family information in this introduction is drawn from this source.
3 Bean Papers, AWM, Personal Records 7447 (3rd Series), folder 6.
4 *British Australasian*, Oct 1914.
5 CEWB to Effie, 30 Aug 1917 or 1918 (year not stated). Bazley Papers, AWM.
6 'Position of the assistant correspondent AIF and duties of the Australian War Correspondent', 12 Dec 1917. Bean Papers, AWM, folder 268.
7 CEW Bean, *Gallipoli mission* (Canberra 1952) p. 25.
8 CEWB to Mother, 4 Oct 1914. Bean Papers, AWM, Personal Records 7447 (3rd series), folder 6.
9 *Gallipoli mission*, p. 25.
10 CEWB to Mother, 4 Oct 1914.
11 AW Bazley Diary, 6 Jan, 5 May, 22 June 1917. AWM 2 DRL 215.
12 PFE Schuler, *Australia in arms* (London 1916) p. 10; press cutting from Sydney *Sun*, Murdoch Papers, NLA MS 2823/80; *Bulletin*, 19 Aug 1915, p. 41.
13 N Lytton, *The press and the General Staff* (London 1920) pp. x, 119–20.
14 'Position of the assistant correspondent AIF. . .', 12 Dec 1917.
15 *Commonwealth gazette*, 8 June 1915, p. 1092.
16 *Bulletin*, 7 Oct 1915, p. 26.
17 Years later, Bean accounted for the vast wealth of information he had recorded at the war in terms of it being collected 'by a trained investigator, mainly at the time of events, and in most cases from the actors themselves'. CEW Bean, 'The Writing of the Australian Official History of the Great War — Sources, Methods and Some Conclusions.' *Royal Australian Historical Society: Journal and Proceedings*, Vol 24 (2), 1938 p. 100.
18 Bean Papers, AWM, folder 760.

1 Australia Will be There

1 Charles's brother, Monty, was residing at this St Kilda boarding house. Charles had stayed there since coming down from Sydney late in September to prepare for embarkation. Their parents travelled over from Hobart to farewell Charles.
2 The threat from German warships made it imperative that local censorship guidelines be rigorously adhered to during this period. Yet, through a series of blunders in the office of the Chief of the General Staff, details of the names and sailing dates of convoy vessels were freely available. The press, particularly in Melbourne, widely published articles describing the departure of the convoy. On 30 October, in response to these indiscretions, the Minister for Defence ordered Customs officials to ensure that no newspaper was allowed to leave Australia for a fortnight.
3 Vaccination against smallpox and inoculation against typhoid was made compulsory for all men enlisting in the AIF. These treatments, though comparatively common by this time, were still regarded with suspicion by many people, including some doctors.
4 Peter Schuler was special correspondent for the Melburne *Age*. CP Smith travelled with the second convoy as the *Argus* special correspondent. These appointments had been confirmed by the outgoing Liberal Government in September before GF Pearce, Labor's Minister for Defence, decided that one pressman should represent all the Australian press. Schuler and Smith subsequently were not allowed to accompany the AIF at the Gallipoli landings. They based themselves and Alexandria and compiled stories from the official despatches and inter-

views with the evacuated wounded. In July Sir Ian Hamilton personally authorised them to visit the Peninsula.

5 He wrote separate articles (each number consecutively) for the morning and evening papers. His account of the *Sydney–Emden* battle appeared in the Australian press on 4 December.

6 During the four months which the AIF spent training in Egypt venereal disease incapacitated over 2000 of its troops.

7 In making these observations, Bean reveals himself as typifying the popular values and prejudices of the period. A more objective assessment of Australian–Egyptian relations is provided by Suzanne Brugger in her book *Australians and Egypt 1914–1919*.

8 Lord Kitchener and the War Office were highly suspicious of reporters and bluntly refused to allow any newspapermen near the Western Front. Instead, they appointed a so-called 'Eyewitness' to convert the army's official daily reports into journalese. The appointee, Colonel Ernest Swinton, formerly the Assistant Secretary to the Committee on Imperial Defence, had no journalistic experience. His constant stream of stories highlighting plucky Allied chivalry led one paper to label him 'Eyewash'. Sir Max Aitken was the Canadian 'Eyewitness'.

9 Compulsory military training had been introduced to Australia in 1911.

10 The question of Bean's licence was mishandled so badly by these offices that when the Australian Government complained on 19 May at the lack of information emanating from the Peninsula, the Admiralty informed the Colonial Office that the Australian and New Zealand correspondents had not yet arrived at the front. (PRO CO 616/24/424).

11 The causes of the riot are scarcely any clearer today. Bill Gammage (*The broken years* pp. 39–40) claims it developed in response to 'real or imagined grievances' amongst the troops against 'the bad drink and diseased women sold in the area'. Suzanne Brugger agrees with this appraisal. She adds (p. 146) that by 2 April most soldiers knew they were soon to leave Cairo, thus 'those with scores to settle had a limited time in which to do so'.

2 *Into Battle*

1 The postponement was caused by the strong winds.

2 The first Australians landed at 4.30 a.m.

3 Probably an error in writing. 4.55 seems a more likely time.

4 Bean often preferred this spelling to the now accepted Gaba Tepe.

5 Their surprise was understandable, as the landings had not been made at the site designated in the plan. Strong local currents and, possibly, faulty navigation had pushed the first group of landing craft one mile north of the proposed landing point. The troops had expected to meet low sandbanks when they came ashore; instead they faced steep cliffs.

6 By early evening it had become clear to the senior ANZAC officers ashore that the Gaba Tepe landing had failed. Their forces had established a beach-head but the possibility of achieving the desired break-out seemed remote. Those troops who had not been killed or wounded were exhausted after long hours of fierce fighting. It seemed highly probable that next morning the Turks would mount a fierce counter-attack and overwhelm the depleted and fatigued ANZAC ranks. Therefore, at about 10 p.m. General Bridges requested that Birdwood come ashore to discuss the possibility of evacuating the entire force. By about midnight, after the seriousness of the situation had been laid before him, Birdwood had had the request signalled to GHQ. Hamilton rejected the plea, essentially because he was advised that an evacuation could not be organised in the time available.

7 The Australian submarine, *AE2*, had indeed slipped through the straits and sunk a small Turkish cruiser. The sinking was of marginal strategic significance to the campaign, however, and Hamilton probably passed on the news in order to bolster the apparently flagging morale of those ashore. Five days later the submarine was sunk by a Turkish torpedo boat in the Sea of Marmara.

8 This was part of a general Turkish counter-attack launched that day with the aim of driving the Allied force back into the sea.

9 No instance of mutilation, Larkin included, was ever proven, but Bean and most of his companions remained sceptical regarding Turkish treatment of prisoners.

10 A mix up by British officials at Alexandria held up the cables until 13 May. Consequently they did not appear in the Australian press until 14 May, six days after Ellis Ashmead Bartlett's famous despatch had described the landing to the world.

11 Bean had attended Clifton College, England,

from 1886 to 1889. Old boys of the school included the British generals, Douglas Haig and William Birdwood, and both sons of WG Grace, the cricketer.

12 This collier had been used to land 2 000 troops. The plan was for the ship to be beached and for the men to pour out from special openings cut in its sides. The ship nosed ashore at 6.20 a.m., 25 April, but when its doors were opened the Turks directed murderous machine-gun fire against it. So great were the ensuing British casualties that the sea was soon stained red.

13 Bean was recommended for the Military Cross for this act of bravery. However, being a civilian, he was deemed ineligible to receive it. He was mentioned in despatches for his work in assisting the wounded during this night.

14 'Dugouts' was the colloquial term used for old soldiers brought out of retirement.

3 Life and Death

1 On 14 May Birdwood had a lucky escape when a fragment of bullet grazed his skull. Next day Bridges was mortally wounded by a bullet through his right thigh as he was inspecting positions at the head of Monash Valley.

2 The Deal Battalion, Royal Marine Light Infantry, had landed on 29 April. The unit had suffered heavy casualties in the defence of Antwerp (October 1914) and thus came to Gallipoli with many raw recruits in its ranks.

3 A sap was a defensive ground work, similar to a trench, but dug forward from an existing trench.

4 42 000 Turkish troops had been assembled for the offensive. The Allied forces defending Anzac Cove numbered only 17 356. During the day the Turks attacked along virtually the entire ANZAC line.

5 Explosive 'dum dum' bullets were outlawed by the Hague Convention, 1899, but as Turkey was not a signatory it was not bound by its conventions.

6 The British armies in France and the Mediterranean both laboured under a shortage of artillery ammunition at this time, largely because of the still amateurish manner in which the War Office was controlling the war effort.

7 The British battleship, *Triumph*, had been sunk by a German U-boat off Anzac Cove on 25 May. The seventeen troop transports had already been withdrawn to the safety of Imbros Harbour on 11 May. With the supporting naval fire power withdrawn and the local seas now virtually deserted, the Anzacs had good reason to feel that High Command had forgotten them.

8 Hamilton had decided to concentrate his major offensive effort at Cape Helles.

9 Support bases had by now been extablished on both Imbros and Lemnos Islands. GHQ was situated on Imbros.

10 Ordinary newspapers were at least several weeks old by the time they reached the Peninsula so GHQ regularly published this news-sheet and had it posted at the headquarters of most units. It was edited by the MEF censor, Captain Maxwell.

11 Bean's account of the landing appeared in Australian papers on 14 May.

12 Malcolm Ross, the Official New Zealand War Correspondent, had arrived on the Peninsula on 24 June.

13 Bartlett had had to return to England after all his kit went down with the battleship, *Majestic*, sunk by a German U-boat on 27 May. While in London he had discussed the Gallipoli campaign with Prime Minister Asquith and the Secretary for War, Lord Kitchener.

14 This film, *Heroes of Gallipoli*, with titles written by Bean specifically for Australasian audiences, was shown widely in Australia and New Zealand in 1916.

4 A Losing Battle

1 The fault, in fact, lay with the Royal Navy. It had stopped the bombardment seven minutes earlier than planned. As a result, four lines of Australian lighthorsemen were cut down by a wall of Turkish bullets. By 5.15 a.m. 234 Australians lay dead in an area little larger than a tennis court. The charge at the Nek is remembered as the most futile sacrifice of the entire campaign.

2 This was the strongest criticism Bean had levelled against any Australian officer. The comments seem less than fair and might, perhaps, stem in large part from the painful wound Bean suffered, and his consequent frustration at being unable to be in the trenches witnessing what seemed the most crucial moment yet reached in the entire Gallipoli campaign.

Because of his wound, Bean had gained most accounts of Monash's operation secondhand. Had he been able to observe the action or interview the participants as was his normal practice, he would have realised that Monash had been set an almost impossible task. The 4th Brigade and the Gurkhas were expected to move four miles on the darkest of nights through unreconnoitred country, aided only by poor maps. When the

New Zealand Mounted Rifles took longer than expected to clear the foothills, the local guide tried to make up lost time by taking a short cut. The change in route proved disastrous as the new path was narrow and extremely rugged, hence the rate of progress slowed still more. As morning came the brigade was still several hours' march short of its objective so Monash ordered his by now exhausted troops to dig in. Later historians have concluded that no troops could possibly have reached 4th Brigade's objective, especially after so much valuable time was lost through factors outside its control. Bean himself admits in the *Official history* (Vol. 2, p. 663) that 'the country in front of the 4th Brigade appeared to be more difficult than any against which Australian infantry was elsewhere sent. So rugged was it that from the supposed starting line ... the climbing of Abdel Rahman Bair, even in daylight and in peaceful manoeuvres, would have taken troops, though at the acme of fitness and health, longer than the time allowed for the whole operation'. Bean had probably revised his assessment of the march and Monash's subsequent actions after he personally inspected the ground in 1919.

Monash consolidated his line on 7 August, then next morning renewed his attack. The Turks soon counter-attacked fiercely. The 4th Brigade withdrew, suffering 750 casualties in the process. The heavy toll in lives can be blamed more on the general failure of the Allied assault and the tactical difficulties this created, than on supposedly poor leadership by Monash.

3 Controversy still surrounds the bombardment, with some historians asserting that it was naval fire, and others maintaining that it came from a battery in the old Anzac area which, not unnaturally, assumed the stream of men must be Turks. By the time he wrote the *Official history*, Bean subscribed to the latter school. Whoever fired the shells, the incident was most unfortunate but it seems unlikely that it turned the battle as Bean suggests. New Zealand, British and Gurkha units had established a fragile grip on Chunuk Bair and nearby Hill Q during 9 August, but the fighting remained fierce throughout the day. Early on 10 August the Turks delievered a determined counter-attack. They suffered heavy casualties but succeeded in driving the weary Allied remnants off the peaks.

4 It is not known why these correspondents were not permitted to remain. Certainly, the Australian Government did not approve of unofficial correspondents visiting the Front. In November 1915 it asked the British authorities to prohibit such visits as they 'result[ed] in value of Government press service being discounted'.

5 The military police had boarded Murdoch's ship at Marseilles and forced him to surrender the letter.

6 This speculation about possible new Allied offensives in the Balkans was well founded. The Germans knew that Turkish reserves of manpower and munitions were dwindling fast. Germany, on the other hand, had inflicted a series of crushing defeats on Russia in 1915 and was now in a position to transfer a large portion of her forces away from the Eastern Front. Early in October the Allies landed two divisions at Salonika in neutral Greece to try to arrest the situation. The Central Powers duly invaded Serbia and, on 15 October, war was declared between Bulgaria and Great Britain. The Serbian armies were soon overrun.

7 Bartlett lectured in Britain, then toured the United States and Australasia, December 1915–April 1916, generally drawing large crowds to his meetings.

8 In response to his rise to comparative public eminence, new editions of three of CEW Bean's books, *The dreadnought of the Darling, Flagships three*, and *On the wool track*, were published in 1916 by Hodder and Stoughton.

9 The *Aragon* was a lavishly appointed vessel which had been hired as headquarters for the Lines of Communication staff. Those aboard lived in indecent luxury when compared with what had to be endured ashore. Officers and soldiers alike were embittered by the ship's presence and the seeming disregard for others displayed by its residents.

5 *Evacuation*

1 Kitchener had visited Australia in 1910 to advise the Government on defence matters.

2 The title finally chosen was *The Anzac book* (London 1916).

3 His contributions to the book were: two poems ('Non nobis' and 'Abdul'), a water colour painting ('The silver lining'), and a host of sketches and photographs.

4 The Allies feared that if the Mediterranean Expeditionary Force had to be evacuted or remained pinned down by only a small Turkish force, the Turks might direct a large army against Egypt.

Biographical Notes

These notes were compiled from: biographical cards and newspaper cuttings, AWM; *Official history of Australia in the war of 1914–18*; *Australian dictionary of biography*, Vols 7 & 8; *National dictionary of biography*; *Army list*; L Wigmore, *They dared mightily* (Canberra 1963); J Rydon, *A biographical register of the Commonwealth Parliament 1901–1972* (Canberra 1975); *Who was who*; *Who's who in Australia*.

Rank cited is the highest held during the Gallipoli campaign. All units are AIF unless otherwise indicated.

Anderson, Capt JSS 1891– . Staff Capt, HQ 1st Bde. University student of Sydney and Inverell, NSW.

Aspinall, Lt-Col CF 1878–1959. GSO, MEF. Officer in British Regular Army. Active service in Ashanti 1900, Sth Africa 1901–02, Mohmand Expedition 1908.

Austin, Major CD 1872–KIA 6.8.1915. Quartermaster, 3rd Bn.

Bartlett, E Ashmead 1881–1931. Press correspondent for the London daily newspapers. Served in Sth African War. Vastly experienced; had reported on six wars 1907–13. Late 1915–16 lectured in Britain, USA, Australasia on the Dardanelles campaign. Appointed press correspondent to French Army, Western Front 1916. Wrote: *Despatches from the Dardanelles* (London 1918); *The uncensored Dardanelles* (London 1928).

Bazley, Pte AW 1896–1972. Batman to CEWB. Clerk of South Yarra, Melbourne. Enlisted 5.10.1914, RTA as S/Sgt 1.4.1919. Secretary and assistant to Bean 1919–39; Chief clerk & librarian, AWM 1939–43; Acting Director, AWM 1943–48; officer in Dept of Immigration, 1948–64.

Bean, Edwin 1851–1922. Father of CEWB. Schoolmaster. The family lived in Hobart throughout the war years, with Edwin teaching part-time at Hutchins School.

Bean, Major JWB (nicknamed 'Jack' and 'Jock') 1881–1969. Medical Officer, 3rd Bn. Brother of CEWB. Enlisted 20.8.1914. Served in Egypt, Gallipoli, France. RTA Nov 1919. Medical officer with Queensland Department of Education 1926(?)–1939. In 1939, after the death of his wife, he moved to Tasmania as medical officer with Department of Defence. General secretary, Australian Theosophical Society.

Bean, Lucy M (née Butler) 1852–1942. Mother of CEWB and his two younger brothers, Jack and Montague (Monty).

Bennett, Lt-Col HG 1887–1962. CO 6th Bn. Employee of AMP Society, Melbourne. GOC 8th Div 2 AIF.

Birdwood, Lieut-Gen Sir WR 1865–1951. GOC ANZAC. Acting GOC AIF May–June 1915. GOC AIF Sept. 1915–19 (appointment conferred Sept 1916 but backdated). Officer of Indian Army. Had served in North West Frontier campaigns and Sth African War. See: *ADB* Vol 7.

Blamey, Major TA 1884–1951. GSO (Intelligence) 1st Div. Officer in Australian Permanent Forces. C in C Australian Army 1941–45. See: J Hetherington *Blamey: controversial soldier* (Canberra 1973).

Bolton, Col WK 1860–1941. Comd 2nd Inf. Bde. Commonwealth Senator 1917–23. See: *ADB* Vol 7.

Boyle, Capt the Hon ADEH 1871–1949. Captain of HMS *Bacchante*.

Braithwaite, Maj-Gen WP 1865–1945. CGS, MEF 13.3.1915–23.10.1915. British Regular Army. Served in Sth African War. Commanded 62nd Div. 1915–18.

Braund, Lt-Col GF 1866–KIA 4.5.1915. CO 2nd Bn. Merchant and politician. See: *ADB* Vol 7.

Bridges, Maj-Gen Sir WT 1861–DOW 18.5.1915. GOC 1st Div. Served in Sth African War. Chief of Intelligence, CMF 1905–09; Commandant, RMC Duntroon 1911–14; Inspector-Gen, CMF May–Aug 1914. See: CEW Bean *Two men I knew* (Sydney 1957); CD Coulthard-Clark *A heritage of spirit* (Melbourne 1979).

Brooks, E. British Official Photographer. Arrived on Peninsula early July.

Brown, Lt-Col ES 1875–DOW 8.8.1915. Adjutant, 3rd Bn 19.8.1914; CO 3rd Bn 5.5.1915. Aust. Perm. Forces, of Haberfield, NSW.

Butler, Pte JH 1894–1924. Signaller, 2nd ALH Regt. Cousin of CEWB. Jackeroo of Hobart, Tas. and Darling Downs, Qld. Enlisted 19.8.1914. RTA Dec 1918.

Butler, Major SS 1880–1964. Intelligence officer, ANZAC. British Regular Army. Served Sth Africa; King's African Rifles 1905–08, Egyptian Army 1909–15.

Casey, Capt RG 1890–1976. ADC to GOC 27.2.1915; to 1st Inf Bde 4.7.1915; to HQ 1st Div 26.7.1915; Staff Captain HQ 3rd Inf Bde 18.8.1915. Engineer. MHR (Corio) 1931–40; (La Trobe) 1949–60. Held various ministerial portfolios. Governor-General of Australia 1965–69.

Cass, Lt-Col WEH 1876–1931. Bde Major 2nd Inf Bde 18.8.1914; AA & QMG 2nd Div 6.8.1915; CO 2nd Bn 7.8.1915. Teacher. See: *ADB* Vol 7.

Chamberlain, Pte C 1889– . Batman to Brig-Gen JW M'Cay, 2nd Inf Bde. Gardener of Eaglehawk, Vic.

Chambers, Capt RW 1890– . Medical Officer, 2nd Field Ambulance. Medical practitioner of Sandringham, Vic.

Chauvel, Col HG 1865–1945. Comd 1st ALH Bde. GOC Desert Mounted Corps 1917–19, CGS 1923–30. See: AJ Hill *Chauvel of the Light Horse* (Melbourne 1978).

Clarke, Major CW 1876– . 4th ALH Regt.

Cox, Major-Gen Sir HV 1860–1923. Comd 29th Indian Inf Bde 31.10.1914–25.11.1915. Comd 4th AIF Div 2.2.1915–28.1.1917. Indian Regular Army.

De Bucy, Major SMER de L 1864–1929. APM, 1st Aust Div 18.8.1914–23.2.1915; Acting Commandant, Australian Base, Egypt 1915. Served Matabele and Bechuanaland, 1896–97; Sth Africa 1899–1902.

de Lisle, General Sir B 1864–1955. GOC 1st Cav Div 10.10.1914–25.5.1915; GOC 29th Div (British Army) 4.6.1915–14.8.1915, 24.8.1915–11.3.1918; temp GOC 9th Corps 15.8.1915–23.8.1915. British Regular Army. Served in Sth African War.

Delmé Radcliffe, Major. British staff officer sent from England early Aug "to take charge of all War Correspondents" attached to MEF. For a time he took over Maxwell's duties as censor but the complaints of the correspondents led to Maxwell being reinstated (E Ashmead Bartlett *Uncensored Dardanelles*).

Dowse, Major R 1866–1955. AQMG, 3rd Military District (Vic.). Served in Sth African War. See: *ADB* Vol 8.

Embelton, Capt. DM 1887– . Medical officer 3rd Field Ambulance. Medical practitioner of Northcote, Vic.

Evans, Lt TH 1881–KIA 26.5.1915. Machine gun officer, 3rd Bn. Machinery agent of Sydney, NSW. Recommended for VC.

Foott, Lt-Col CH 1876–1942. AA & QMG, 1st Div. Aust. Perm. Forces officer. See: *ADB* Vol 8.

Foster, Major WJ 1881–1927. ADC to Major-Gen Bridges; later, Bde Major 2nd ALH Bde. Aust. Perm. Forces. See: *ADB* Vol 8.

Freame, Sgt WHK 1885?–1941. Scout, 1st Bn. Merchant seaman and adventurer. See: *ADB* Vol 8.

Gellibrand, Lt-Col J 1872–1945. DAA & QMG, 1st Div; DAA & QMG 2nd Div, Aug 1915; CO 12th Bn, Dec 1915. Orchardist of Risdon, Tas; formerly of British Regular Army. See: *ADB* Vol 8.

Gibbs, Major SG 1886–KIA 20.9.1917. 1st ALH Bde 1.11.1914; transferred to 2nd Div 26.7.1915. Mining engineer.

Giblin, Lt-Col WW 1872–1951. CO 1st Aust. Casualty Clearing Station. Evacuated sick 1.9.1915. Medical practitioner of Hobart, Tas.

Glasfurd, Lt-Col DJ 1873–DOW 12.11.1916. Operations staff, HQ 1st Div. Formerly of British Regular Army; Director of Military Training, CMF 1912–14.

Glossop, Capt JCT 1871–1934. Captain of HMAS *Sydney*. Royal Navy officer.

Godley, Lt-Gen AJ 1867–1957. GOC NZ & A Div 1914; GOC ANZAC 25.11.1915. British Regular Army. Served in Sth African war. With NZ Military Forces 1910–14. GOC NZEF Aug 1914–March 1919.

Goold, Major RH 1880– . Signals officer, 1st Div; transferred to No. 3 Signals Coy, 2nd Div 27.7.1915. Evacuated 19.9.1915. Engineer of Elsternwick, Vic.

Grace, Capt HE 1876–1937. Captain of HMS *Grafton*.

Griffiths, Major T 1865–1947. DAAG, 1st Div. Aust. Perm. Forces. Administrator of German New Guinea 1920–21, 1932–38; of Nauru 1921–27; Acting Director, AWM 1927; War Pensions Entitlement Tribunal 1929–32.

Hamilton, General Sir I 1853–1947. C in C, MEF, 12.3.1915–16.10.1915. Active service in Afghanistan 1879; Natal 1881; Egypt 1884; Sth Africa 1899–1902; official observer at Russo-Japanese War 1904; toured Australia 1913–14 as adviser to Commonwealth Government on defence matters. Wrote: *Gallipoli diary*, 2 vols (London 1920)

Hankey, Col MPA 1877–1963. Secretary, Committee of Imperial Defence. Formerly in Royal Marines. Wrote: *The supreme command* (London 1961).

Hastie, Lt T 1894– . 5th Bn. Grocery manager of Clifton Hill, Vic.

Hobbs, Brig-Gen JJT 1864–1938. Comd 1st Div artillery; temp Comd 1st Div 13.10.1915. Architect of Perth, WA.

Howell-Price, Major OG 1890–DOW 4.11.1916. 2nd Lt, 3rd Bn 27.8.1914; Adjutant 25.4.1915; temp CO 3rd Bn 5.9.1915. Farmer.

Howse, Col. NR 1863–1930. Assistant Director, Medical Services 28.12.1914; DDMS, ANZAC 11.9.1915; DMS & temp Surgeon General 22.11.1915. With NSW Medical Corps in Sth African War; VC. MHR (Calare) 1922–29. Minister for Defence & for Health 1925–27, for Home & Territories 1928, for Health 1928–29. See: L Wigmore *They dared mightily*.

Hughes, Lt-Col JG 1866– . CO Canterbury Inf Bn, NZ & A Div.

Hunter-Weston, Lt-Gen AG 1864–1940. GOC 29th Div, British Army; GOC 8th Army Corps 1915–18. Formerly CO British 11th Inf Bde in France, 1914.

Keyes, Commodore RJB 1872–1945. Chief of Staff, Eastern Mediterranean Squadron, Royal Navy. Wrote: *The Fight for Gallipoli* (London 1941)

Kitchener of Khartoum, Earl 1850–1916. British Secretary for War 1914–16. Active service in Egypt 1882, 1884–85; Sudan 1886–89, 1896–98; Sth Africa 1899–1902. Visited Australia & NZ in 1910 to advise on defence matters. See: GH Cassar *Kitchener: architect of victory* (London 1977).

Larkin, Sgt ER 1880–KIA 24.5.1915. 5th Bn. Policeman. MLA (Willoughby, NSW) 1913–15. Secretary, NSW Rugby League 1909–13.

Lawrence, L. Reuters News Agency press correspondent attached to MEF.

Legge, Major-Gen JG 1863–1947. GOC 1st Div June–July 1915; transferred to Egypt 26.7.1915 to establish 2nd Div. Returned to Anzac 6.9.1915. Fell ill in October and evacuated to Egypt. Aust. Perm. Forces, of Melbourne, Vic. Aust representative at War Office, London, 1912–14. CGS 8.8.1914–May 1915.

Lesslie, Brig-Gen WB 1868–1942. AA & QMG, ANZAC Corps 1914–Aug 1915; Aug 1915 appointed Chief Engineer at Anzac. British Regular Army. Had previously served as instructor at RMC Kingston & in Indian Army.

Lowing, Lieut. BM 1881–1937. 12th ALH Regt 31.10.1914; 6th ALH Regt 29.8.1915. Grazier.

M'Cay, Major-Gen JW 1864–1930. Comd 2nd Inf Bde. Lawyer of Melbourne, Vic. MLA (Castlemaine) 1895–99, 1900. State Minister for Public Instruction & Commissioner for Trade & Customs 1899. MHR (Corinella) 1901–06. Minister for Defence 1904–05. Lieut Governor, Vic. 1920.

McGlinn, Lt-Col JP 1869–1946. Bde Major 4th Inf Bde 23.9.1914; Public servant of Sydney & West Maitland, NSW. 1923–30 Member of Commonwealth Public Service Board.

MacLaurin, Col HN 1878–KIA 27.4.1915. Comd 1st Inf Bde. Barrister of Sydney, NSW.

MacNaghten, Lt-Col CM 1879–1931. 4th Bn; CO 4th Bn 14.7.1915; Camp Commdt, Tel-el-Kebir 1.2.1916. AIF appointment terminated 7.9.1916. Re-enlisted as a private, 9th Bn 19.10.1916. Solicitor of Sydney, NSW.

McNicoll, Lt-Col WR 1877–1947. 7th Bn 28.8.1914; CO 6th Bn 3.4.1915. School teacher. MHR (Werriwa) 1931–34. Administrator, Mandated Territory of New Guinea 1931–41.

Malone, Lt-Col WG 1859–KIA 8.8.1915. CO Wellington Bn, NZ Inf 1914–15.

Mathison, Capt GCM 1883–DOW 18.5.1915. Medical Officer 2nd Field Ambulance, 5th Bn. Medical practitioner of Elsternwick, Vic.

Maxwell, Gen Rt Hon. Sir JG 1859–1929. GOC, British Army in Egypt, Sept. 1914–March 1916.

Maxwell, Capt. W *d.* 1928. Press Censor, MEF. Formerly press correspondent at Sudan campaign, Sth African War, Balkan War. In Aug. 1914 had been *Daily Mail* correspondent in Luxembourg & Liege.

Maygar, Lt-Col LC 1872–DOW 1.11.1917. 4th ALH Regt 20.8.1914; CO 8th ALH Regt 17.10.1915. Grazier of Longwood & Euroa, Vic. Served in Sth African War; VC. See: Wigmore *They dared mightily*.

Milner, Lord A 1854–1925. Prominent British Unionist parliamentarian & outspoken critic of the Government's Dardanelles strategy. Joined coalition War Cabinet 8.12.1916.

Milner, Capt. JT 1881– . 11th Bn. Station manager of WA.

Monash, Brig-Gen J 1865–1931. Comd 4th Inf Bde. GOC 3rd Div 1916–18. May 1918 promoted Lt-Gen and succeeded Birdwood as GOC Aust. Army Corps. Civil engineer of Melbourne, Vic. Chairman, State Electricity Commission of Vic, 1921–31. Vice Chancellor, University of Melbourne, 1923–31. See: AG Serle *John Monash: a biography* (Melbourne 1982)

Monro, Gen Sir CC 1860–1929. C in C, MEF, 17.10.1915–18.1.1916. Served in Sth African War 1899–1901.

Murdoch, KA 1886–1952. Australian journalist,

visited Peninsula en route to England to take up appointment with United Cable Service. See: D Zwar *In search of Keith Murdoch* (Melbourne 1980).

Murphy, Lt FP 1879– . Aust. Automobile Corps, 1st Div HQ. Grazier of Melbourne, Vic. Discharged to British Army 16.11.1915.

Nash, Pte RGB 1886– . 11th Coy AASC. Railway night officer of Young, NSW. Contributed two articles to *Anzac book* under nom de plume N. Ash.

Nevinson, WH 1856–1941. Press correspondent for *Manchester Guardian*. Vastly experienced war correspondent. On 21 Aug 1915 a bullet hit his helmet but caused only a slight flesh wound. With British Army in Salonika & Egypt 1916; in France & Germany 1918–19. Wrote: *The Dardanelles campaign* (London 1918).

Newcombe, Major SF 1878–1956. Intelligence officer with Egyptian War Officer 1914–15; CRE 2nd Div 1915–16. British Regular Army. Sth African War 1899–1900; with Egyptian Army 1901–11.

Nicholson, Major EJH 1870–1955. 1st Div Artillery HQ 5.9.1914; Staff Officer HQ 1st Div 26.7.1915. Mineral buyer of Claremont, WA.

Noonan, Sgt FWS 1887– . 6th Bn Clerk of Kew, Vic.

Onslow, Lt-Col GMM 1875–1931. 2 I/C., 7th ALH Regt. Estate manager & grazier of Menangle, NSW.

Osborne, Lieut. JB 1892–KIA 15.10.1918. 4 Bn. Farmer and grazier of Sydney, NSW.

Owen, Lt-Col RH 1862–1927. CO 3rd Bn 20.8.1914; temp Comd 1st Bde 15–20.5.1915 then rejoined 3rd Bn. Bank officer of Sydney, NSW.

Paddon, Major CJSW 1875– . NZ Otago Mounted Rifles. Active service at Matabele War 1893–4, Sth African War (1899–1901). Wounded 7.8.1915.

Pain, Capt JHF 1893–1941. 2nd Bn. RMC Duntroon graduate, of Sydney, NSW.

Patterson, Lt-Col WG 1862–1916. DAA & QMG 15.8.1914; AA & QMG, 1st Div HQ 13.1.1915. RTA 3.7.1915. Aust. Perm. Forces, of Sth Yarra, Vic.

Phillips, Major OF 1882–1966. CO 4th Field Artillery Battery. Aust. Perm. Forces officer of Sydney, NSW.

Pinwill, Lt-Col WR 1873– . Staff Officer, NZ & A Div 27.3.1915–21.7.1916, then rejoined British Army.

Plugge, Col A 1878–1934. CO Auckland Bn. Schoolmaster of Auckland, NZ.

Pope, Lt-Col H 1873–1938. CO 16th Bn 13.10.1914; temp Comd 4th Inf Bde 9–17.10.1915. Commissioner of Railways, WA 1919–29.

Price, G Ward 1886–1961. Press correspondent at Dardanelles & with Salonika Army. Formerly special foreign correspondent with Turkish Army at First Balkan War, 1912. Wrote: *The story of the Salonika Army* (London 1917).

Ramsay, Capt RA 1869– . Auto Corps Div. Staff 9.9.1914; DAAG, 1st Div 21.8.1915. Grazier of Birregurra, Vic.

Reid, Sir GH 1845–1918. First Australian High Commissioner in London 1910–16. Premier of NSW 1894–99; Prime Minister 1904–05; MP (House of Commons) 1916–18.

Rosenthal, Lt-Col C 1875–1954. Comd 3rd Field Artillery Bde 1914–16, 4th Div Artillery 1916, 9th Inf Bde 1917–18, temp Comd 1st Aust. Div 1918, 2nd Aust. Div 1918–19. Architect of Sydney, NSW.

Ross, Major AM 1879–1933. Orderly officer to Comd 3rd Inf Bde 15.8.1914; Staff Capt 5.1.1915; Bde Major 16.5.1915. British Regular Army.

Ross, M *d.* 1930. Official NZ press correspondent. Journalist of Wellington, NZ. Assisted with preparation of Sir CP Lucas *The Empire at war* 5 Vols (London 1921–26).

Schuler, PFE *d.* 1917. Special correspondent, Melbourne *Age*. Journalist of Hawthorn, Vic. Son of GFH Schuler, editor of *Age*. Wrote: *The battlefields of Anzac* (Melbourne 1916); *Australia in arms* (London 1916).

Simpson, Capt AJG 1888– . 4th Bn. Articled law clerk of Hunters Hill, NSW.

Sinclair-MacLagan, Brig-Gen EG 1868–1948. Comd 3rd Inf Bde 1914–17. British Regular Army.

Skeen, Brev Lt-Col A 1873–1935. BGGS, A & NZ Army Corps. Chief of Staff to Gen Birdwood. Indian Army officer.

Smith, Capt. AG 1873–1953. Naval Transport Officer to 1st convoy. Royal Navy officer on loan to RAN 1913–17.

Smith, CP 1879–1963. Special correspondent, Melbourne *Argus*. Journalist of Melbourne, Vic. Managing editor, *West Australian* 1927–51 & director 1931–51.

Smyth, Col NM 1868–1941. Temp Comd 1st Inf Bde 20.5.1915–23.6.1915; Comd 2nd Inf Bde 20.7.1915; HQ 1st Inf Bde 26.7.1915. British Regular Army officer of Marazion, Cornwall.

Stopford, Lt-Gen Sir FW 1854–1929. GOC 9th Corps, British Army, June–16.8.1915. Active service in Egypt 1882; Sth Africa 1899–1902.

Swinton, Col ED 1868–1951. British 'Eyewitness'

on W. Front, Sept 1914–July 1915. Formerly Assistant Secretary to Committee of Imperial Defence. Wrote: *Eyewitness* (London 1932).

Thompson, Capt CW 1882–1941. Medical Officer, 1st Bn. Medical practitioner of Bathurst, NSW.

Tyrrell, Lt-Col GE 1871–1917. Chief of Intelligence, GHQ, MEF, Sept 1915–Jan 1916. British Military Attaché, Constantinople, 1909–13.

Villiers-Stuart, Major CH 1874–KIA 17.5.1915. Intelligence officer, A & NZ Army Corps. Indian Army officer.

Wagstaffe, Lt-Col CM 1878–1934. Staff officer (Operations), A & NZ Army Corps 12.12.1914; AA & QMG, A & NZ Corps 5.10.1915–6.12.1915. British Regular Army.

Walker, Major-Gen HB 1862–1934. BGGS, A & NZ Army Corps 12.12.1914; GOC 1st Inf Bde 24.6.1915; GOC 1st Div 1915–18. British Regular Army.

Wallace, Col R. 1864–1915. Commdt, 3rd Military District 1.6.1914–7.10.1915. Officer of Aust. Perm. Forces, of Melbourne, Vic.

Wanliss, Lt-Col DS 1864– . CO 5th Bn; temp Comd 2nd Inf. Bde 18.5.1915–8.6.1915, 6.7.1915–20.7.1915. Barrister of Ballarat, Vic.

Ward, Lt-Col MCP 1869– . General Staff Officer, GHQ, MEF, March–Sept 1915.

Watson, Capt SH 1887– . 1st Div. Signals Coy 20.10.1914; 3rd Signals Coy, 2nd Div 27.7.1915. Draftsman of Plympton, SA.

White, Brig-Gen CBB 1876–1940. BGGS, 1st Anzac Corps and Aust. Corps; CGS 1920–23, 1940. Served in Sth African War, then in Aust. Perm. Forces. Bean claimed (*Official History*, Vol I, p. 75) White "was more than any other the moulder of the Australian Imperial Force". See: CEW Bean *Two men I knew* (Sydney 1957).

Whyte, AS 1880– . Journalist with Melbourne *Argus*, previously with *SMH*. Gen Sec Victorian National Federation. Close personal friend of CEWB.

Woods, Sgt HV 1889– . 4th Field Ambulance. Carpenter of Adelaide, SA.

Woodward, Brig-Gen EM 1861–1943. Deputy Adjutant General (in charge of personnel), MEF. British Regular Army.

Select Bibliography

Manuscripts

Bazley Papers, AWM
Bean Papers, AWM
Murdoch Papers, NLA

Secondary

The Anzac book (London 1916).

Bartlett, E Ashmead *The uncensored Dardanelles* (London 1928).

Bean, CEW *Gallipoli mission* (Canberra 1952).

—— *The official history of Australia in the war of 1914–1918*. Vols. I and II (Sydney 1921, 1924).

—— *Two men I knew* (Sydney 1957).

—— *What to know in Egypt . . . a guide for Australasian soldiers* (Cairo 1915).

—— 'The writing of the Australian Official History of the Great War — Sources, methods and some conclusions', *Royal Australian Historical Society Journal and Proceedings* Vol. 24 Part 2 1938

Brugger, S *Australians and Egypt 1914–1919* (Melbourne 1980).

Butler, AG *The Australian Army Medical Services in the war of 1914–1918*. Vol. I, *The Gallipoli campaign* (Melbourne 1930).

Gammage, B *The broken years* (Canberra 1974).

James, RR *Gallipoli* (Sydney 1965).

Laffin, J *Damn the Dardanelles*! (Sydney 1980).

Moorehead, A *Gallipoli* (illus. edn) (Sydney 1975).

Other

Fewster KJ 'Expression and suppression: aspects of military censorship in Australia during the Great War', unpublished Ph. D. dissertation (UNSW 1980).

Index

Illustrations are signified by bold type